W9-AFZ-753

Extraordinary praise for Joshua Cooper Ramo's

THE AGE OF THE
UNTHINKABLE

"A great read, a wondrous and unexpected journey through a world that keeps getting more complicated. Joshua Cooper Ramo has a brilliant mind and a beautiful pen, and both are evident in this stimulating book."

—Fareed Zakaria, author of *The Post-American World*

"Full of engaging vignettes.... Ramo uses his anecdotes to make some sharp observations."   —*The Economist*

"Ramo certainly gets you thinking in ways you had not considered before. And for me, that's the true test of a good book."

—Evan Newmark, *Wall Street Journal*

"A poignant, informed, and optimistic book."

—Michael Maiello, Forbes.com

"Thought-provoking.... Ramo questions conventional thinking and provides fresh ideas—something we deeply need these days."   —Walter Isaacson, author of *Einstein*

"Ramo pushes the reader into uncomfortable yet exhilarating places with controversial ways of thinking about global challenges.... Ramo's revelatory work argues that there must be some audacity in thinking before there can be any audacity of hope."   —*Publishers Weekly*, starred review

"Mr. Ramo argues in these pages that today's complex, interconnected, globalized world requires policy makers willing to toss out old assumptions (about cause and effect, deterrence and defense, nation states and balances of power) and embrace creative new approaches. Today's world, he suggests, requires resilient pragmatists who, like the most talented Silicon Valley venture capitalists on the one hand or the survival-minded leadership of Hezbollah on the other, possess both an intuitive ability to see problems in a larger context and a willingness to rejigger their organizations continually to grapple with ever-shifting challenges and circumstances....In drawing upon chaos science, complexity theory, and the theory of disruptive innovation, Mr. Ramo does a nimble job of showing how such theories shed light on the current political and economic climate while avoiding the worst pitfalls....He has managed, in this stimulating volume, to make the reader seriously contemplate the alarming nature of a rapidly changing world."   —Michiko Kakutani, *New York Times*

"*The Age of the Unthinkable* may be one of the grains of sand that causes that much-needed avalanche."
                    —Reagan Upshaw, *San Francisco Chronicle*

"A fascinating study of the way the world really works....*The Age of the Unthinkable* sparkles with insight and imagination. You'll learn more about foreign policy from this text than you would in most university courses....Ramo seamlessly fuses the bird's-eye and worm's-eye views to render a compelling picture of global security threats....As a new generation of leaders maps out America's course in the world, Ramo's navigational skill will surely be in high demand."
                    —Josh Burek, *Christian Science Monitor*

"The formula on display here—reported vignettes, grand theorizing, surprising juxtapositions—will be familiar to readers of Thomas L. Friedman and Malcolm Gladwell, and Ramo executes it with verve." —Gary Rosen, *New York Times Book Review*

"A beacon for those who have been looking for straight talk about our current economic crisis and how you and I, everyday people, can move forward."
—Christa Avampato, *San Francisco Examiner*

"A good example of Ramo's challenge of the status quo is his criticism of Joseph Nye's soft power theory. Soft power theory says that if the 'enemy' likes our culture he will stop being our enemy. As Ramo shows, it is possible for terrorists to listen to our music, watch our movies, dress like us and still...want to blow us up....Ramo shows us how talking to the enemy and learning from the enemy can be a better strategy than spending trillions trying and failing to destroy it. But before getting carried away here is my advice: Buy the book and come up with your own opinion. It's worth it."
—Martin Varsavsky, huffingtonpost.com

"Ramo entertainingly examines subjects as diverse as fish ecology and Hezbollah guerrilla tactics." —*The New Yorker*

"Elegantly written....Ramo's analyses offer interesting lessons for executives, especially during a recession."
—Reena Jana, *BusinessWeek*

"Ramo's cinematic narrative is breathless....His wake-up call has done us a service." —Lionel Barber, *Financial Times*

ALSO BY JOSHUA COOPER RAMO

No Visible Horizon

THE AGE OF THE
UNTHINKABLE

· · ·

WHY THE NEW WORLD DISORDER CONSTANTLY SURPRISES US AND WHAT WE CAN DO ABOUT IT

JOSHUA COOPER RAMO

BACK BAY BOOKS
LITTLE, BROWN AND COMPANY
New York Boston London

For my mentors

Copyright © 2009 by Joshua Cooper Ramo
Afterword copyright © 2010 by Joshua Cooper Ramo
Reading group guide copyright © 2010 by Joshua Cooper Ramo and
Little, Brown and Company

All rights reserved. Except as permitted under the U.S. Copyright Act of 1976,
no part of this publication may be reproduced, distributed, or transmitted in
any form or by any means, or stored in a database or retrieval system, without
the prior written permission of the publisher.

Back Bay Books / Little, Brown and Company
Hachette Book Group
237 Park Avenue, New York, NY 10017
www.hachettebookgroup.com

Originally published in hardcover by Little, Brown and Company, March 2009
First Back Bay paperback edition, June 2010

Back Bay Books is an imprint of Little, Brown and Company.
The Back Bay Books name and logo are trademarks of Hachette Book Group, Inc.

Library of Congress Cataloging-in-Publication Data
Ramo, Joshua Cooper.
   The age of the unthinkable : why the new world disorder constantly
surprises us and what we can do about it / Joshua Cooper Ramo. — 1st ed.
      p. cm.
   Includes bibliographical references and index.
   ISBN 978-0-316-11808-8 (hc) / 978-0-316-05651-9 (int'l. ed.) /
   978-0-316-11811-8 (pb)
   1. United States — Foreign relations — 2001–2009.   2. United States —
Military policy.   3. World politics — 21st century.   I. Title.
   E902.R3588 2009
   973.931 — dc22   2009000854

10 9 8 7 6 5 4 3 2 1

RRD-IN

Printed in the United States of America

Contents

Forgive my vehemence, which has deep causes in my hope for the future. This is my subject. I know, or partly know, what I want. I know, and clearly know, what I fear.

—JOHN MAYNARD KEYNES TO DEAN ACHESON,
AUGUST 1941

PART I

• • •

The Sandpile Effect

CHAPTER ONE

The Nature of the Age

1. Split Screen

The thick coffee, in two small gilt-edged cups and with that bitter bite of near-burnt Arabic chicory, has gone cold. We are sitting more or less in silence, each of us thinking, staring idly at a muted television nearby. It is the early fall of 2008, and the headlines, even on the station we are watching—Al Manar, the TV channel of Hizb'allah here in Lebanon—are about the global financial crisis. Fouad and I have a settled peace about us at the moment, the slow calm of an early afternoon, each of us getting ready to return to our respective lives. He will, when he leaves, go back to his work as a chief of information technology for Hizb'allah, the guerrilla and terror group that is, as one Israeli general has said, "the greatest in the world" at what it does.

Fouad and I have had a long conversation about the Koran, about the demands of martyrdom, about his sense of himself as "already dead," simply walking the earth doing the work he is meant to do before ascending to heaven, probably at some moment chosen in Tel Aviv. We've talked about his children and his brothers and sisters. He has asked me questions about China, which is where I live and is a place he wants to understand better. I had come to see Fouad because, in all my dealings with Hizb'allah over the years, I had found myself particularly fascinated and intrigued by their capacity for creativity and innovation, even in the pursuit of shocking ends. Their obsession with finding better ways to fight and survive under the full pressure of Israeli attack seemed to me a signpost of sorts, but I had always struggled to figure out what precisely it marked. It meant, at the least, a record of defeat for the Israeli army. In 2006, for instance, fewer than 500 Hizb'allah fighters had frustrated a 30,000-man Israeli attack, including one of the most extensive air campaigns in Middle East history. Hizb'allah, to prove their point, had made a show of firing the same number of missiles on the last day of the war as they had on the first.

In trying to understand how our global order is now working and changing, I knew I needed to be intimate with the ideas Fouad carried around, no matter how repellent they might be. In a way, the passion for innovation and the geeky curiosity of fighters like Fouad reminded me of friends of mine who had started great Internet companies or people I knew who were managing gigantic hedge funds. They were mostly around my age, in their thirties and forties. And if I had encountered them first in my role as foreign editor of *Time* magazine, these people had remained interesting and fascinating to me once I left journalism precisely so that I could better feel how our world was changing, instead of merely observing its shifts and lurches from a reportorial distance. The instinct for change, an eager fluency with the tools of serious disruption, I had noticed, seemed particularly alive in my generation. This was the generation that had built the Web into something useful and revolutionary, that had assembled huge and unregulatable financial firms churning out billions in profits while creating trillions of dollars of risk. It was a sense you could also find in many people I knew in China as they struggled to build an economic and political order against the unpredictable demands of constant newness. Change is at the center of all of their lives. They seek it out and, when change is proceeding too slowly, accelerate it. They operate with the self-regard and courage of people who believe that the tide of history is on their side, bringing us closer to whatever dream they find most exciting, whether it is fast universal connections to data or wholly new types of government. They see this process as one in which destabilization of the existing order is not only necessary but inevitable.

You don't dare draw a moral equivalency between the crimes of Hizb'allah and, say, the innovations of Google, but you can see in each the workings of a powerful energy: the imbalance of 500 fighters against 30,000 soldiers or two university students remaking the whole Web from a dorm room. These hot cells of innovation draw the very best minds of a generation: quantitative-math geniuses to hedge funds, computer savants to tech startups and, well, darker corners. "Our e-mail is flooded with CVs," Fouad told me. "But of course some people don't have the courage to be on the terrorist watch list, even if it is to serve a sacred cause."

When I thought of these rebels I knew in the context of other friends of mine, such as the suits working in the National Security Council or the U.S. Army or IBM or Time Warner, I realized that there was no chance those conservative places could ever compete. They were locked, from top to bottom, from young to old, and in every level of their bureaucratic life, in a vision of the world that was out of date and inflexible. As a perplexed Alan Greenspan confessed to Congress about his own thinking in 2008, just a few weeks after Fouad and I watched financial news together: "I have found a flaw. I don't know how significant or permanent it is. But I have been very distressed by the fact." The congressman questioning him asked, "In other words, you found that your view of the world, your ideology, was not right. It was not working?" Greenspan replied, "Absolutely. Precisely. You know that's precisely the reason I was shocked. Because I have been going for forty years or more with very considerable evidence that it was working exceptionally well."

You probably didn't need to hear it from Greenspan to have a sense of the confused navigation of our leaders. How can the president of the United States declare a war won just as it becomes more violent? Why are Russian bombers flying off American coasts again? How did China, a country with an average daily income of $7 per person, amass nearly $2 trillion in U.S. debt in less than a decade? How is it that the secretary of the treasury of the United States, a near-billionaire financier, can say that the worst of a crisis is over in May and then find himself in August furiously battling to save the global financial system? Why is it we can agree on an immense collection of problems, such as global warming or the spread of nuclear weapons, that must be solved now—and then make no real progress or only move backward?

After I left Fouad, I recalled a conversation I had had a week earlier with a friend who has a key role in the Chinese banking system. He explained to me how he had locked down his own financial institutions in 2007 to avoid just the sort of crisis now sweeping the globe. He was shocked, he said, that the United States had not seen it coming, had not acted. He had seen it, had *felt* this incipient crisis. It began to dawn on me that what Hizb'allah, China, and those friends of mine working in places like Google shared was something more than just ambition for change. Remember how, in advance of the tsunami in 2004, animals all around Indonesia and Thailand and Sri Lanka ran uphill well before the waves that killed 250,000 people arrived, how they were responding to some instinct for cataclysm, one now comforted out of existence in our own psyches. Well, I realized that afternoon with Fouad that he and the other people I had been talking with had somehow rediscovered this instinct, had mastered it. In every twitch of their keyboards or investments or suicide bombs there was the mark of a much larger change that they knew was, even now, surely rolling toward us.

The night before I was with Fouad, Hizb'allah's deadly and charismatic leader Hassan Nasrallah had exulted that the U.S. government had told the Georgian military they should study Hizb'allah to learn how to fight the Russians more effectively. The White House recommending the tactics of Hizb'allah as a study text? It was impossible, given the rumor mill that is Beirut, to know (or even hope to verify) if such self-inflating gossip was true. But even if it wasn't, *should* it have been? Was there something to learn from Fouad and Nasrallah and their few-thousand-man unholy army? Anyhow, if you were sitting in Beirut on that fall 2008 day, watching allegedly unbreakable billion-dollar financial institutions snap on one TV channel and Nasrallah celebrating his imagined endorsement from Washington on another, this much at least was obvious: we had arrived firmly in an age in which the unthinkable had become, frankly, inevitable.

2. The Cascade

We are now at the start of what may become the most dramatic change in the international order in several centuries, the biggest shift since European nations were first shuffled into a sovereign order by the Peace of Westphalia in 1648. This change is irresistible. It is infectious. It will spread to every corner of our lives, to our businesses, our bank accounts, our hopes, and our health. What we face isn't one single shift or revolution, like the end of World War II or the collapse of the Soviet Union or a financial crisis, so much as an avalanche of ceaseless change. It is change that will render institutions that look unshakable weak and unstable; it will elevate movements that look weak into positions of great power. As much as we might wish it, our world is not becoming more stable or easier to comprehend. We are entering, in short, a revolutionary age. And we are doing so with ideas, leaders, and institutions that are better suited for a world now several centuries behind us. On the one hand, this revolution is creating unprecedented disruption and dislocation. But it is also creating new fortunes, new power, fresh hope, and a new global order. Revolutions, after all, don't produce only losers. They also—and this is the heart of the story I want to tell here—produce a whole new cast of historical champions. This book isn't the tale of our inevitable doom. It's a guide to how we can save ourselves. What you'll find on the following pages is meant to be a decoder ring for the perplexities of our current world, for the dangerous magic that seems to be unspooling everywhere. And it is also, once you've understood it clearly, a way for anyone, from eight to eighty, to begin to see what this world means for you—and to see what you can do about it.

Unfortunately, whether they are running corporations or foreign ministries or central banks, some of the best minds of our era are still in thrall to an older way of seeing and thinking. They are making repeated misjudgments about the world. In a way, it's hard to blame them. Mostly they grew up at a time when the global order could largely be understood in simpler terms, when only nations really mattered, when you could think there was a predictable relationship between what you wanted and what you got. They came of age as part of a tradition that believed all international crises had beginnings and, if managed well, ends. They share as background a view in which the spread of capitalism is good and inevitable, in which democracy and technology produce an increase in general stability. Such a view represents a shared consensus of elites, the best-mind conventional wisdom of our day, found everywhere from Geneva boardrooms to Whitehall corridors to Washington war rooms. These ideas fail both tests of good science: they neither predict nor explain our world. But too many of our leaders are incapable of confronting this disconnect. They lack the language, creativity, and revolutionary spirit our moment demands. In many cases, they have been badly corrupted by power, position, and prestige. We've left our future, in other words, largely in the hands of people whose single greatest characteristic is that they are bewildered by the present.

The sum of their misconceptions has now produced a tragic paradox: policies designed to make us safer instead make the world more perilous. History's grandest war against terrorism, for instance, not only fails to eliminate terrorism, it creates more dangerous terrorists. Attempts to stop the spread of nuclear weapons instead encourage countries to accelerate their quest for an atom bomb. Global capitalism, intended to boost the quality of life of people around the world, claws the gap between rich and poor ever wider. Decisions taken to stem a financial crisis appear, in the end, to guarantee its arrival. Environmental techniques engineered to protect species lead to their extinction. Middle East peace plans produce less peace. We stare now at a long list of similar looking-glass problems, challenges in which our best intentions and their terrible results exist in a horrific mirror-image dance. The integrity of our leaders, our ability to trust that they understand what we are confronting—or, for that matter, that they are telling us the truth about it—is leaching away. Why should we believe what they say about the war on terror, the safety of our food, the global financial crisis, or any of a dozen essential issues when, over and over, their policies endanger us?

Little in the current discussion of our shared problems suggests the radical rethinking our world requires. There is now hope and even the first hints of substantial changes in policy, but the basic architecture of ideas and theories necessary to back up such difficult work remains profoundly underdeveloped. No debate about terrorism, global warming, destructive weapons, economic chaos, or other threats can make sense without a grand strategy, though this is the thing most obviously missing today. Instead, the most likely course for our future is the most dangerous: minor adjustments to current policies, incremental changes to institutions that are already collapsing, and an inevitable and frustrating expansion of failure. And this will happen fast. Among the things our leaders seem to be missing is a comprehension of the staggering speed at which these change epidemics occur: one bank fails, then fifty; one country develops an atom bomb, a dozen try to follow; one computer or one child comes down with a virus, and the speed of its spread is incomprehensible. The immensity of the challenges we now face, the disturbing failures that likely lie ahead, and our inability to deal with problems effectively with old ways of thinking will assuredly lead us to question many fundamental values of our society. It will put even the nature of our government and our democracy into the debate. These discussions are important and legitimate. But they should occur only on a basis of security and confidence. Today we have neither, and that fundamental uneasiness could lead to some awful betrayals. It would be nice if we lived in a time when technology or capitalism or democracy was erasing unpredictability, when shifts could be carefully mapped and planned for using logic that originated centuries ago. This is the world that many politicians or foreign and financial policy experts have been trying to peddle to us.

It bears very little resemblance, really, to the future we do face.

3. Virtuosos of the Moment

This book is the story of a new way of thinking. It is one that takes complexity and unpredictability as its first consideration and produces, as a result, a different and useful way of seeing our world. It explains why unthinkable disasters are blossoming all around us and—as important—what we can do about them. The main argument of the book is not particularly complicated: it is that in a revolutionary era of surprise and innovation, you need to learn to think and act like a revolutionary. (People at revolutions who don't act that way have a particular name: victims.) When I say the ideas here are useful, it's because all of them are already at work in the hands of people who are thriving in this new order. The concepts have been field-tested in places where the consequences of ignoring the rules of the new power physics are often catastrophic: bankruptcy, social chaos, even death. As we travel from Hizb'allah guerrilla camps in Lebanon to the offices of billionaire investors in Silicon Valley, as we listen to a brilliant spymaster and a game-changing innovator in Kyoto, you'll see that what marks them all is a relentless urge to avoid models of the world built with the language of the past.

One of the lessons of this new model is that we can harness the change we see all around us, and if we do so, we shall gain a clearer sense of what sort of nation America should be. In a way, the most ambitious goal of any international policy—improving as many lives as possible around the world while securing our own safety—is more important than ever. But our only real chance of delivering such a result, our only hope of guaranteeing the human rights and moral decency this world demands, is radically new language and thinking. Today we are generally neither secure nor decent. This is, profoundly, not a moment to abandon decency for pure power, not the time for cold and brutal calculations that treat states like gears and humans like lubricant. This poses some hard questions on subjects like rights and the uses of national power.

In the days of classical foreign policy, back when the old rules seemed to make more sense, the best statesmen, the honest ones, admitted that they were always trying to manage a physics that lingered beyond real control, that confounded old ideas pretty quickly. This is the sense, a sort of bashfulness in the face of history, that emerges from the private letters and diaries of men like Metternich or Castlereagh or Eisenhower or Bismarck (or the testimony of a former Fed chairman). This isn't simply the natural worry of brilliant men who have found the limits of their intelligence. Rather, it is an instinctive sense of the weird, impenetrable, and complex magic that seems to linger in global politics, marking the line between triumph and disaster. It is an awareness that enforces a constant alertness—an eagerness, even, to discard old models for new ones. August Fournier, one of Metternich's more arch biographers, once derisively labeled him *ein Virtuoso des Moments*—a virtuoso of moments. It's hard to imagine that the Austrian prince would have been offended; mastery of the passing instant is often the most that even the best statecraft can hope to deliver. As the great seventeenth-century statesman François de Callières wrote: "There is no such thing as a diplomatic triumph." Even when you think you've reached the end of a problem, you are usually simply at the start of new troubles.

Louis Halle, an American diplomat and strategist of the 1950s, once observed that foreign policy is made not in reaction to the world but rather in reaction to an image of the world in the minds of the people making decisions. "In the degree that the image is false, actually and philosophically false," Halle warned, "no technicians, however proficient, can make the policy that is based on it sound." Our image of the world now, constructed by people we once thought we could rely upon for such work, is false, actually and philosophically false. It's time to replace it with an image that actually works. What we need is a framework for the sort of change that fits our world—and that lays a foundation for the widespread personal involvement of millions of people that will make such change useful, durable, and sustainable. Without these two elements, hope for change will dissolve quickly into lethargic frustration at best and, at worst, panic.

4. Looking out the Window

In the physical sciences, dramatic shifts to very different ways of thinking are common. In fact, they are regarded as essential. Every once in a while a big idea will arrive, thundering in from a great genius or slipping quietly in from an obscure research corner, to replace all of the old thinking in an instant. Albert Einstein started such a revolution with his theories of relativity. James Watson and Francis Crick did the same when they described the double helix of DNA. The fundamental challenge of adapting our old thinking about power to this new world is similar. It resembles nothing so much as the problem physicists confronted in the twentieth century when they found that Isaac Newton's physics failed to explain how things worked at a subatomic level. It didn't mean junking Newton altogether but, rather, augmenting his ideas with a set of theories that fit a complex subatomic landscape. Moving into that smaller world required a revolution in thinking, creative concepts so inventive that they appeared at first blush to contradict much of what was assumed to be true in conventional physics. Einstein's theory of relativity showed that Newton's laws had to be modified for objects moving at high speed; the same might be said of our international system. The old laws of power, confronted with a faster-moving and more intricately ordered system, are now in need of modification.

Such a paradigm shift isn't easy. It certainly wasn't simple for physics. As the Danish physicist Niels Bohr once told friends, "If quantum mechanics hasn't profoundly shocked you, then you haven't understood it." The goal of this book is not to give stylized, simple answers—what honest thinker would hope to answer questions that are still being created and that exist outside our current language? Rather, it's to explore a new way to think about problems as they arise, to develop new instincts. Some of the ideas here or those you may dream up as you read should shock you at least a bit— *Stop trying to create a peace agreement as a way to make the Middle East more peaceful? Redesign much of the State Department? Let illiterate farmers manage complex health-care programs?*

Understood fully, however, the same forces now making our world more dangerous contain the ingredients we need to make it safer. In every roadside bomb in Tal'Afar, in every death from drug-resistant tuberculosis, in each hiccup of global financial markets, we can see the workings of powerful forces that, once mastered, offer hope at the same time they present new dangers.

It is difficult to overstate the difference between our world today and that of just one hundred years ago, when many of our ideas about nations and global politics originated. We may think of 1900 as the modern era, but in fact the world was then struggling hugely with the demands of the simplest aspects of modernity. Sixty percent of Europeans and Americans were still essentially preindustrial, living off the land and just beginning the earliest march of urbanization. Factories and assembly lines were new and tenuous inventions that created wealth for some and a new sort of wretchedness for others. The unrest that resulted helped plant the seeds of economic dislocation, which blossomed into socialism and fascism. Yet, that shift from agrarian to industrial was also accompanied by an acceleration of interconnection, transportation, and education. These forces in turn helped drive a vast increase in productivity, which, combined with our more recent shift from industry to information and service, means that economies now double in size about every thirty-five years, quadruple the rate of a century ago. But perhaps nothing has changed so much as the speed with which we can transmit information. A letter carried on horseback 150 years ago would have moved information at a rate of about .003 bits per second (the average note carrying, say, 10 kilobytes of data, though of course that measure didn't yet exist). As late as the 1960s those same 10 kilobytes might have moved at 300 bits per second. Today global telecom cables transmit at a rate of billions of bits per second, a many-billion-fold increase in speed over 150 years.

All of these trends follow what Internet watchers like to call a "hockey stick" curve: they start slowly and then rapidly accelerate. And while we might feel as if we're at the end of some historical process called "modernization," for most of the world it is just beginning. Today only ten of the world's fifty largest cities are in Europe or North America. And all around us, new actors are streaming one after another into the mix once optimistically described as the global order. States matter less, interconnections make it very hard to trace simple lines between cause (home mortgages) and effect (declining oil prices), and, as we've seen, our smartest-looking policies backfire over and over.

Scientists speak of systems like this as "complex" because their internal dynamics confound easy description and often defy prediction. Change in complex systems, whether they are ecosystems or stock markets, often takes place not in a smooth progression but as a sequence of fast catastrophic events. Not surprisingly, these systems are very hard to manage or design from the outside. They also stump the classical approach of physics, the one we associate with Newton or Aristotle, which relied on the idea that you could reduce the world to building blocks and then assemble everything from them.

Complex-systems scientists, when asked, "What's a complex system?" usually just reply: "Look out the window!" Clouds, mountains, rivers, the whole jumbled and surprising landscape of our world, are expressions of what results from unpredictable interactions. Per Bak, a magnificent scientist whom we'll meet in a bit, once explained the importance of complexity by saying, "Most phenomena around us seem rather distant from the basic laws of physics." He meant that what you see out your window usually can't be explained by the rules of energy or motion that most physicists rely on. They require a leap into a more complex, buried logic. Bak used to tell a joke popular among more rebellious scientists, about the dairy farmer who hired a theoretical physicist for help raising cows that would produce more milk. The physicist came to the farm, spoke with the farmer, disappeared for several years, and then returned with the good news that he had found an answer. "Imagine," he began, "a spherical cow..." Bak's frustration with old ways of seeing the world in science was that they too often began with these sorts of assumptions and simplifications. We'll spend more time with complex systems as this book progresses, so there's no need to be exhaustive here, but keep in mind that their most marked feature is a departure from the idea that our world can be reduced to simple models, that the real dynamics of the world make prediction nearly impossible and demand a different way of thinking. They demolish poor Alan Greenspan's hope that even forty years of experience is a reliable guide to the future.

"Complex systems," as Bak wrote, "can exhibit catastrophic behavior where one part of the system can affect many others by a domino effect. Cracks in the earth's crust propagate this way to produce earthquakes, sometimes with tremendous energies." That is our world now, filled with propagating cracks and surprising energy. Radical change in one area produces radical change elsewhere. Simple interactions, easy-to-map dynamics — they are as common as spherical cows. But this infectious energy of change now exploding around us *can* be harnessed. In fact, it can be understood and used by each of us. It's true that we can no longer rely only on our nations or companies or armies to guarantee our security, that we have to take this responsibility at least partly into our own hands. But as we'll see, such a shift also offers a chance for a profound improvement in how we live and in the sort of planet we'll leave behind. I'm guessing that if you've felt nervous about how little comprehension our leaders seem to have of our financial or security order, you've also felt at least a twinge of moral worry as well: how is it that the most basic problems of human decency are so hard to solve? Well, as we will see, a really dynamic and accurate view of power now can offer a way to engage our world that is not only more reliable but also — and this is crucial — more decent.

Before making this jump to a new model, I want to turn to the underlying physics of our world. We'll begin with a look at where our old ideas about power come from and where they have led us and then move to a different model, one that better incorporates inevitable dynamism and newness. With that done, we'll look around to get a clearer picture of the dangers and possibilities that suddenly become visible, the *unthinkable* made *thinkable*. Then we'll turn, in the second half of the book, to an approach to our future I call "deep security." This is a way of seeing, thinking, and acting that takes the best ideas from the playbook of revolutionary forces and combines them with the demands and responsibilities that our established power places on us. It is a revolutionary approach for a revolutionary age, one whose goal is a return to real safety and prosperity. What we need now, both for our world and in each of our lives, is a way of living that resembles nothing so much as a global immune system: always ready, capable of dealing with the unexpected, as dynamic as the world itself. An immune system can't prevent the existence of a disease, but without one even the slightest of germs have deadly implications. The idea of deep security as an immune system is useful also because the stakes here could not be higher. The problems we are failing to confront now, from nuclear proliferation to global climate change to the rise of new and angry powers, are on a historic scale, and their cost will ultimately be weighed in the lives and deaths of tens of millions of people.

Shortly after World War II, George Kennan, arguably the greatest geostrategist of the last century, holed up at the National War College for a year simply to sit and think and lecture. Kennan had a full, adventurous life, but he later said that no time was as exciting as the year he spent in his Fort McNair office, looking out the window and trying to come to terms with a world whose order was only just becoming apparent. "Today you cannot even do good unless you are prepared to exert your share of power, take your share of responsibility, make your share of mistakes, and assume your share of risks," he said in one of the thirteen magnificent lectures he gave that year. He saw, he said, the phenomenal urgency of finding a new way to think about power. This, in a sense, is where we sit again today, in need of fresh large-scale ideas. I don't propose the instant junking of ideas and institutions—such a move would yield yet more problems. But urgent, steady, ceaseless reform and innovation must begin immediately so that in five years, or at most ten, we will have a new, revolutionary architecture of financial, environmental, and national security built with fresh language and stocked with new minds. This is the most exciting possible moment to be working in international affairs, to be thinking deeply about the forces now violently reordering the globe, to try to change the corporations where we work or the communities where we live. Decades from now, much about how we engage the world will be different as a result of the tsunami whose vibrations I was feeling that day sitting with Fouad sipping coffee. Ahead of us is the invigorating possibility of discovery and reinvention.

CHAPTER TWO

The Old Physics

1. CSI Heidelberg

There was a moment, sometime in the early spring of 1961 or 1962, when The Idea began to crystallize in Dean Babst's mind and he decided, with the kind of certainty that grabs a man sometimes, that he had to get it out into the world. If The Idea seemed unlikely to Babst at first, it was even more unlikely coming *from* Babst, who was a criminologist at the New York State Narcotics Addiction Control Commission. The Idea needed to breathe in more rarefied air than was usually found among criminologists. The Idea was nothing less than a notion designed to drift among the highest rafters of the church of political philosophy, a place generally reserved for the immortal music of men like Immanuel Kant and Niccolò Machiavelli, men who wrote hymns that broke nations, made history. Dean Babst spent his days worrying about why Mexican heroin was weaving its way up the East Coast and into New York's cities or explaining the statistical patterns of marijuana use among hazy-brained rural teenagers. Babst was a man who believed in the power of science to explain the world better than it had ever been explained before. Machiavelli, Kant—their ideas had roots spread back as far as the Athenian agora. But The Idea emerged from a purely modern mindscape, a scientific view of life, and from ways of seeing and calculating that surpassed what even the greatest minds of antiquity might have dreamed up. *We are living in a technological age,* everyone said. Shouldn't that one unmissable fact of modern life, a fact that flavored CBS and Chevrolet and General Electric and every other part of 1960s America, inform our philosophy as well?

As much as any other academic discipline, political philosophy, the work of thinking the grandest possible thoughts about history and power, was a kind of aristocrats' club. Hans J. Morgenthau, then America's giant in theories of political and international relations, occupied his office at the University of Chicago almost as if it were a birthright—which it pretty nearly was. Morgenthau was a German-born intellectual whose eyes seemed to project the very spirit of Kant when he entered a classroom. When he introduced himself, the very cadence of his name was like a hammer of European intellectual righteousness: *Hans. J. Morg-en-thau.* As comfortable quoting the Chinese philosopher Mencius as Machiavelli, he almost seemed to carry with him, like some precious treasure, the last pure DNA of European intellectual history. He had sprinted out of Germany in 1935 as Hitler was rising, and he had been, for decades, one phone call or telegram away from a dozen great statesmen who relied on his judgment. Dean Babst, by contrast, was a forty-three-year-old statistician in midcareer, the kind of figure you'd have been more likely to spot buying a round of Pabst Blue Ribbon at the local Elks club than staring down at you from a gold-rimmed portrait in some library in Heidelberg.

None of this bothered Babst. It wasn't that he didn't know

about Morgenthau and the gentlemen's club. It was that he thought they were out of date, like men using fourteenth-century maps to find their way to Ohio. Babst knew that The Idea, if he could prove it with his criminologist's tools, would be ideological magic. It offered an unimpeachable answer to the noise of the Soviet premier Nikita Khrushchev's famous "We will bury you!" verdict on the question of whether American democracy or Soviet communism, one hundred years hence, would rule the globe.

2. Disney Peace Theory

Babst began by categorizing every major war since the eighteenth century, conflicts as different as the 247-day First Schleswig-Holstein War (6,000 dead) and World War II (2,176 days, 56 million dead). He filed the data in a computer program usually used to track pot and heroin. And he reached this remarkable conclusion: "No wars have been fought between independent nations with elective governments between 1789 [and] 1941." Democracies, the results seemed to suggest, never went to war with one another. Although often engaged in thrashing it out with totalitarian or authoritarian states, countries with elected governments banded into alliances, worked out their problems over tabletops, not battlefields, and never went after each other. Thus, The Idea: democracy equals peace. It was a notion that, in general terms, had roots going as far back as Kant, but until now, Babst thought, it had not had *scientific proof.* Two years after he began his research, Babst put his conclusions into a paper he hoped would remake the debate about how nations danced with one another on the stage of history, a paper that would use science to do to political philosophy what it had already done to armies, to polio, and was even now, President Kennedy promised, about to do to space flight. But where Babst had to publish his paper — *The Wisconsin Sociologist* — told you something about how seriously his ideas were taken in 1964, about how far it was from upstate New York to the corridors of power. He might just as well have chosen the *Journal of the American Veterinary Society*. When, nearly a decade later, Babst reprised his argument in the only slightly less obscure pages of a journal called *Industrial Research* (a step up on the establishment ladder, the intellectual equivalent of a move from a windowless basement studio apartment to one with a window), he was still on the fringes of foreign policy, light-years away from Hans J. Morgenthau.

Yet as political philosophy evolved into political science, something curious happened. The Idea, it turned out, had a quirk that made its rescue from obscurity very nearly inevitable: the texture of real science. Babst had bypassed the usual slow, foreign-accented routes to truth in political philosophy and reached instead for the American tools, *speed tools*, of science and technology. Starting with that list of wars Babst had compiled, it was possible to use computers and math to press into a world of history that you could treat like algebra, to divide time and conflict in thousands of different ways. History became data; the future became output. Political science and international relations could no more resist the arrival of technology than the phone company or your local brain surgeon. All those doctors of political science needed patients to operate on. Babst's axiom was an ideal candidate, a perpetual source of Ph.D.s, offering limitless chances to explore an essential debate. Budding political scientists, following a path well worn by data-happy economists, sociologists, and even anthropologists, now split their time between history books and computer labs. They studied periods of war for all sorts of twitches and spikes. Who started the war? How did it end? Were alliances involved? Could the computer tell you the answer? Learning to program in Fortran became, in some corners, as essential as mastering German or Russian.

So, slowly at first, The Idea, born in Babst's upstate New York home, advanced to the very center of the debate about international affairs. Along the way, it acquired a new name, one sufficiently detached from its origins to make it credible in places like Oxford and New Haven: Democratic Peace Theory. The "Theory" at the end was a nice touch, hinting at scientific rigor and evoking a logical chain that bound Isaac Newton to Immanuel Kant to Albert Einstein to...well, if not Dean Babst, at least to the halls of the universities where The Idea was in vogue. And when, twenty-five years after Babst proposed The Idea, the Soviet Union collapsed, Democratic Peace Theory got a vital boost—one accelerated by the arrival at the highest levels of the U.S. government of political scientists who had studied and admired The Idea. By 2002 Democratic Peace Theory, carried along by what seemed to be the force of history, became the central premise of the foreign policy of the most powerful nation in history. Speaking to an audience of West Point cadets in 2003, President George W. Bush equated American security with global democracy, a theory he was about to test with their blood. America would be secure when the rest of the world became democratic, the president said. (Or, barring that, when it was *made* to be democratic.) Condoleezza Rice, as Bush's secretary of state, realigned the work of the State Department around the mission of promoting democracy, turning American diplomats from mere representatives of their governments into enthusiastic franchise peddlers for democratic revolution. The story of

Dean Babst's Idea rising up out of Albany played like a Disney movie, in which the pudgy junior-high hockey coach is pulled out of retirement and begged to suit up for the Olympics, where he leads his team to a gold medal.

Disney, by the way, would have been the perfect home for such a tale, for Democratic Peace Theory was at heart as much an encapsulation of every triumphalist American dream as Mickey Mouse. Democratic Peace Theory held in its DNA the notion that what was true and sacred about America was the very thing the planet needed most, that the whispered sound of the American Constitution was on the lips of every suppressed soul on earth. By making the world more, well, more American, the United States could not only guarantee its own security but also elevate those poor masses to a world they surely dreamed of, one that looked very much like Phoenix—even if they lived in Peshawar or Tashkent or Beijing.

3. Glass-House Dangers

But, elegant as Democratic Peace Theory looked on paper or on some computer screen, it often stumbled when confronted with reality. In 1999, American bombers struck at the democratically elected government of Serbia in Belgrade—a reminder that ballots were as capable of generating horror as they were of producing allies. In fact, once you got out of your political science department—or walked away from your hobbyist spreadsheets—you inevitably began to find ways in which The Idea fell apart.

Part of the elegant logic of Democratic Peace, for instance, was something like this: if your country is open and democratic,

then my open and democratic country can see what you are thinking. You can see what we are thinking. So we should be able to get
along. International relations scholars Bernard Finel and Kristin
Lord have called this "positive transparency," the idea that more
clarity should mean more stability. So a big, open, transparent,
democratic world should, according to this reasoning, be the most
stable we could hope for. (This argument is echoed in another
classroom-lovely and real-world-deadly notion: that an interconnected global financial system should be more stable, since it
allows easier movement of money and goods. Did more markets
really mean more stability? Not quite. In fact, as we'll see, more
markets only made finance more confusing and dangerous.)

Imagine for a moment that political transparency actually
runs the other way. What if seeing into other nations makes you
more nervous rather than less? What if it confuses your policy making? If your neighbor's house was transparent and you
could watch him polishing his gun collection, would this make
you more nervous or less? What if you just watched him doing
nothing at all, simply watched him while he watched you? In
fact, when Finel and Lord studied a number of historical conflicts, they concluded that a "negative transparency" was often at
work. Openness made countries nervous, confused their leaders,
and quite often made crises worse rather than better.

Once we think about it, this idea of "negative transparency"
may not be all that surprising. Democracies are extremely chaotic and messy. This isn't a judgment about whether they are
good or bad, but a reflection of the fact that democracies have
been defined as the most unpredictable form of government in
the world. And certainly the process of *becoming* truly democratic, as we've seen in places as different as Russia and Taiwan
and Iraq, never follows a smooth path. Without a basis of eco-

nomic development, without a culture of politics that fits democratic discourse, becoming democratic was often a guarantee of instability. Democratizing Arab countries, for instance, might not make them less militant—particularly given cultures that tended to thrive on violent conflict.

And even if countries could manage the transition to democracy, national policy in an elected government can change dramatically, even unrecognizably, from one month to the next. This ebb and flow of open politics might create so much unpredictability that any sane enemy would decide that the safest thing to do is to assume the worst. This is probably the best way to explain why the United States, worried that its interests were at risk, decided to manipulate democratic processes in Iran, Guatemala, Indonesia, British Guiana, Brazil (twice), Chile, and Nicaragua over a period of about forty years. Even if some of these interventions were vitally important to American national interests in the face of Cold War dangers, the record hardly suggests that democracy alone created a stable basis for trust and cooperation. This isn't simply a historical matter: elections in Gaza, Russia, and Iran in recent years all challenge the notion that a democratic process delivers a reliable ally.

Finel and Lord also found numerous examples of "good" traits of democracies that often accelerated conflict instead of easing it. A free press? A magnificent feature of open systems but given at times to war-speeding jingoism. The transparency of democratic systems? An essential part of what makes democracy great—but makes it difficult to conduct secret negotiations that can forestall or shorten conflicts. Responsive democracies, when you begin to look at the tensions and problems that animate national life, at the many-sided virtues that come with a vote, might make the globe more confusing rather than less.

4. The Naturalist of Power

If there was one man who had worked hardest and with the most inventive spirit on the problem of making global power into something more scientific it was Morgenthau, and it is worth understanding the nature of his genius, not only because of his huge influence but also because he represented a very particular way of thinking, one that put states first, assumed countries were rational, and made the bet that pure power was the solution to any problem. Morgenthau was trying to shuffle all the quirks of the global system into some sensible order, to explain wars with the precision that Darwin, say, had brought to biology or Newton to physics.

The idea that international relations could be thought of in such a scientific way had roots in some of the oldest concepts of Western thought, and particularly in the beautifully architected ideas of men like Kant, Hobbes, and Machiavelli, whose voices echo in Morgenthau's work. All were men who prided themselves on developing systems and guidelines. On paper, Morgenthau's ideas looked very similar to that other historical work. But Morgenthau was also very much a man of his turbulent times. You can still feel, on every page of his books, the slow ticking of his psychology: the refugee's demand for pragmatism over daydreams, an inescapable belief in the logic of might and right—and the hope that this sort of brutal calculus could defend against chaos of the sort that had demolished his German childhood. When he sat down to write his masterwork, *Politics Among Nations: The Struggle for Power and Peace,* in the days when World War II was ending, he wanted to put on paper an empirical guide to how the world worked, a handbook that could do for statesmen what the periodic table did for chemists. It became the most influential book in international affairs for fifty years.

To begin with, Morgenthau defined himself as a "realist," a thinker of a school that set store in what he considered to be purely practical, "realistic" theories of policy instead of an ideology, like Nazism or Communism. You should pick ideas and make choices because they worked, because they were practical, and not because you dreamed, as Hitler or Lenin had, that they fit into some larger historical process. The international system, Morgenthau believed, was defined by nation-states ceaselessly wrestling in a contest for security. Idealism, the notion that history should be moved by moral principles such as justice or humanity, struck Morgenthau as a poor basis for policy. Who, after all, was to say what was "moral" and what was not? "The realist," he wrote, "parts company with other schools of thought before the all-important question of how the contemporary world is to be transformed. The realist is persuaded that this transformation can be achieved only through the workmanlike manipulation of the perennial forces that have shaped the past as they will the future." Morgenthau's statesman faced the present with a set of reliable, time-worn tools that he could use to engineer and manipulate what he had in front of him. And nearly every decision of national life could and should be run through this crucial filter: "How does this affect the power of our nation?"

5. The Hat on the Floor

For Morgenthau, national power was something you could apprehend at a fast glance, as you might check the weather outside or the level of your swimming pool. It was *the* ingredient that mattered most, the measure of security whose absence or presence was most obvious. At one point in *Politics Among Nations*, Morgenthau refers to a story from European history, the so-called Dresden interview, a famous meeting between Napoleon and Metternich in late June of 1813. At the time of the meeting, Napoleon has been master of Europe for more than a decade. He has known and even liked Metternich for years. But now, following a humiliating defeat in Russia, the French emperor, then just forty-three, finds himself face-to-face with the forty-year-old Austrian minister of state. The interview lasts for nine hours. Napoleon tries to dissuade Metternich from placing Austria in a coalition intent on demolishing France's place in European power politics. The emperor leans hard on Metternich, sputtering with threats, reaching for all kinds of psychological and emotional tricks, like a cop trying to extract a confession. "Our conference," Metternich wrote later, "consisted of the strangest farrago of heterogeneous subjects, characterized now by extreme friendliness, now by the most violent of fury." At one point Metternich insults the exhausted, drained French army. The soldiers are, he says offhandedly, "no more than children." The emperor explodes. "You are not a soldier," he screams. Napoleon flings his hat into a corner—part theater, part pure rage. He waits, expecting Metternich to pick up the hat. He is, after all, an emperor. The prince does not move. The hat sits on the tiles of the Marcolini Palace like some sad symbol of lost power. Napoleon finally bends over to pick it up himself. "Sire," Metternich says, "you are a lost man." The next day Metternich places Austria in an alliance against France. Less than a year later, Napoleon is exiled to Elba.

Morgenthau's brilliance was to develop an entire physics of global affairs based on the idea that power worked in such direct and almost predictable ways. His statesmen saw their interests clearly. The very word *states-men* told you a lot: these were men who thought, moved, and acted on the scale of nations. Diplomacy was work for wood-paneled rooms, ideally insulated from the pull of domestic tension, an idea known as *das Primat de Aussenpolitik,* or the primacy of foreign affairs. And national power could be tracked with the clarity of that thrown hat: Metternich's refusal to stoop for the emperor told you all you needed to know about the history unfolding there. Sure there were unpredictable moments in battle or in diplomacy, but generally the system should be predictable, since its actors were all rational. Was Napoleon's tantrum irrational? No, it was simply the calculated act of a leader looking for an edge and a man who believed he could achieve face-to-face what his armies might not be able to achieve on the field of battle. Realism, Morgenthau wrote, "shares with all social theory the need, for the sake of theoretical understanding, to stress the rational elements of political reality." He saw his statesmen as working out balances in a system of power that reflected the physics of Newton: capable of equilibrium, predictability, linearity. Using realist precepts, great men like Metternich and Castlereagh could see and measure the threats they faced, could balance them one against the other.

This view of the global stage as a kind of workshop was revolutionary. It was an attack on ancient, persistent schools of thought that saw the progress of history as a result of divine forces, for instance, or saw in history an inevitable working out of some ideological magic, whether it be the natural right of Nazi fascism to rule the planet or the economic inevitability of Marxism. It was an answer as well to the ideas of men like Woodrow Wilson, who had thought that with the right institutions, such as a League of Nations, it would be possible to fashion a stable, peaceful global order that appealed to the higher instincts of men. Morgenthau dismissed such views as fantasy. He ran his world order on that old refugee calculus that power equals survival, and violence is inevitable. In the end, he said, for men and nations alike, only one instinct mattered: the twitch toward mastery of others.

With his "workshop" view of the world, Morgenthau established, more or less, the whole discipline of international relations as a science of sorts. Seventy years after he published *Politics Among Nations*, realist theory still dominates international-relations thinking in most universities. It shapes everything from how we make alliances to how we build institutions that are supposed to control everything from disease to financial panic. And its fundamental premises and language inform even competing schools of thought such as liberalism, internationalism, or bureaucratic-politics theory; they serve as the basis for a Scrabble board of similarly named ideas like *defensive realism* and *neoclassical realism*. Frankly, you can't even begin a serious discussion of international relations without reference to Morgenthau, which is part of the reason I've introduced him here.

Politics Among Nations is one of those rare books of politics that is as beautiful and inspiring as it is sharp. You can see in every sentence why Morgenthau bewitched presidents, diplomats, and theorists. But there is also, on nearly every page, something else: a gnawing sense that he knows he is proposing a way of looking at the world that, like those elegantly naive models of Dean Babst, simplifies the international order to the point of near-irrelevance. Sometimes you only glimpse this wistfulness in passing, buried in footnotes. Moving your eyes from page to footnote and back again in *Politics Among Nations*, you sometimes feel you are reading a pharmaceutical ad, in which a miracle treatment is offset by a host of potentially lethal complications, listed in fine print. Morgenthau will make an expansive and promising and reasonable statement—"The greater the stability of a society, the smaller are the chances for collective emotions to seek an outlet in aggressive nationalism"—only to balance it out with a footnote warning that there are many situations in which this might not be true. Richer, more stable countries should be free from the internal dangers that pushed places like Germany and Japan to insanity and war. But, he says in a note, that assumes such nations are free from "class struggle, revolution, urban violence and civil war"—the very forces that do make history.

Morgenthau knew better, and his worries leak out in his speeches and in the most personal passages in his writing. He had, after all, lived with the Nazis, had lived the costs of those footnoted forces. You could no more edit such dangers out of your models than you could out of your life. "Political reality," he confesses, not without some sense of frustration, "is replete with contingencies and systemic irrationalities." And he knew the limits of using science to model humans, a tension he had explored with masterful fluency in an earlier book, *Scientific Man Versus Power Politics*. The truth was, he wrote, the world wasn't a math problem. It wasn't simply replete with contingency and irrationality; in some ways it seemed to be nothing but contingency and irrationality. Yet in their eagerness to bring some sense of order to that reality, many of Morgenthau's more enthusiastic acolytes pushed these dynamic parts of the system off to the side.

6. The Price of Simplicity

"Systematic irrationalities" have always tripped up simplicities like Democratic Peace Theory, have always challenged policy

makers, whether they are American presidents or Roman generals. This is one of the reasons that, when they finally do get their
hands on real power, many foreign-affairs academics or economic
masters are quick to leave their beautiful scholarly ideas behind.
Lawrence Summers, the Harvard economist who became secretary of the treasury under Bill Clinton and then head of the
National Economic Council under Barack Obama, once said to
me that the most important thing he had learned from Robert
Rubin, his predecessor at the Treasury and a rigorously practical former Goldman Sachs trader, was to "adopt a probabilistic
view of the world and discard the black-and-white models that
make for success in academia." During talks with the Chinese
premier Zhou Enlai that reestablished U.S.-China relations, for
instance, there was a memorable exchange in which another former Harvard professor, Henry Kissinger (then national security
advisor), said to the Chinese leader that many of the ideas the
two of them were discussing were almost exactly the opposite of
what the theories he once taught would have suggested. Lovely
as they were in the classroom, those Cambridge models were
largely useless in reality.

The complex physics of our world now makes this even more
apparent. The more beautiful a theory is in the lab or those Heidelberg halls or some guy's basement, the less it seems to hew to
a reality in which, to give just one example, states and their leaders aren't always rational. (Or they may be rational in a way we
think is crazy—a conundrum captured in a popular quip about
Iran at the turn of the millennium, that the country needed to
decide "if it was a nation or a jihad.") The idea that two nations
could ever see their interests in the same way assumes a sort of
objectivity that's impossible. And the allegedly clear, stable,
knowable interests of states are often none of those things. They

change and move as rapidly as our personal idea of our "interest" changes as we age, confront crises, strike it rich. National interest can be jarred and reshaped in an instant. Pearl Harbor transformed many Americans' view of the country's position in a single morning. That day, Senator Arthur Vandenberg sadly remarked, "ended isolationism for any realist." September 11 was a similar shock. The old line that "there are no permanent friends in international relations, only permanent interests," got it half right. Even interests themselves can be refigured with incredible speed.

Realism now falls down in other ways, too. It famously assumes, for instance, that states have a monopoly on violence. But in this age of computer hackers, terrorists, and drug cartels, that's certainly no longer entirely accurate. And, confronted with the peculiar nature of a financially interconnected world, where danger, risk, and profit are linked in ways that can be impossible to spot and manage, theories that involve only armies and diplomats don't have much use. Political power is spreading more widely than it did when Morgenthau wrote. More than 90 percent of the nongovernmental organizations in the world were created in the past ten years, for instance. And recall Morgenthau's line about the uselessness of morality, that only might made right? Even if such an assumption were honest enough, because it can be hard to say who is right or wrong in a moral argument, some of the most energetic modern forces, as different in their decency as Hizb'allah and Greenpeace, draw power from an explicitly ethical worldview. You might disagree with the morality of such groups, it might look twisted when lined up against your own, but their followers are unquestionably driven by lively ethics as much as by a lust for power. The classical models shuffled such worries into the footnotes because they were too hard to model. Unfortunately, these worries are now among the most important parts of the system.

7. Who's in Charge?

The revolutionary physics of our world now has the effect of taking what might have been idle curiosities in one era—the charming but simple ideas of journalists, say, or the theories of criminologists who were history buffs—and turning them into dangerous weapons of self-destruction, as if one tried to use Newtonian physics to control a nuclear reactor. But this is an important reminder before we move on. When confronted now with "experts" giving advice about the international situation or proposing to conduct diplomacy on your behalf, it is not unreasonable to ask about their background. What are they rounding out or footnoting in their own thinking that they might not even be aware of? In the past we might have believed that the best preparation for a career in foreign policy was a fluency with European history, an ability to speak Russian or French, an understanding of the roots of world order. The future demands a different résumé. Today the ideal candidates for foreign-policy power should be able to speak and think in revolutionary terms. They should have an expertise in some area of the world—be it China or the Internet or bioengineering—where fast change and unpredictability are the dominant facts of life. They should have experienced the unforgiving demands for precision and care that characterize real negotiation—as well as the magical effect of risk-taking at the right moments. They should have mastered the essential skill of the next fifty years: crisis management. And they should be inclined toward action, even action at times without too much reflection, since at certain moments instinct and speed are more important than the lovely perfection of academic models. The recent history of American foreign policy is filled with tales of academic or journalistically trained bureaucrats who were paralyzed instead of energized by the demand for what Churchill used to call "action this day." Most of all, however, we need policy makers and thinkers who have that intuitive revolutionary feel for the inescapable demands of innovation. We need early adopters, men and women who touch newness and change as an almost totemic reminder of what is possible in the human spirit and who are honest about the fights and struggles that lie ahead. Believing, for instance, that the triumph of democracy and capitalism is inevitable should disqualify you immediately from a serious position in foreign policy.

Today our global policy is largely conducted by elites who are descendants of Morgenthau and disciples of Babst. By definition such people make pretty poor revolutionaries. Why change a system that's been working well for *you?* This makes it vitally important that they learn to think in terms that can correct the blindness that a Harvard education or decades of living in Washington, D.C., seems to produce. At a time when the major international issues were contests between nations, when those hat-dropping Metternich moments turned the pages of history, putting the winners in society in charge of policy might have been reasonable. Anyhow, it was probably inevitable. (Though it still led to many bloody confrontations.) But in an era when many of the most dynamic forces in society come from outside elite circles, from geeks who in the past might have been thought of as "losers," such an approach is an error of catastrophic proportions.

It isn't easy to accept that the world is being shaped by forces

you don't understand and can't agree with. It requires a willingness to master some of that strangeness instead of simply labeling
it as "mad" or trashing it as "evil." It means getting comfortable
with the attitude that Niels Bohr once described as an inevitable
part of a quantum view, that tickling "are you kidding me?" feeling as you try something a bit nuts only to discover that it works
wonderfully. Building a bureaucracy that can do that, populating
it with minds capable of such leaps, is going to require a heroic act
of reimagination on our part. But, as I think you'll see by the end
of this book, there's no reason to think we're not capable of it.

8. "The Pretence of Knowledge"

In December 1974 the Austrian economist Friedrich August von
Hayek received one of the very first Nobel Prizes in economics. Hayek was a prince of the same European intellectual court
that had produced men like Morgenthau. A genius economist,
he had been among the first to describe how central banks could
use money to influence the expansion and contraction of economies. On the afternoon of December 11, delivering the traditional Nobelist's lecture, Hayek first remarked what a privilege it
was to receive the award. The addition of a Nobel in economics
to those given for hard sciences such as physics, chemistry, and
medicine was, he said, a sign of the field's graduation from black
art to real social *science*. The Nobel Prize, he began, "marks a
significant step in the process by which, in the opinion of the
general public, economics has been conceded some of the dig-
nity and prestige of the physical sciences."

But, Hayek said, he was wondering just how much of that
prestige was really justified. "Economists are at this moment,"

he continued, "called upon to say how to extricate the free world from the serious threat of accelerating inflation, which, it must be admitted, has been brought about by policies which the majority of economists recommended and even urged governments to pursue. We have indeed at the moment little cause for pride: as a profession we have made a mess of things." Thus Hayek began what was essentially a twenty-minute apology for winning a Nobel Prize.

Hayek titled his speech "The Pretence of Knowledge," and what he had to say was important not simply as a set of observations about economics. To treat complex phenomena as if they were simple, to pretend that you could hold the unknowable in the cleverly crafted structure of your ideas—he could think of nothing that was more dangerous. "There is much reason," Hayek said, "to be apprehensive about the long-run dangers created in a much wider field by the uncritical acceptance of assertions which have the appearance of being scientific." And if you insert "foreign policy experts" or "financial gurus" for "economists" in Hayek's remarks, well, you have a sad, disturbing summary of the state of our world at the moment.

Concluding his Nobel speech, Hayek warned, "If man is not to do more harm than good in his efforts to improve the social order, he will have to learn that in this, as in all other fields where essential complexity of an organized kind prevails, he cannot acquire the full knowledge which would make mastery of the events possible." Politicians and thinkers would be wise not to try to bend history as "the craftsman shapes his handiwork, but rather to cultivate growth by providing the appropriate environment, in the manner a gardener does for his plants."

To see the world this way, as a ceaselessly complex and adaptive system, requires a revolution. It involves changing the role we imagine for ourselves, from architects of a system we can control and manage to gardeners in a living, shifting ecosystem. For hundreds of years now we have lived in our minds as builders: constructing everything from nations to bridges, heedlessly grabbing whatever resources we've needed in pursuit of a dream of some imagined palace of global prosperity. This mode of existence, which delivered amazing progress, is no longer suitable. The world is too complex, its resources too limited, and its internal dynamics too unstable to accommodate much more of this mania. It is now delivering the opposite of what we intend even as it presents us with new and insoluble problems. In a revolutionary age, with rapid change all around us, our architects' tools are deadly. It is time for us to put them down and follow Hayek's injunction to live and to think as gardeners.

CHAPTER THREE

The Sandpile

1. Mussel Shoals

Shortly after September 11, 2001, the National Academy of Sciences called together a group of American scientists and presented them with a question: could science and technology combat terrorism? With great minds hustling from lab to Pentagon and back again, the meetings had a sort of 1950s smell to them, reminiscent of the early Cold War, a time when the firm knot of American technology and policy seemed to promise the greatest security. In meeting after meeting, the eight subcommittees the academy had assembled imagined all sorts of potential disasters and tried to outthink them. The teams were a Who's Who of modern American science: plucky Nobelists, directors of some of the largest labs on earth, professors so brilliant they would never have to teach a single class. In a reflective moment, you might have pictured this battle of minds as a contest between science and fundamentalism, sketched out in the lives of Americans and the country's enemies, except that there were moments (too many of them, if you wanted to ask) when science and technology appeared to be on the side of terror. In the days after the National Academy began planning these gatherings, someone mailed envelopes filled with military-grade anthrax spores to the offices of the *National Enquirer.*

Of course, none of the scientists who would later make up the biological-risks committee needed this particular bit of news to begin thinking about the world's vulnerability to chemical or bioweapons. "Simply enormous," one of the committee members told me when I asked him about America's exposure to the dangers of bioviolence or bioaccident. Such worries had haunted these scientists for years, with the mental constancy that you or I might devote to worrying about a sick family member or an impending exam we fear we are bound to fail. Anthrax letters mailed by a rogue lab rat were a small threat compared to the list the bioscientists carried around in their heads: mutant genes directed at American wheat, say, or superpersistent versions of viruses such as Ebola, distributed via suicidal, self-infected human biobombs. By the end of 2006 it was possible to download the complete genetic recipe for smallpox from the Internet; you could order or make most of the deadly virus's base pairs with similar ease. Within a few years it would likely be possible to build a homemade, vaccine-resistant version of smallpox for about the cost of a used car. Earlier in 2001, some of those same scientists at the National Academy meeting had participated in a war game called Dark Winter, an epidemiological horror show in which a simulated smallpox outbreak, starting with a single infected patient, killed millions in the span of a few weeks. The results were so upsetting that the Pentagon pulled the plug before the simulation had run its course. A special presidential panel would warn a few years later, in 2008, that a bioattack by 2013 was probably inevitable.

As the biological-risks committee was working through the

usual list of suggestions—stockpile vaccines, develop air sniffers, distribute medical-crisis kits to American hospitals—one member, a Princeton professor named Simon Levin, sat watching the proceedings unfold, a quiet worry working up in his mind, ever louder. Levin is an ecologist, but an unlikely one. A mathematician by training, he had stumbled into ecology when his passion for the environment led him into the particularly complex, hard-to-model systems that abound in nature. The result was a set of groundbreaking 1970s studies based on his research in mussel shoals off the coast of Washington State with Robert Paine (a man so fond of remote places and bivalves that he earned a reputation as a sort of Edmund Hillary of wild mussels). Though Levin confesses to having "the opposite of whatever a green thumb for fieldwork is," his particular genius was the ability to take Paine's fieldwork—extensive data that rarely fit elegantly into the usual equations of natural science—and develop models in which math was less a straitjacket than a comfortable robe.

We all remember Charles Darwin for explaining the process of evolution, but his notebooks also contain pages of failed attempts to bring math to bear on the chaos of ecological development, a reminder that even genius hits a wall from time to time. Levin was one of the first thinkers to get past Darwin's wall. Starting in those mussel shoals, he began developing numerical pictures of nature that had an impressive fidelity, particularly when describing what happens to ecological systems that are hit by an unexpected shock. The models changed the face of ecology. Yet for all his fame among environmental scientists, Levin retains the geeky demeanor of a mathematician: long silences punctuated by koan-like insights, an equal penchant for both intellectual rigor and conversational digression. His Patagonia vests and Birkenstocks are often the only hint of the ecologist's energy that animates his thinking.

As Levin listened to the discussions at the National Academy of Sciences meetings, to the lists of things that needed to be planned and positioned against the most reasonable of paranoias, he became convinced there was a deeper, more fundamental problem that no one was talking about. Whatever he and the other minds on the committee could think of, Levin concluded, the terrorists could think of something else. "We could build up stocks of every known vaccine on the planet," he later recalled. "But it wouldn't matter. They could just engineer something we had never seen before." As soon as civil defense planners stored up protection against one biothreat, Levin suspected, terrorists would simply uncork a different, more horrible, more surprising test tube. Or perhaps they would unleash something we *did* know how to deal with, but only to exhaust our doctors and hospitals and soldiers before releasing, hours later, some horror we had never imagined. "This wasn't some dumb game-theory model you were playing with," he told me one afternoon as we sat in his office at Princeton. "It was an *adaptive* enemy. Whatever you did, they still had an ability to think around it and surprise you. There was a limit to how much you could prepare." War planners used to look at threats around the world, hundreds of potential nightmares, and, as bad as they all were, they could at least be numbered, ranked, monitored, anticipated. "Is there anything we haven't thought of?" they might ask. And they could feel with some certainty that there was not. But this new world? With destabilizing dangers which emerged not only from crafty enemies but also from the day-to-day technology that we needed to survive—airplanes or genetic engineering or commodities markets—it was very hard to find a spot where our normal lives ended and risk began.

Levin noticed something else that worried him. Complex problems like the ones the bioterror team was staring at have a particularly eerie characteristic: they tend to become more complex as time goes on. The systems never get simpler. There was no moment at which they would evaporate or condense into a single, easy-to-spot target such as the USSR. The 1979 Islamic revolution in Iran, for example, was a single very knotty event that, in turn, gave birth to hundreds of jihadist groups, each of which developed different methods of terror, particular techniques of attack and destruction, which themselves were always changing and evolving. It was like a cruel scientific version of the old Middle Eastern quip that "friends come and go; enemies accumulate." Complexities accumulated. This was a security problem that could never be solved by traditional security alone.

Levin was suddenly very interested.

Recall that Levin's most brilliant work had not involved the easy, everyday math of natural systems but rather those moments of radical change, the big shifts caused by storms, extinctions, or new life. And what three decades of mussels, mathematics, and other science had convinced him of was that when the system changed, you had to change the way you thought about it, or else even carefully assembled data would appear to be meaningless mush. This was exactly the sort of problem Louis Halle described when he talked about the dangers of making foreign policy with an image that was out of date and wrong.

One afternoon, as Levin and I were sitting together after lunch at the Princeton Faculty Club, we began wondering if we might use the models he and others had developed to think about international affairs, to navigate the change to a more complex, revolutionary world. I began spinning his own insights back to him, but with small changes: "international system" instead of "nature," "terrorists" instead of "viruses," and so on. Levin nodded. The question he and I were facing together is the one I want to turn to now: is there some model, some intellectual picture, that does a better job of capturing the dynamics of the complex world around us than the models we saw in the last chapter? Can we find a way of understanding this revolutionary age that doesn't require us to do all the rounding and footnoting that doomed the old models?

This isn't an easy challenge, but Levin was quick to point out that it was exactly the sort of evolution that science itself had made in recent years. The economist Brian Arthur, a friend of Levin's who noticed similar phenomena in his field, framed the problem this way: "The story of the sciences in the twentieth century is one of a steady loss of certainty. Much of what was real and machine-like and objective and deterministic at the start of the century, by mid-century was a phantom, unpredictable, subjective and indeterminate." Of course, during that same time, science had made more progress than it had in all of human history. It wasn't just Werner Heisenberg injecting uncertainty into quantum physics. It was Alfred Tarski bringing unpredictability to mathematics, Kurt Gödel bringing incompleteness to logic, Benoit Mandelbrot doing the same for fluid dynamics and Gregory Chaitin for information theory. They all proved that once you made the leap to a new model—if it was the right model—then accepting uncertainty and indeterminacy allowed you to make sense of parts of the world you had never understood before. Problems that seemed unapproachable by old methods became explainable: radioactivity, antimatter, the movement of light. "Sometimes in science," Levin said to me, "we find that we have reached the end of the bookshelf. Then it is time to write new books."

2. The Sandpile

The Thomas J. Watson Research Center in Yorktown Heights, New York, is testament to the fact that since the founding of the International Business Machines Corporation, IBM has always tried to produce ideas, not just boxes with plugs. In a way, the lab is a giant, campus-sized expression of Watson's famous admonition, once plastered on corporate walls all over the world: "Think." One of the virtues of working at the Watson lab is that you can chase down pretty much any idea that seems interesting, whether or not it has much to do with computers or databases or anything that will ever be sold to anyone. The Watson lab is a place for "pure" research, which generally means "free from commercial use." And somehow, despite all the ups and downs in the computer business, it has held on to this mandate.

The main building at the lab is a giant white limestone crescent that sits atop a small hill and affords a commanding view of the surrounding Hudson River valley landscape. The Watson Center contains a mix of offices and labs, and the spirit of fellowship makes it feel more like a university than a company. When I recently visited, the experiments under way in the labs included everything from studies about how frogs think to why clouds "decide" to rain. The office of Glenn A. Held, a physicist with a specialty in materials science, was for many years on the second floor. (Held left recently to join a hedge fund, a switch from science without commerce — *Think.* — to its more lucrative opposite — *Earn!*). Held is a small, graying man with a visibly strong natural curiosity. He is the sort who would, as he once did with me, take you to lunch and then drag you into a lecture on cellular electrical communication under the (incorrect) assumption that even if you didn't understand a word, it would still be interesting.

In the late 1980s, a few years after he had joined IBM, Held began noticing a great deal of discussion among scientists about a conjecture made by a Danish physicist and biologist named Per Bak. Bak's idea had to do with one of those things in science that seem simple on the surface but that in fact contain many layers of complexity, layers that go far beyond what current knowledge can explain. With Galileo, for instance, those famous balls he dropped off the Tower of Pisa to measure gravity's pull represented such a case: simple on the surface but loaded, in reality, with deep problems. Why *did* a heavy ball and a light ball take the same amount of time to reach the ground? This was a puzzle, one of those one-sentence questions that take centuries to answer. The problem that fascinated Bak also appeared, on the surface, simple enough: if you piled sand, grain by grain, until it made a cone about the size of your fist, how would you know when that tiny pyramid would have a little avalanche? After all, as the pile got taller, and the sides became steeper, it was inevitable that some sand would slide off. Could you predict when? Could you predict how much? Simple question, terribly hard to answer.

Bak, who died in 2002 at age fifty-four, was called by one of his friends "the most American of Danish scientists." What his friend meant was that Bak liked arguing and inventing, preferably at the same time. The idea Bak had invented for his sandpile was a radical one, a new way of looking at physics that, if he was right, had dramatic implications. Bak hypothesized that after an initial period, in which the sand piled itself into a little cone, the stack would organize itself into instability, a state in which adding just a single grain of sand could trigger a large avalanche—or nothing at all. What was radical about his idea was that it implied that these sand cones, which looked relatively stable, were in fact deeply unpredictable, that you had absolutely no way of knowing what was going to happen next, that there was a mysterious relationship between input and output. You could see the way physics struggled against the very limits of language when confronted with such a concept: *organized* instability? Bak wanted to know what exactly caused an avalanche to occur at any given moment. This was, it emerged, very difficult to say—at least through traditional science. "Complex behavior in nature," Bak explained, "reflects the tendency of large systems to evolve into a poised 'critical' state, way out of balance, where minor disturbances may lead to events, called avalanches, of all sizes."

What Bak was trying to study wasn't simply stacks of sand, but rather the underlying physics of the world. And this was where the sandpile got interesting. He believed that sandpile energy, the energy of systems constantly poised on the edge of unpredictable change, was one of the fundamental forces of nature. He saw it everywhere, from physics (in the way tiny particles amassed and released energy) to the weather (in the assembly of clouds and the hard-to-predict onset of rainstorms) to biology (in the stutter-step evolution of mammals). Bak's sandpile universe was violent—and history-making. It wasn't that he didn't see stability in the world, but that he saw stability as a passing phase, as a pause in a system of incredible—and unmappable—dynamism. Bak's world was like a constantly spinning revolver in a game of Russian roulette, one random trigger-pull away from explosion.

Scientists call systems like the sandpile or the universe "nonlinear," precisely because their internal dynamics routinely disrupt the idea that you can expect a given action to produce the same reaction every time. If you could find a way to model these systems, you might gain some insight into how and why they evolved over really long periods of time—exactly the sorts of problems, puzzles of the "where did we come from and where are we going?" variety, that had stumped even the most advanced theories. But no one had mastered the ability to model them with any accuracy, even though they were so central to science that physicist and mathematician Stanislaw Ulam once observed that calling any part of science "nonlinear science" was like calling any part of zoology "non-elephant zoology." Most aspects of the world, Bak insisted, and maybe the most important parts of the universe, were defined by being poised out of balance, moving not in a smooth line but in fits and starts. Geology provided the easiest analogy for such thinking: southern California, after all, looks very stable most days.

3. Power Laws

The idea of a sandpile and its avalanches began as a "thought experiment" of the sort that scientists, particularly big-idea scientists like Bak, loved: you did the math in your mind or on a computer, playing with the variables as much as you wanted without ever having to actually step into a lab. Glenn Held, however, was an experimental scientist, so when he read what Bak and others had written, he asked himself, "Well, what would happen if we tried this in real life?" How often *would* those sand avalanches occur? Were the ideas in Bak's head also true in the lab? Bak had first suggested the idea in a theoretical journal; he didn't seem to have much of an intention to test it in reality. Could it be done?

How do you build a sandpile grain by grain? No one had ever attempted it. So Glenn Held decided to give it a try.

To begin with, Held needed grains that were more or less the same size, since clumps of sand would distort the evenness of the pile. In pursuit of something reliably sandlike, he began experimenting with grains of aluminum oxide, but he eventually discovered that beach sand, collected on weekend trips to the shore, was more than sandlike enough. Held filtered what he collected to get grains of more or less the same size. He made sure that the grains were all dry (any moisture would have altered their weight and interfered with the experiment). Then he placed the sand in a jerry-rigged machine that looked sort of like an automatic pepper mill connected to (of course) an IBM PC. The computer controlled how fast the mill turned and how many grains trickled out on each rotation. This allowed Held to drop the grains precisely onto a palm-sized plate. He put the plate on a scale so he could measure how much sand was falling on and off the pile (each grain weighed .0006 ounce) and then propped the scale inside a Plexiglas case so stray air-conditioning breezes wouldn't disturb his pile. Building the device took him about ten hours. Then Held turned it on.

The first sandpile, which took a day to build, the grains dropping carefully one at a time, was about two inches across on the bottom. Just as Bak had predicted, during an initial period the pile shaped itself into a cone, an example of what physicists call "self-organization." No one was telling the grains where to go; the intrinsic physics of falling sand just meant that, over time, they sorted themselves into a nice even pile instead of spraying all over the place.

Once a pile reached a certain size, Held saw, it entered that strange "critical" state Bak had anticipated. Sometimes one additional grain would cause an avalanche; other times Held could add thousands of grains before the sand started sliding off. Held discovered a surface pattern to the avalanches, something scientists call a "power law," which also applies to the distribution of other nonlinear natural phenomena, such as earthquakes. (Charles F. Richter, the father of the Richter scale, teased the pattern from centuries of earthquake data: large earthquakes occur exponentially less frequently than small ones. This is called a "power-law distribution.")

But the most interesting thing about the sandpile was its fundamental unpredictability. You couldn't take your eyes off it for an instant. The power law told you the general chances of getting an avalanche, but would that next grain of sand set one off? Traditional science saw the sandpile as stable, in an equilibrium state, something that might have an avalanche when disturbed by some strong outside force or when the number of grains reached a particular quantity. But Held's sandpile behaved quite differently. There was no magic number. One additional grain of sand was as likely to start an avalanche as a dozen. What happened *within* the pile, the shifting and sliding of the grains, was as important as what happened *to* the pile. There was no explicit link between how you hit the pile and how it responded, no "proportionality" between cause and effect. Just as Bak had theorized, the sandpile was a system that could "break down not only under the force of a mighty blow, but also at the drop of a pin."

Held wondered how you might model such a system. Frankly, this was a difficult puzzle. Every grain on the pile was, in a sense, linked by invisible webs of pressure and tension to every other grain. So the full dynamics of sand physics grew in complexity a millionfold every second. New grain of sand? Okay, you had to remap *everything*. No computer could work that fast. The nature of this expanding complexity demolished the concept of prediction. "As one attempts to make predictions further and further into the future," Bak had speculated, "the amount of information one needs to gather about the initial conditions increases exponentially." And this is exactly what Held saw inside that Plexiglas case. While you might be able to predict how one or two or even a hundred grains would interact, by the time you got to a thousand grains, it was impossible to measure every little detail you'd need to even try to guess what was going to happen next. Such a world was beyond the scope of even the most complex forms of Newtonian physics. In Bak's mind there was almost no limit to how far you might extend this logic. Any complex system likely expressed the same dynamics: the earth's crust, ecosystems, stock markets, international politics. Past a certain point, the internal dynamics of these systems were simply, bewilderingly unknowable.

Held tried making piles on larger and larger plates and found that, after a certain size, even the power-law distribution of avalanches disappeared. The systems became so complex that no rules offered even a general sense of how often a grain of sand would lead to catastrophe. You just had to sit there and watch, grain by grain, and wait. And while you sat there, you could think about this: nothing in the history of physics or mathematics could tell you what was going to happen next.

Bak's world wasn't stable or well ordered. The chaos, the random, hectic shifting and shuffling of Held's microscopic beach particles, was an expression of energy of a sort, energy just as likely to create as to destroy. The sandpile was in a continuous state of change; it never stood still long enough for any one set of equations to describe it fully. If Bak was right about his theory, it should be as true outside the lab as inside—and that would demand nothing less than a complete revolution in how the scientists around him thought. There was something profound and amazing in the dynamics of the piles, he thought: their ability not only to translate order into chaos, but also to translate chaos into order. Sand grains, stocks, pieces of the earth's crust—these moved not according to some simple input and output formula but rather because of a complex logic, where dense internal forces were as important as any outside forces. Avalanches and earthquakes expressed that logic, but what got Bak excited was that the same physics was also at work when the sandpiles produced California from pebbles, or great fortunes from the movement of markets. The sandpile seemed to *make* things, maybe even most of the world.

Bak liked to pass along a quote from the nineteenth-century French novelist Victor Hugo as a prescient summary of the idea: "How do we know that the creations of worlds are not determined by falling grains of sand?" What if the real world was like this, precariously unbalanced between stability and chaos? Bak wondered. If the logic of such a complex system could be penetrated, even a little bit, there might be no limit to what you could create. The world wasn't a slew of senseless randomness; it just required new and different ways of calculating. If you could manage to discover those new ways, even the most difficult problems would open up. This had happened before—repeatedly—in science. But if the system remained opaque? If the logic stayed buried in those shifting sand grains? Well, then, science would continue chasing the phantoms that had undone every model for the universe ever created. The logic of the world, even while expressing an immense inner order, would continue to appear to us as a senseless riot.

4. Saint-Tropez

One morning in July 2007, the investor Bill Browder woke up in his vacation house in the south of France. It was Browder's habit to write a letter to investors in his $2 billion Hermitage Fund once a month, not only updating them about the state of the fund and its investments but also expressing his thoughts about the markets more generally. Browder had started doing this more than a decade before, when he was launching Hermitage with a small investment from Edmond Safra, the legendary Lebanese banker. Hermitage was a fund that invested in one of the most unstable markets in the world—Russia—and Browder's ups and downs there had made him a legend in the world of investing. (A legend not a little burnished by the fact that he was the grandson of Earl Browder, a former head of the American Communist Party.) Browder's investment model at Hermitage wasn't just to buy and sell Russian stocks. It was to buy shares in the most corrupt, worst-run Russian companies and then press them to change. A company whose shares traded at $1 because it was overseen and looted by goons could be worth $10 a share if it was managed even slightly better. Buy, agitate, sell: this was Browder's strategy. And, given the people he was dealing with, between "agitate" and "sell" he made sure he had plenty of security if need be.

Working in Russia over the years had accustomed Browder to the fact that markets could snap in ways that are largely unimaginable, susceptible to sandpile-type forces that are invisible until they strike. In 1998, for instance, Hermitage had almost been wiped out when the Russian stock market lost 93 percent of its value in a matter of weeks. Was this avalanche triggered by some

terrible Russian problem? Some deep hole in his investing strategy? No, the root cause was a confidence crisis that had begun
more than a year earlier. In Thailand.

Browder had been through a number of such neck-snapping
"how did *that* happen" crises, and they had sharpened how he
thought about markets. "When you've been in a market that
really can go to zero, it changes the way you think afterward," he
told me. "The main lesson is that just because something is too
terrible to contemplate doesn't mean it's not going to happen." At
heart Browder was someone who believed that markets could be
well run and efficient. After all, the whole premise of Hermitage
was that if you could clean up companies, they could attain their
real value on the Russian exchanges. But the lesson of his years
in Russia was that as solid as the foundations of a market might
look at any given moment, they were, in fact, made of sand. And
if you forgot that for even an instant, you would end up like the
dozens of his fellow investors Browder had seen broken and
bankrupted over his decade and a half in Russia.

In that summer of 2007, Browder was in the midst of a very
good quarter—his fund was up some 30 percent in the past few
months—but this habit of living on his toes, of looking for any
sign that the landscape around him was about to avalanche away,
drew his attention to a news item in the papers that July morning. In New York an auction of debt from leveraged-buyout deals
had failed to draw enough bidders and was shut down. To most
of the investing world this looked simply like a small hiccup in
an otherwise well-functioning financial system. But Browder
recognized it for what it was: a sign that the world had run out
of the ability to absorb new debt. It was the end of a Ponzi-like
scheme and, he knew, the start of an avalanche that might reach
a historic, tragic scale. Having been through this before, in

Russia, he knew exactly how bad the markets could get. It gave him a very clear sense of what was perhaps about to happen to global markets. No preparation could be too much. "This is it," he told me a few days later, as we were catching up by phone. "This is the end. And it will now all start to unravel."

Writing to his investors that week, Browder explained that he had seen what a $40 billion hole in the Russian balance sheet had done to that country (demolished its financial system) and that from where he sat, "a US$300-billion problem is simply a lot larger than a US$40-billion problem, and the implications for world markets will be similarly greater." And, he cautioned, the final price tag on what would come to be known as the subprime-mortgage crisis was likely to be much bigger than $300 billion. Almost immediately, he began stockpiling cash, reducing his exposure to stocks as much as he could, and moving his and his investors' money into any safe haven he could find. He began to pioneer what he called an "off-the-grid" investing style. "The analogy is an electrical black-out," he wrote his investors. "Those working in an office building get paralyzed, but those living in a cabin in the mountains hardly notice. We want to achieve the financial markets' equivalent of living in a cabin in the mountains." Or, if you wanted to put it another way, he was trying to outrun a tsunami.

One of the lessons of international finance is that from time to time large economic storms come along and wipe out huge pieces of the global economy. And our modern trading systems often seem to be self-fulfilling disaster machines in this regard. "The problem with global financial markets," Larry Summers mused to me at the height of the 1997 Asian economic crisis, "is that they are like modern jet planes. They get you where you need to go faster, but the crashes are far, far worse." This was what happened to some degree in the 1987 U.S. stock market crash, when an accumulation of small factors led to a sudden systemic change that tore up years of market value. It happened again during the Asian crisis that in 1997 and 1998 lopped Browder's fund by 75 percent. In each case the markets had simply become unglued from any normal rules of behavior, had gone "nonlinear," as the hedge-fund jockeys liked to say. None of the tools used to predict or explain what was happening worked. With no better reason than that *everyone else is getting out,* investors dumped and ran. "In crises like this," Browder said, "people sell first and ask questions later." Sometimes these ripples of unknowable economic physics hit only a few innocent bystanders — the arrogant yuppies tagged by the 1987 crash, a poorly educated Mexican treasury hit in 1995, the random unlucky Thai real estate developer nailed in 1998. But every once in a while the physics come along and munch away decades of civilized life, the way the 1929 stock market crash tightened Europe's downward economic spiral, helping to elevate Hitler and the whole horrible historical train wreck that came afterward. Looking at what was happening in 2007 and then into 2008, Browder asked himself, *Is this another one of those historic crises?*

A unique kind of panic emerges at such moments. If you went to one of the hastily called meetings in the wood-paneled rooms of the Council on Foreign Relations or if you sat with the best financial minds in the City in London or at a Starbucks in Greenwich, you could see a strange and creeping fear. It was weird in a way, because these were investors who had made fortunes from instability and volatility in markets. They had devised instruments to capture and contain and profit from it. Even to *encourage* it. But when what they thought of as the usual rules didn't apply, they became, very quickly, like Greenspan in his fall 2008 congressional testimony: humbled, perplexed, and worried.

Browder never made a decision without thinking about the downside—not just once but constantly. He knew this was the only safe approach in markets that could, like one of Bak's sand-piles, collapse under the pressure of a pin. Change in such a system would come fast and would be merciless to anyone who was not flexible and prepared. What Browder saw in 2007 was that the real dynamics of the world were about to assert themselves.

By the time most of the planet understood what Browder had realized on that summer morning, however, thirteen crucial months had passed.

5. Way out of Balance

Our world, whether we are looking at financial markets or nuclear proliferation, now resembles Bak's sandpiles in many nervous-making ways. To begin with, it is defined by the two explosive bits of physics that interested him most: increasing numbers of players and connections between them. If you'd like, you can think of these two effects as *granularity*—the unstoppable tumbling of fresh grains of sand onto our pile—and *interdependence*—the surprising connections that link one part of the pile with another. But what matters is that these two effects represent a revolutionary change in the physics of power, a change that has to inform every strategy or policy we make from now on. When Bak described the "tendency of large systems to evolve into a poised 'critical' state, way out of balance, where minor disturbances may lead to events, called avalanches, of all sizes," he could have been speaking about the Middle East, relations between the United States and China, the oil market, disease, nuclear proliferation, cyberwarfare or a dozen other problems of global affairs and security. Every day now, new players and forces are trickling onto the pile of our world order as if they were dropping from a beaker in Held's lab: viruses, NGOs, new inventions, Indian peasants moving to cities. And these are all connected one to another by ties of contact and technology that we can't fully map or monitor. What is true for Bak's piles is true for our world now. We are, in many ways, organized into instability.

This dynamic sandpile energy demands that we accept the basic unpredictability of the global order — one of those intellectual leaps that sounds simple but that immediately junks a great deal of traditional thinking. It also produces (or should produce) a profound psychological shift in what we can and can't expect from the world. Constant surprise and new ideas? Yes. Stable political order, less complexity, the survival of institutions built for an older world? No. Recall that Morgenthau's entire calculus of power was based on being able to measure who stood where, who did or did not pick up the hat. But in a fast-changing revolutionary world, you can't map power so easily. Writing about a similar transformation in his field, the economist Brian Arthur explained it this way: "In the standard view of the economy, which has an intellectual lineage that goes back to the Enlightenment, the economy is mechanistic. It is complicated but can be viewed as a series of objects and linkages between them. Subject and object — agents and the economy they perform in — can be neatly separated." But in a complex order, Arthur explains, "subject and object cannot be neatly separated. And so the economy shows behavior that we can best describe as organic, rather than mechanistic. It is not a well-ordered, gigantic machine. It is organic. At all levels it contains pockets of indeterminacy." This new physics demolishes the idea that somehow we can use simpler, older tools to manage the international political or financial system toward a stable equilibrium. But it doesn't mean complete chaos either.

Complex systems are not incomprehensible. If complexity were unmanageable and simply reduced to chaos in the end, we would have no Internet, no organized healthy ecosystems, no functioning immune systems or financial markets. In a summary of his study of various complex systems, the ecologist C. S. Holling identified dozens of systems capable of managing the demands of a changing environment with surprising ease: wild grasslands, futures markets, entrepreneurial businesses. All of these systems are confronted constantly with unsuspected risk, but each has found ways to thrive. More worrisome, however, Holling and a team of mathematicians and biologists also found examples of the opposite sorts of systems, filled with what he called a "perverse resilience," that insisted on preserving bad ideas. In such "maladaptive systems," Holling explained, "any novelty is either smothered or its inventor ejected. It would represent a rigidity trap." Such systems might look good for a while, but when they are hit with the unexpected, they react in ways that doom them. They simply can't shed their wrong ideas fast enough. Sound familiar?

Once, a few years after he first proposed the idea of a sandpile experiment, Per Bak was having dinner at Churchill College, Cambridge, with a group of British scientists. Something about the setting, all the formality and the stiff necks, brought out the American side of Bak that delighted and bewildered his fellow Danes. A few glasses of wine into dinner, his contempt for the "big science" he saw around the table began to slip out. Bak liked to observe that multibillion-dollar science programs almost never produced meaningful discoveries. They were cash furnaces. Nobel Prizes were won by scientists who had made extraordinary breakthroughs by themselves or working in teams of two. Big universities, where conservative and riskless views of the world were the norm, where the future of mankind always seemed to be one more billion-dollar atom smasher away, set Bak's teeth on edge. Science, in his mind, was about taking a hammer to the glass walls of old, wrong ideas. Here at dinner he had a sense of a group of guys who spent their time polishing those glass walls.

Bak popped. "Why is it that you guys are so conservative in your views, in the face of the almost complete lack of understanding of what is going on in your field?" he asked. To Bak, the fact that science still explained so little demanded constant radicalism, the sort of creative imagining that has inspired great scientific leaps throughout history. In intellectual terms, he felt, the constipation of a place like this couldn't possibly be justified when there was still so much amazing science left to do. The Cambridge scientists responded that they didn't see another choice. "If we don't accept *some* common picture," they said, "there would be nothing to bind us together as a scientific community." Bak was astonished. The explanation for this shared wrong view—you had to call it a *delusion,* really—was social rather than factual. People agreed because they wanted to be part of the community more than they wanted to be right. It was a situation you could find echoed around the world in foreign policy or finance in 2008: a set of shared, wrong ideas, clung to loyally by people who couldn't quite see past their illusions or the imagination-killing need to agree and fit in. Bak knew that if you wanted to truly understand the world, these commonly held ideas were absolutely blinding. But he had seen what his revolution in thinking was already making possible. He was just one guy in a lab, the Cambridge dons chided him. But those were the sorts of guys, Bak knew, who made history.

CHAPTER FOUR

Avalanche Country

1. Snowman

I have sat with him before and the eyes remain the same as ever—lucid, clear, a bit soft. His head nods now at times, just slightly. Mortality's creep. But the famous face is unchanged, its strong lines as unforgettable as when they graced television sets and magazine covers. He has a way of listening, cocking his head forward like a curious bull, that bespeaks a funny mixture of impatience and decency, a polite urgency that can set you off again on all the old debates in your mind. What was it that in the end did him in? The politeness? The urgency? Both? At home I have a photograph of him that I once asked him to sign. It shows him, hat in hand and bundled in an overcoat, standing calf-deep in snow in a barren pine forest near his house. You can see the footprints in the snow that lead to where he stands. The immensity of the forest makes him appear small and human, a scale that is unusual for him, a man usually presented as so much larger. Still, he looks comfortable in this awkward position. He was always that: a man who could deal gracefully with the uncomfortable. The portrait of him alone in the snow tells a great deal.

We are sitting quietly now, the easy topics exhausted—his health, recent travels, what we have read and are thinking about. I recall our last meeting; he discusses his decision to slow down his travels. But these are small matters. I have sat with him before, but one question, the one I most want to ask, I have never raised directly. I have read what he has written on the subject, pages of justifications and explanations. How even to ask it? What causes a nation to crumble? What does it feel like to have 250 million lives and hopes run through your fingers like so much wheat? I take a sip of tea, look at him directly. I ask: "As you look back on it now, why did it unravel?" He shifts in his chair, rubs his hand across his face, fingers his water glass, and smiles. Then, slowly, Mikhail Gorbachev begins his answer.

2. Failure to Crystallize

The end of the Soviet Union was one of those sandpile avalanches that, like the 1929 stock market collapse, demanded a complete remapping of the world. Its collapse was a permanent modification to the landscape of power. At the time, the Soviet Union was one of two centers of global power. The country's scientists and engineers were among the best on earth; its artists and musicians were celebrated overseas; its military was the closest match on the planet for the forces of the United States. The USSR put men and women in space, gave billions in aid to other countries, had a philosophy of politics and a dream of society that had seduced men as different as Nelson Mandela and Fidel Castro. And then, in a historical instant, the whole ornate system was simply gone. It was, in short, Per Bak in Red Square.

The Cold War had to end someday, of course. But how?

Nuclear holocaust? Truce? And when? These questions had been pondered at the cost of billions of dollars. They had underpinned the careers of generals, spies, economists, and diplomats, consumed entire lifetimes in hurried conferences, secret briefings, cables and photos and leaks scrutinized for meaningful hints. In a rather pointed "ahem" directed at his own profession, the Yale historian and political scientist John Lewis Gaddis once observed that the end of the Cold War "was of such importance that no approach to the study of international relations claiming both foresight and competence should have failed to see it coming. None actually did so, though." And it wasn't just the Ph.D.s who missed the clues. All those generals, all those spies, all those diplomats — they were just as blind.

Why, twenty years after the USSR split open in front of its astonished audience like some clever magic trick, do we really care what happened? Isn't it enough to have seen the trick at work, to have watched how, under some sort of historical pressure, the collective apparatus that ordered the lives of millions simply sighed, split, died, and baffled the experts? Maybe. But the collapse of the USSR is useful for us too as a study of how the wrong way of seeing can hide the real dynamics of the world, why the end of the USSR stunned the same minds who would later be stunned by 9/11 or the financial collapse of 2008 and who, I assure you, will be stunned again before long. The USSR was — as Gorbachev himself may have been shocked to discover — one of those poised critical systems that Bak described. It was organized into instability. Of course, when the Soviet Union tumbled, there were naturally a few theories about *why* it tumbled (inked out, of course, by the same folks who had missed the collapse in the first place). But few of these theories, and none of the ones that became most popular, accepted the real and, for us, *useful* sorts of lessons a more complex way of looking at the world really suggested. Before we can move on to addressing the main problem of this book, which is about how we can best navigate an increasingly complex international order, we need to clear up an important question that remains unanswered: why, despite our overwhelming material and military superiority over the rest of the world, do we still have this creeping and evidently justified sensation of insecurity? My argument so far has been that it is because many of our best minds, blinded by optimism and confusion, are using out-of-date and unrealistic models of the world. This is why our uneasiness about resting our future in their hands is inevitable. Despite their good intentions, most of our foreign-policy thinkers today resemble students who arrive to take a test that is composed in a language they do not speak.

Yet before we move on to discuss a new idiom that should make our world more comprehensible, if not more predictable, it is vital that we understand the sources of this confusion. Only by examining these fractures, by feeling out the rough edges of our old ideology, can we assemble a new theory of how to think about the world. And there is no better place to begin than the moment at which the old models completely failed. What happened in the USSR was revolutionary, to be sure, unthinkable in almost every sense. The lessons we learned from that collapse, however, weren't revolutionary enough. Worse, they blinded us to the future we do face.

It is my contention that Bak's avalanche law has an important implication that we have to master so we can see the world clearly, honestly, as it is—an essential precursor to creating a new approach to our security. You remember the first part of Bak's theory: small things can trigger a big change. Well, this also means that when a big change occurs, it isn't always the case that something big is responsible. We all saw the USSR implode and thought, wow, something *giant* must be behind that. We figured that the giant force was the end of history, the arrival of a global era of democracy and capitalism, or a result of our unmatchable defense spending. It was seen as a sign of the triumph of our ideals—more than the triumph, the *rightness* of those ideals. President George W. Bush, in the 2002 *National Security Strategy of the United States,* the document that is supposed to capture the most essential ideas of American security, explained it this way: "For most of the twentieth century the world was divided by a great struggle over ideas: destructive totalitarian visions versus freedom and equality. That great struggle is over." But was it? Did the end of the USSR really prove that?

To many of the people who were part of it, the collapse of the USSR was and still is baffling. Even Gorbachev has never quite delivered a compelling explanation. Gaddis, the Cold War historian, calls his memoirs "voluminously unreflective," which was more or less the same caliber of answer I got when I asked him directly. It was as if he had no language to describe what had occurred. In a way, that's not a surprise. Almost by definition, most status-quo power figures can never quite make sense of revolutionary energy, even after it has unzipped and discarded them. This is as true for blame-shifting Wall Street CEOs watching their banks collapse as it is for overthrown political leaders. Revolutionary ideas threaten everything most great men prize: how they think, where they make their fortunes, their sense of identity, often their very lives. Gorbachev was educated and raised with a whole taxonomy of thoughts about the nature of power that made understanding what happened around him impossibly difficult.

Once you start to unpack the details of the Soviet collapse, you discover that the real lesson is a lot more complicated—and frankly a lot more interesting—than the linear "input Western ideas, output implosion" explanations that make up the bulk of our thinking. It turns out that the end of the USSR wasn't the story of some historically inevitable process but, rather, the result of a complex and unpredictable set of interactions that could have shot off in any number of directions. Was the country facing certain economic failure in the 1980s and 1990s? Well, the economy was a mess, but the Soviet Union had been exposed to periods of far greater economic and social pressure without imploding. And badly performing economic and political systems, many far sicker than the USSR in the late 1980s, have been reformed, not overthrown: 1930s America and 1970s China, for instance. If the political system was so deeply fragile and rotten, then why had the entire predictive superstructure of Soviet *and* foreign experts missed the signs? Why, in a democratic referendum less than nine months before the USSR imploded, had more than 75 percent of its citizens said they wanted it to remain intact?

Why, when you talked to people, like Gorbachev, who had stood inches away from this collapsing behemoth, did each one tell a different, more complicated story? Did American defense spending really bankrupt Moscow? Then why did Soviet officials later observe, as diplomat Anatoly Dobrynin wrote, "Increased defense spending provoked by Reagan's policies was not the straw that broke the back of the evil empire....In fact, if [Reagan] hadn't abandoned his hostile stance towards the USSR, Gorbachev would not have been able to launch his reforms." Most everyone agrees that the USSR was creaky, slow, and morally broken on a vast scale. But no serious Russian scholar born and raised in the Soviet era would tell you twenty years later, "Yes, it was inevitable." They would openly laugh at suggestions that the U.S. military threat, smuggled *samizdat* propaganda, mimeographed newsletters, or popular discontent had finally tipped the USSR over. Those features, they were quick to remind you, had been a part of Soviet life for decades.

In the mid-1990s, two Western researchers on the USSR set out to answer the question of what brought the USSR down — and to do so without assuming that the final result was inevitable. David Kotz and Fred Weir, both Russian experts who had lived and worked in the USSR, interviewed hundreds of senior Soviet officials, men and women who had been in the halls of Russian power as the empire peeled away from them day after day. "Great powers have declined in history," they later wrote, "but never so rapidly and unexpectedly." Kotz and Weir's research concluded that the USSR didn't collapse because of popular pressure upward from the grass roots of Soviet life — pressure that could have been suppressed at any time — but largely because of the ruthless power math of Soviet elites themselves and some terrible miscalculations by Gorbachev. Politburo members like Gorbachev certainly held sway on the macro level, but the Soviet *nomenklatura*, a label that means "list of names" in Russian, actually ran the country. The *nomenklatura* were the army officers, professors, and officials who had managed the day-to-day work of the USSR since the 1917 revolution. These elites were a very small percentage of the Soviet population. But, Kotz and Weir found in their discussions, the *nomenklatura* decided, once Gorbachev began reforming a system that had protected their rights and privileges, they had more to gain by letting the USSR fracture than by holding it together. If you were sitting on top of the empire when it fell down, the *nomenklatura* logic went, you would surely be in the best place to pick up the pieces. This was a cold, selfish decision. It was also, fatally, one that Gorbachev hadn't anticipated in full.

"The ultimate explanation for the surprisingly peaceful and sudden demise of the Soviet system," Weir and Kotz wrote, "was that it was abandoned by most of its own elite." Had the USSR collapsed in the face of a real revolution, like the one that created the Soviet Union in 1917, it would look very different today. After all, the mark of a true people's revolution is that the old leaders are shot, exiled, or forgotten. But two decades later, all across the former USSR, the top leaders, the richest billionaires, and the most powerful politicians were usually the same men who had lingered near the top of the system in the old days. Was Vladimir Putin, the two-term Russian president who followed Boris Yeltsin, some up-from-the-streets ideologue? No. He was once an elite KGB agent, a prince of the old order.

The idea that the *nomenklatura* sold out their own system is important, not least because it shows us how many small variables conspired in the downfall of the USSR. Changing even one of them—higher oil prices to boost the economy, a more ambitious military commander or two, Gorbachev getting sick—could have produced a very different and possibly a more violent world. The end of the USSR was a case of internal implosion due to faults, twists, and kinks in the society that even today we cannot map clearly. All the more reason that we need to abandon the idea that our "triumph" in the Cold War was inevitable. Even Gorbachev offers at least this guidance: "It is a mistake," he writes, "to think that the West won the Cold War."

The great physics error of the collapse of the USSR involved an assumption that the internal tensions of the Soviet system would be predictable or at least manageable once the overpowering force of freedom was released. The USSR would snap into alignment and eventually come to resemble the USA, with a smooth and controlled stream of wealth and democracy. But the internal dynamics, as Bak might have warned, proved hard to predict. Gorbachev made his system more complex and unstable rather than less. *Perestroika* means "restructuring." But the sort of refurbishment Gorbachev got was, in the end, very different from what he had in mind. And in the difference between a "move the chairs around" redecoration and a "tear the house down" demolition, there is an encyclopedia of lessons about what happens when you misanalyze the world. Gorbachev's story is, yet again, one of those unnerving reversals of intention and outcome (fight terrorism, get more dangerous terrorists) that should be familiar by now. He set out to reform the USSR, but in the end he helped destroy it.

The collapse of the USSR wasn't a proof of determinism (input democracy, get stability) but rather proof of the opposite (input democracy, get the unimaginable). And it's this lesson that is useful as we look at places as different as the Middle East and China. Change produces unpredictability and surprise. That means that any time we push for change — and my contention is that we need even more change than we have today — we have to prepare ourselves for the fact that much of what we'll get is unpredictable. This inherent instability has to change how we make policy for our nation or how we plan our own lives, the problem we'll turn to in the second half of the book. Of course it also makes the game of pushing for radical reform in any society an uncertain proposition. Americans who press political liberalization on China, for instance, usually assume that what would emerge would be a democratic, pro-American government. But there's at least as much evidence that a sandpiled

China might avalanche to the lowest common denominator of nationalist identity, emerging from radical change as virulently anti-American.

There's a temptation, of course, to jam all this complexity into tightly constrained models. Actually, it's more than a temptation: it's a habit suggested by every intellectual twitch since Aristotle began classifying actions and reactions. In discussing U.S. policy toward Russia, President Bill Clinton once complained to Deputy Secretary of State Strobe Talbott, "You've still got to be able to crystallize complexity in a way people get right away." He added, "The operative problem of the moment is that a bunch of smart people haven't been able to come up with a new slogan, and saying there aren't any good slogans isn't a slogan either....We can litanize and analyze all we want, but until people can say it in a few words we're sunk." Clinton and his team never found such a model. The lesson of sandpile dynamics is that you can't really crystallize, because that implies freezing a picture of a world that can be profoundly shifting even as you try to fix its most basic dimensions into some sort of map. It's far better to speak and think and, as Clinton said, "litanize" in terms of dynamism.

The constant shifting and adjusting of our world, the unpredictable clashing of internal forces, didn't end in 1989. Today our sandpile order is churning out new ideologies as fast as it produces new computer software: Islamic fundamentalism, Indian caste capitalism, Venezuelan charismatic democracy, Putin-style centralism, and dozens of others we have not yet seen enough of to name or understand. As it becomes ever clearer that the idea of capitalist democracy is failing to deliver on its promises — and, in many cases, is delivering the opposite of what was intended — new ideas will explode into view. "Our job," Secretary of Defense Robert Gates said in 2008, "is to prevent the emergence of another '-ism.'" But the emergence of a new -ism is inevitable. And there won't just be one. There will be thousands.

In the middle of 2008, as the global financial crisis was just getting rolling, Simon Levin—the geeky Princeton mathematical ecologist you'll remember from the post-9/11 biological-risks panel—sat down with two other colleagues and penned a short article called "Ecology for Bankers." Too much of what he was seeing in finance reminded him of natural systems he had seen slip into uncontrollable chaos—the chaos of the "take out one species, destroy the ecosystem" variety, a small change triggering huge disaster. His goal in 2008 was to draw a few connections between the complexity of environmental webs and the dangers that lurked in an interconnected financial system. In particular, he said, he wanted to discuss "regime shifts," which is the term ecologists use to describe rapid, usually unexpected, reorganizations. (A regime shift was what happened to Mikhail Gorbachev.)

"For banking and other financial institutions," Levin wrote, "the Wall Street Crash of 1929 and the Great Depression epitomize such an event. These days, the increasingly interlinked financial markets are no less immune." What triggers these collapses, Levin said, often has little to do with big outside forces. Rather, he wrote, "catastrophic changes in the overall state of a system can ultimately derive from how it is organized, from feedback mechanisms within it, and from linkages that are latent and often unrecognized. The change may be initiated by some obvious external event, such as war, but is more usually triggered by a seemingly minor happenstance or even an unsubstantial rumor. Once set in motion, however, such changes can become explosive."

We've now seen clearly that Levin and his colleagues were right: our financial markets are rigged so that rapid fundamental change is possible. They are organized, as Bak would have said, into instability. But many other parts of our world may be as well. This suggests that we need to constantly examine the world around us for hidden faults and connections, for other lurking regime shifts. Levin's message for us (Gorbachev's too, in a way) is that we may have underestimated the cracks, faults, and tensions of our own system, the other disasters that may now await us if we don't plan properly. Addressing these risks fully will require radical new thinking and commitment—national energy at a historic level. But before we turn to that, it's worth looking at another example of how, inevitably, wrong ideas have led us to some very dangerous, very wrong choices.

3. Soft Thinking

I am in Beirut. There's a funny trick to the light at this hour, a way in which a Mediterranean haze thickens sunlight as it settles like paint onto rooflines and gathers in corners. You feel you are seeing the city a thousand years ago. It is the sort of peaceful pause that both deepens your love for Beirut and makes you wonder at the arch particulars of its historical fate. I am relaxing at a rooftop café, watching the sun drop into the ocean, that last light settling into bullet scars and blast marks on the seaside buildings. Lena is sitting next to me, and she too makes you startle a bit at the collision of history and spirit here, makes you fall in love with the city even as she perplexes you. She has dark eyes, an elegant smooth neck stretching out of a turquoise silk blouse, and a ready smile. She has been shopping at the record store downstairs, picking up the latest albums by Madonna and Gwen Stefani. Lena is smoking hand-rolled cigarettes, complaining a bit in passing about work, the small annoyances of a job at a Lebanese TV station. The subject of our conversation turns to Lena's hatred of the United States and of Jews. With great passion, in between pulls on the cigarette, Lena is talking about the dream of destroying Israel.

One of the most appealing notions that emerged from the Soviet collapse was the idea that what B-52s, ICBMs, and years of economic and political pressure had been unable to do, *Dallas* episodes, Michael Jackson, Levi's, and Coke had done in the space of a couple of years. Give Lena Madonna, and her heart would follow. The idea was given an academic blessing by the then-dean of the John F. Kennedy School of Government at Harvard, Joseph Nye, who labeled it "soft power" in an influential 1990 essay. "Hard power," Nye explained, was guns and armies and fighter planes. "Soft power" meant, in language only a political scientist could love, "the ability to establish preferences." Soft power was carried not in bombs but in television shows, music, and the dream of what a nation stood for. Hard power killed people; soft power seduced them. And America, Nye said, had plenty of it. In fact, American cultural dominance seemed in some ways more uncontestable than her military strength. Other nations had aircraft carriers and cruise missiles, but who else had *Monday Night Football* and Disney World? The country's cultural superiority, Nye suggested, should help guarantee its security for decades.

But there was a problem: soft power was one of those beautiful academic ideas that failed a lot of tests of practical foreign policy, not simply the little paradoxes in places like Lena's handbag, where Madonna albums and anti-American propaganda nestled comfortably. Soft power felt right, *sounded* right to American ears—all the more so because it confirmed our suspicions about the superiority of our way of life and bolstered our natural hopes for a peaceful future. It became, like Democratic Peace Theory, one of those vague, unprovable notions that triggered a whole set of foreign-policy misfires. When, after all, had soft power ever really stopped a war? Europe's history is filled with tragic examples of countries that shared resonant values tearing vengefully into one another with a loathing that no opera or philosophy or ballet could mitigate. "A conquering army on the border will not be stopped by eloquence," Bismarck—a Paris-lover who besieged the city—once observed. And armies weren't stopped by even the deepest cultural affinity. It was hard to see much soft power at work, for instance, as Japanese generals used Chinese characters to ink page after page of orders to incinerate Chinese cities in World War II—before sitting down to a rice-heavy dinner consumed with chopsticks in a spirit of Bushido that owed not a little to Chinese Ch'an Buddhism.

Listening to Nye's stories of soft power at work, you could find yourself in some uncomfortable intellectual backbends. "Nicaraguan television broadcast American shows even while the government fought American-backed guerrillas," he wrote at one point, eager to show soft power at work. "Similarly, Soviet teenagers wear blue jeans and seek American recordings, and Chinese students used a symbol modeled on the Statue of Liberty during the 1989 uprisings." If you wanted to, you *could* read the irrepressibility of American culture into these observations: "Even as they waged war against us, those crazy Central Americans still watched our TV shows!" you might chuckle as you sat in Boston or Washington. "They couldn't fight their real love for our way of life, hard as they tried." But you could also read this more simply and pick up a message that was impossible to miss if you had actually spent any time in Managua or Moscow or Beijing with the people Nye had in mind. It was possible to watch *C.O.P.S. and* kill American proxy-army soldiers. You could spend your morning applying to Harvard and your afternoon—as happened in Beijing in 1999 after U.S. missiles hit the Chinese embassy in Belgrade—stoning the U.S. embassy. The North Korean leader Kim Jong Il grew up watching Clint Eastwood movies. Shiites may like Madonna. Bosnian soldiers murdering civilians while wearing Nikes are not some weird historical anomaly—*How can they like the Houston Rockets and also murdering children?* Rather, they are highly personal expressions of the way in which collisions of power and modernity produce unpredictable results. Soft power sounds good, it reassures us that there must be *something* great about our own way of living, but it doesn't really make much sense if you think about it. Those murderous Bosnians in their Air Jordans are an expression of the diversity that awaits us and that we have to plan for—not some weird exception.

The illusion of soft power has led to some disastrous miscalculations. Through several U.S. presidencies, for instance, American foreign-policy leaders were seduced by the idea of a "moderate Iran" that needed only time and the gentle application of soft power in order to emerge, like a butterfly sleeping inside a cocoon of fundamentalist hate. For most of the 1990s, Iran's support for terrorism and its relentless quest for an atom bomb were written off as soon-to-be-forgotten peculiarities of a still-evolving nation. *Let soft power do its work,* the thinking ran. The United

States pursued a policy of light pressure and incessant flirting, entranced by the idea that Tehran's hard-line mullahs would be pillowed into submission as mobile phones, Wi-Fi, and teenaged Iranian girls wearing lipstick under their hijabs worked their magic.

Iran, meanwhile, did evolve—just not in the way it was supposed to: it started refining more uranium using better technology, and it expanded its ties to Hizb'allah, deepened its connection with Syria, encouraged all sorts of mischief in Gaza and Iraq. Opinion polls showed that even moderate Iranians thought the country should keep working on a nuclear bomb. As Iran patiently accumulated the tools of regional influence and luxuriated in the power vacuum brought on by U.S. destruction of its neighbors Afghanistan and Iraq, it developed both the tools and the trenchant mentality of a Shia superpower. It hardly mattered whether the United States and its allies had been tricked or deluded. The result was settled: in substituting Levi's for reality, America and Europe had squandered a decade of opportunity to pry into Iran's weakness.

Something interesting and important had been going on inside Iran. But, because we were looking at it the wrong way, through a lens of soft-powered inevitability, we missed it. It would have been far better to have a policy that pushed in hard and inventive ways on many fronts at once instead of hoping historical forces would work in ways we thought we could predict. Later on we'll see how surrounding a problem like Iran, swarming it with different policies, presents a radically new kind of diplomatic pressure that is both responsive and flexible, that doesn't count on any certainties. "Iran *will* become more moderate" is not a good basis for policy; it's hardly a good basis for a wager. We can't ever know for sure what is going to happen inside the complex sandpile of Iranian politics and religion, so we've got to explore policies in multiple creative ways all at once. It's the difference between a linear "first we'll sanction them, then we'll wait for history to work, then we'll watch the government collapse" narrative and a campaign better suited for a nonlinear world. We're not baking cookies here; we're trying to stress and press a complex system in many ways.

Of course, it's distressing when we find our enemies ignoring what we thought were those surefire post–Cold War rules, those *just add cell phones* recipes for modernity. When researchers find that the vast majority of suicide bombers come from nonreligious, educated middle-class families, we often have a hard time squaring the facts with the images of the world that we carry around. When voters in Venezuela or Gaza choose governments different from our own in elections, we want to believe they've been misled or cheated. But really these choices are signs of the strange interactions that have always existed and that now simply accumulate faster and in stranger combinations. The end of the Cold War wasn't proof that our way of life was inevitable. Rather it was the clearest possible demonstration of the opposite, of the way that the smallest quirks can mark out great differences—and of how hard we now must work to maintain the ideals and values we believe in.

The good news, as we're about to see, is that this same energy offers tremendous hope. The world isn't being paved over by a smooth, universalized system. And that very ability to evolve systems that fit the needs of different peoples and cultures and to encourage real diversity in thinking will help us solve many of the problems we face. Of course all of this has to be constrained in a framework of basic rights, which we'll discuss as a crucial part of deep security. In a way, the most gripping part of Gorbachev's own story was that he saw the hope that sandpile forces could bring, even though he could never quite figure out how to master them. It's not going to be easy to change ourselves or our ideas enough to take full advantage of these forces either, not least because we'll be trying to do so even as we are faced with a world that feels ever more chaotic, out of control, and threatening. But this is precisely why we've got to abandon the easy idea that history is somehow "on our side" and that the end of the USSR showed that all we need to do is wait. Those thousand flowering -isms now on the way will challenge our values. And if we don't accept the need to move now, to act, to change our ideas, well, then, there's a good chance we'll end up like Gorbachev in the photo that hangs in my house—alone, deep in the wilderness, staring at the footsteps that led us here and finally knowing the answer to that haunting question: *what is it like to lose an empire?*

CHAPTER FIVE

Budweiser

1. The Killing Box

In the fall of 2002, at a military fair in the southern Chinese port city of Zhuhai, you could find for sale, near the stands that were selling miniature plastic helicopter toys and harmless general-aviation seats, a small box that promised, for the cost of tens of thousands of dollars, to undo many billions of dollars of weapons development and about forty years of military history. If you saw the box for sale there, stared at the little collection of transistors and transmitters inside, and you didn't know any better, you might simply have figured that it was the mild and friendly dream invention of one of China's eager new entrepreneurs, produced with the same clever enthusiasm as a mobile phone or plastic car parts. You would have been mistaken.

The Zhuhai military show was not a must-attend stop for the heavyweights of international arms dealing. Though China was a rising power, the country was mostly known for its cheap AK-47s, which probably killed more people in conflicts around the world every year than any other weapon—with the exception of off-years like 1995, when the AK's nearest low-cost competitor, the machete, killed nearly a million people in Rwanda. In any event, China wasn't generally known for peddling particularly impressive weaponry. The Chinese military had a doctrine of developing what they called "assassins' maces"—computer viruses, antisatellite weapons, microsubmarines—which would use high tech to knock out bigger powers (read: the United States) that might one day attack China. But those packages were certainly not for sale. Among other things, the assassins' maces were likely packed full of technology that had been lifted from the United States, France, Russia, and other countries, in violation of nearly every national-security export law on the books in those nations. The Chinese, whose country had been invaded by nine different nations between 1839 and 1949, were noticeably, sensibly reticent about sharing much of their way of war. That, in a way, was what made the innocuous little box on sale at the Zhuhai fair so unusual.

Before we can understand the importance of what the box contained and what it means for us in a sandpile world, we need to understand something about modern warfare—or at least the kind of modern warfare that has been fought by the United States and its allies since World War II. From the earliest African battles of that war to the most recent skirmishes in Iraq, America has held as a matter of nearly religious doctrine the idea that war demands control not only of the ground but of the air. This idea was once seen as so absurd that it cost its leading advocate, a forward-thinking army general named Billy Mitchell, his job in the Army Air Service after he suggested in 1919 that airplanes were the future of war (and, in 1925, predicted an eventual Japanese attack on Pearl Harbor). But by the end of World War II, this apostasy had become dogma: the United States was pumping out more than 100,000 warplanes a year and had crystallized a killing doctrine in which the airplane was indispensable. The idea lived on into the Cold War and beyond through ideas like the Pentagon's AirLand Battle doctrine, in which nearly a million men and billions of dollars' worth of machinery were designed (who knew if it would work?) to produce a harmonious concert of airplanes, satellites, and unmanned aerial vehicles. The U.S. military would no more go to war without air superiority than you or I would drive a car without the windshield.

Future military historians will one day write about American airpower in the same tone they use for the Roman legion or the Greek phalanx: an operational innovation that enabled a nearly invincible battlefield dominance. By the end of the Cold War, the United States was spending billions annually building and maintaining the ability to take control of the sky over any piece of earth at any time, in any weather. Training a rookie pilot cost the air force $3 million. Aircraft carriers ran $5 billion apiece. Some individual planes, such as the B-2 bomber, cost more than $1 billion a copy—so expensive that at times war planners hesitated to actually send them into battle for fear one would be involved in combat.

Protecting planes in the air was an entirely separate business. The reason was that for every dollar the United States spent on planes, its enemies and potential enemies spent good money to develop antiaircraft systems to track and destroy them. Every leader on earth had seen in Iraq and Kosovo that letting the United States control the air over your country meant that, inevitably, your country would pretty soon cease to be *yours*. Early surface-to-air missiles used to attack planes, called SAMs in war-fighter jargon, struggled with accuracy problems or were so poorly made that a pilot who waited until the last second and then pulled a sharp turn could cause the missile to arc so hard it would snap. But the missiles got better, and, starting in the late 1960s, when American planes in Vietnam began falling to these improved SAMs, the United States developed a system of high-speed antiradiation missiles—HARMs—in response. (At the Pentagon you sometimes have to wonder which came first, the acronym or the weapons system.) HARMs worked like this: in advance of an air attack, a collection of specially armed planes would fly over the target and wait for the hungry SAM sites (known, perhaps inevitably, as LBADs—land-based air defenses) to turn on their radars and scan the sky. These LBAD radars, which sent out microwave beams and then waited for the return signal, were like miniature television or radio stations broadcasting on a single frequency. The tactic of a HARM attack was simple and deadly: the missile tuned in to that ground-based radar source the way you or I might tune in to a radio station. And then, at about 2,000 miles an hour, it rode the beam directly back to the missile's radar site. And blew it up.

Of course, once you, as a SAM operator, understood this, you were left with one of those fundamental "should I or shouldn't I?" choices that could keep you up at night, finding that there were some corners of your soul where patriotism didn't quite reach. You could either do your job and maybe try to be a bit cagey about it by switching the radar on and off as quickly as possible, or you could decide that the logic of SAM vs. HARM was sharply, ineffably suicidal: broadcast–receive–fireball. By the time of the First Gulf War, the outcome of this collision was painfully obvious. Twenty-four hours into Desert Storm, American pilots discovered that they need only broadcast the call sign of a HARM flight over the radio frequencies Iraqis monitored and the SAM sites would simply power down, as if on command. "Michelob, Michelob!" the pilots would broadcast, or

"Budweiser, Budweiser, inbound!" (The Iraqis had figured out that many of the HARM flights took the names of American brews.) Off went the radars, a ring of defense that Saddam had built at the cost of tens of millions of dollars, rendered toothless by what sounded more like a frat party than a battle plan.

Which brings us back to that innocent-looking package being sold so mildly at Zhuhai, a box about the size of a roll-on travel suitcase. Packed inside were several thousand microtransmitters, and when you plugged the device in and turned it on, it broadcast signals — 10,000 of them — on the frequency of a SAM site. From the perspective of an American fighter pilot — or, more precisely, from the perspective of his HARM missile looking for a "lock" on a SAM radar signal — this meant an air-to-ground picture that looked like 10,001 SAM signals, of which only one was real. And none of your satellites, your own radar, or your pals back on the aircraft carrier could tell you which of those signals mattered and which didn't, even as one of the signals — the real one — sent a missile toward you at five or six times the speed of sound. As you sat there for your last minute in your billion-dollar airplane, before you either bailed out or died — suddenly afflicted by the same logic that had haunted SAM operators for a couple of decades — you might for a moment think of how well that little Radio Shack project sold at Zhuhai encapsulated one of the oldest laws of warfare, that for every new bit of technology there was always an answer.

Chinese commanders liked to fire themselves up by repeating the trash-talking comment of the U.S. admiral Dennis Blair, who insisted in an interview that "we respect the authority of the People's Liberation Army in their mainland. Yet we must make them understand that the ocean and sky [are] ours." The PLA generals harbored a different plan, an ambition to be more like the legendary autumn wind, which, as the Chinese Taoist classic the *Huainanzi* said, "brings frost and decline; all is rendered formless, yet we don't see the effort." This was that deadly roll-on transmitter: it operated with the effortlessness of the seasons, producing the sort of natural surprise in which strength becomes useless. Why was the box for sale in Zhuhai anyhow? Why were the Chinese tipping their hands that they had such a technology—and that it was *for sale?* Well, the analysts and spies who followed the matter agreed, it must be because somewhere else, locked away, they had *another* technology that was even *more* disruptive. But the principle was probably the same, a little device that, for thousands of dollars, undid several billion dollars of American killing power. You could shout "Budweiser!" all you wanted. That box being sold in Zhuhai, it didn't care. It would kill you anyhow.

2. "Hay aquí mucho catolicismo... y muy poco relihion"

There are moments in history when we might idly hope that the age of war has passed or that war has become knowable and manageable. In 1899, for instance, the Polish mogul-intellectual Ivan Bloch argued that the combination of the industrial revolution and the machine gun had made war awful beyond contemplation. Bloch's book about his notion that technology had somehow conspired to produce a peaceful order was a bestseller. It was also wrong: his dream was undone a decade and a half later by the most violent war in human history, which set the stage for the most violent century ever. Fortresses, machine guns, nuclear bombs—all these technologies of violence brought with them an initial hope of peace, of stability. But the progress of violence always reasserted itself. The love of martial life seems to be an unquenchable human instinct and, when combined with new technologies and fresh grievances, it can produce shocking shifts in our safety. George Santayana, the English philosopher, was right: "Only the dead have seen the end of war." Make us poor and we war out of fury; make us rich and we war out of greed. The strange tensions of modern-day violence are bewildering. Two-dollar machetes murder a million people while billion-dollar surveillance satellites watch overhead.

In the last chapter we saw how granular effects can produce big collapses like the end of the USSR and can spin out new ideologies that will challenge our beliefs. Those same forces, we must also accept, are even now eating away at our physical security. There is a great deal in today's international violence to make one nervous: fresh technologies in the hands of thousands of tinkering Chinese box makers, angry new actors who are a Wi-Fi link away from us, countries intent on asserting their place in the world order, and cultures in which warfare is not a means to an end but an end unto itself, a kind of totem, as defining on the streets of Mogadishu or Ramallah as the rhythms of the office and day care are in London or San Jose. At the same time there is a growing list of the failures of large powers like the United States to defeat insurgents or terrorists and, more worryingly, to defeat their ideas. Since the end of World War II, the last great fight of the industrial age, when nations were retooled into giant factories, big industrial powers have faced embarrassment after embarrassment in war: the French in Indochina and Algeria, the British in Kenya, the United States in Vietnam and Iraq and Afghanistan, the USSR in Afghanistan, Israel in Lebanon—no major power has been able to defeat an insurgency anywhere in the world. The total record is something like 22–0 (or 21–1 if you give the British credit in Malaya, which some historians don't). It's a commonplace of military and foreign-policy chatter that at the end of the day terrorists never achieve their goals, that insurgencies are ultimately weaker than any state, that the technological and information edge of the U.S. military can safeguard our homeland, even if it does hiccup from time to time in places like Afghanistan and Iraq (or is mostly useless to deal with emergent challenges like China, pandemics, and terrorism). But the United States was founded by an insurgency. Terrorism helped establish the state of Israel. And in countries such as Vietnam, Algeria, Namibia, China, and Afghanistan, terror and insurgency led to the creation of new nations. It's mostly, after all, the revolutionaries and rebels who make history.

So we are slowly waking from a dream in which we thought we would fight other states, which could be annihilated, to a nightmare reality in which we must fight adaptive microthreats and ideas, both of which appear to be impossible to destroy even with the most expensive weapons. America's hoped-for "information edge"—the seductive post–Cold War promise that our satellites and airpower would give us an all-seeing, all-knowing security—had been reduced to this observation about the state of the Iraq war by Secretary of Defense Donald Rumsfeld in 2003: "We know we're killing a lot, capturing a lot, collecting arms. We just don't know yet whether that's the same as winning." Just as we must resist the temptation of a "We Won the Cold War!" celebration, we can't regard military dominance as a given or as a reliable source of physical safety anymore.

Yet very little of our mainstream security thinking reflects the extreme and urgent demands of this new reality. Even when our leaders do have the gnawing feeling that something is wrong, they often can't figure out what to do about it. In 2008, for instance, Pentagon officials fretted publicly about all those Chinese assassins' maces—computer viruses, antisatellite weapons, secret smuggled dangers we don't even know about—and then offered this chestnut as a solution: buy more long-range bombers. The poet Ezra Pound once observed of life in prerevolutionary Spain, "Hay aquí mucho catolicismo... y muy poco relihion." There's a lot of Catholicism here... and not much religion. We might say something similar of our defense establishment: we've bought a lot of destructive power with our record budgets, but not much ability to defend. You might wonder, then, if the sorts of fresh ideas we've seen in places like Glenn Held's laboratory can tell us anything about our future, about what this strange imbalance between budget and security really means. Well, yes, there are lessons—and mostly they emerged because of one scholar who just like Held took apart one of those simple-*sounding* questions and poked underneath to find the sandpile forces that were, and still are, lethally at work.

3. Misunderstanding the Machine Gun

Let's go back, for a second, to the battlefield question that baffled poor Ivan Bloch and his predictions: what to make of the machine gun. Let me ask you a question, one that probably sounds like something out of a video-game manual rather than a book on revolutionary power. Do you think the machine gun, when it was first invented, was better as an offensive or as a defensive weapon? That is to say, would machine guns be of more benefit to an attacking army (think lead-spraying German troops rushing across a frontier) or to a defense (think dug-in French soldiers)?

This may seem irrelevant, sort of like asking if a tomato is a fruit or a vegetable. But in fact, as we'll see, it is a distinction whose cost was measured in several million lives. It also gives us some insight into how we might go about thinking of our own security in terms of unpredictability and fluctuation—the way in which the same forces now producing a revolutionary order have always, if more slowly, worked on human history.

In January 1978 the American political scientist Robert Jervis published an essay in the scholarly journal *World Politics* that became one of the most cited papers in his field. It tackled one of the more interesting problems in international security, and even though it was dealing with the very biggest of issues—why do countries fight?—it had its roots in the answer to the machine-gun question. Jervis is a nerdy-looking Columbia University professor who has both the air and the facial hair of a hipster. He looks as if he'd be more comfortable behind a drum set in some Greenwich Village bar than serving, as he often does, as one of the most diligent "inside the room" critics of American intelligence operations. Jervis has said that he was born into a left-leaning Manhattan family in which political debate was served with every meal, and that when he sat down to write his formative paper, he was interested in a specific problem of nation-states that he called the "security dilemma." The dilemma went something like this: every state wants to feel secure, but it is doomed in this quest because the very steps it takes to feel more secure almost always make other states feel less secure. The result is a sort of accelerating uneasiness, a trap that ultimately makes everyone less safe. For instance, Britain's nineteenth-century insistence on having a navy larger than the combined navies of any two potential adversaries reflected the view in London that more warships meant more security. But in Berlin or Paris, more warships looked like, well, *more warships.*

In Jervis's mind the heart of the security dilemma was that though all nations sought the common goal of security, they would be unable to actually achieve it. "In domestic society," Jervis wrote, "there are several ways to increase the security of one's person and property without endangering others. One can move to a safer neighborhood, put bars on the windows, avoid dark streets and keep a distance from suspicious-looking characters. In international politics, however, one state's gain inadvertently threatens another." This was a balanced formula for disaster, no small matter at the time Jervis was writing, when a loose détente was all that kept the nuclear superpowers away from Armageddon.

But Jervis had an idea: what if you could find some way to increase your security without scaring another nation? The equivalent of nation-sized bars on the windows? Then, he thought, it might be possible to skirt the paradox. One way to do this might be through weapons or ways of fighting that were purely defensive. But what sorts of weapons are offensive and which are defensive? Thus the machine-gun question.

In advance of World War I, the consensus of most military thinkers was that machine guns were the best offensive technology ever invented. Ferdinand Foch, the general who was often named as the brightest mind in the French military (a compliment of unclear import), laid out the argument in simple terms. "Any improvement in firearms is bound to strengthen the offensive," he wrote. In this view of the world, one bolstered by the performance of early Gatling guns in the one-sided African colonial affairs and the Spanish-American War, more bullets per second had to be a boon for offensive forces. Thus Europe's generals opened their campaigns in the late summer of 1914 with the promise that the speed of machine-gun battles meant the Great War would be a fast sprint, concluded by Christmas. It was only after four years of grinding trench combat—and the arrival of a true offensive weapon in the form of massed motorized tank formations at Cambrai in 1917—that the generals realized their error: the machine gun was a defensive weapon.

In tracking the shift between offensive and defensive weapons through history, Jervis and other political scientists began to notice a correlation. During times of "offensive dominance," when technologies gave the edge to attacking forces, wars were more frequent. At the tail end of the fifteenth century, for instance, when the use of artillery began to spread in Europe, wars became much more common, undoing the period of relative peace that had started with the increased use of unbreakable fortifications in the twelfth and thirteenth centuries. Then in the sixteenth century, fortress architects developed innovations such as the *trace italienne*, a star-shaped defensive work that allowed gunners inside forts to lay down a murderous cross fire on approaching enemies. This helped the defense take the upper hand again. Cities like Venice and Metz were nearly impregnable to artillery fire; siege times lengthened from days to months or years. And, as the theory predicted, fewer wars were fought. At least until, in the early eighteenth century, mobile artillery was perfected, equipped with longer barrels that could accelerate shells to wall-busting velocities—advantage offense, and the start of a very violent several centuries in Europe. This back-and-forth continued through both world wars (World War II opened with an offensive blitzkrieg that pitted panzer tanks against horse-mounted Polish cavalry) and into the Cold War, a period in which nuclear weapons led to a stable dominance by defense. The cost of offense in an atomic age—complete nuclear destruction—was so large as to preclude full-scale war. It was when the offense had a better chance of winning (or when governments or rebels thought it did) that wars burst out. The measure Jervis and other scholars eventually developed for offensive dominance was this: was it less costly to attack or to defend?

The combination of the Nintendo-style American victory in the Gulf War in 1991 and the collapse of the Soviet Union convinced some military theorists that America's military dominance was untouchable. In their eyes, the world was on the verge of a "revolution in military affairs" not unlike the ones brought on by artillery or fortification. This revolution would be led by information technology—an area in which the United States, with its ceaseless loop of IBM-to-Intel-to-Google innovation, had an unassailable advantage. As one analyst observed in 1993 about the future of war, "While precise prediction is out of the question, it appears certain that it will involve great increases in the ability of military organizations to detect, identify, track and engage with a high degree of precision and lethality far more targets, over a far greater area, in a far shorter period of time, than was possible in the Cold War era." An age of push-button conflict suggested a near-permanent shift in the offense-defense balance, to an era in which offense against the United States became impossible since the attacker would immediately be hunted down and destroyed, most likely by some combination of satellites, unmanned spy planes, and high-speed missiles.

And if we weren't living in a revolutionary age, if we lived in a time when technology innovations, for instance, were confined to just one side, to "the good guys," this view might have been correct. Unfortunately, the idea of a point-and-shoot military revolution was an illusion. The video-game wars in places like Kuwait or Kosovo, it turned out, had been only one sort of combat that was possible. And neither conflict had presented a real threat to American security. Saddam Hussein's toy armies, for example, were based on an old model of fighting in which every nation tried to build a miniature version of the American or Soviet military. The belief that such a force could stand the full weight of the U.S. military was absurd—and yielded a predictable result. But it also set our enemies scrambling for new ways to fight. Enter the engineers behind that Chinese HARM-fooling box, to say nothing of a whole band of terrorists, hackers, bioengineers, and nuclear experts. Indeed, the more relevant mid-1990s battles came in 1993, which included both the bombing of the World Trade Center in March and the botched "Black Hawk Down" American intervention in Somalia in October, both precursors to a decade of small, cheap, and deadly terrorist attacks, on the one hand, and shocking, brutal collisions in places such as Rwanda, the Balkans, and, eventually, the streets of Basra and Kabul, on the other. And for countries such as China or Russia, the two Gulf Wars offered priceless lessons about how *not* to fight the United States, if it ever came to that.

Is it now more expensive to attack or to defend? The real math of our present moment yields the opposite answer from what security optimists postulated in the 1990s: attacking is cheap, and, if Jervis is right, it suggests that we'll see more violence in the future rather than less. The 9/11 hijackers spent less than $1 million to attack the United States. The cost to try to prevent a similar attack—in police, airport security, and other systems—runs to a million dollars *an hour* in the United States alone. Any thoughts that somehow a professional military would absorb hits for us, that there is an easy division between military and civilian, are also being scrubbed away. The logic of Hizb'allah's Sheik Nasrallah in relation to Israel, that "in occupied Palestine there is no difference between a soldier and a civilian, for they are all invaders, occupiers and usurpers of the land," can be seen in attacks in places as different as Moscow, Bogotá, Bali, New York City, and Madrid.

As in most every revolution, new technologies benefit revolutionaries the most. And the culture of revolutionaries, that psychology of risk and curiosity and confidence admixed with joy, is custom-built to find ways to wedge into the places where big-ticket power doesn't reach. Today insurgents and terrorists possess underground logistics networks capable of securely spreading money, matériel, and men around the world. Transnational drug smugglers cultivate, distribute, and invest the returns of a multibillion-dollar business, for instance. And mixed with ideology, technology only speeds the spread of revolutionary ideas. Since 9/11, Al Qaeda cells have been found in Italy, Germany, Spain, Britain, Canada, the United States, South Africa, Tanzania, Kenya, Yemen, Albania, Singapore, Malaysia, the Philippines, Jordan, Algeria, Libya, Pakistan, Saudi Arabia, and France. Robert Pape, in his study of suicide bombing, notes that of all such bombings in history, 90 percent have occurred in the past decade. It was a tactic, Martin Kramer writes in "The Moral Logic of Hizb'allah," that "enjoyed such stunning success that leading Shi'ite clerics were prepared to bend their interpretation of Islamic law to sanction it." As Clausewitz wrote in *On War*, "Once barriers—which consist in a sense only in man's ignorance of the possible—are torn down, they are not easily set up again."

So it turns out that the balance-of-violence equation that produced a relatively stable world in the Cold War by ensuring that offense was suicidal was a passing phenomenon. It emerged from the usual tidal rocking of human history. The idea that stability of security is normal—or even reliably obtainable with enough careful thought—is one of those legacy ideas that are frankly lethal in the presence of the sandpile effect. Conflagrations around our planet, the nervous itchings of a rising power like China or a reemerging one like Russia, aren't exceptions to the rule of a globalizing international order. They are not the last gasp of holdouts against American-style modernity. They are a natural expression of the shifting, shuffling energy of global power, energy that will only become more pronounced as the effects of financial fear, demographics, and ideology kick in. Keeping our soldiers at home no matter the circumstances, doing less in the world, minding our own business—none of these will protect us any more than meter-thick fortress walls could protect against long-barreled siege artillery. We're entering a new and dangerous era. The offense-defense balance switch has flipped. We must squarely face the awful fact that our security will become ever more perilous.

4. 21–1

In a painfully frank analysis titled "Why Big Nations Lose Small Wars," written in 1975 as Vietnam wound down, the historian Andrew Mack compiled a list of reasons to explain the inability of superpowers to win small wars. Mack identified the weak joints that undid superpowers. They rarely had their complete survival on the line, unlike guerrillas, who had everything to lose. They were victims of a timetable; guerrillas were committed to fighting protracted struggles, forever if necessary. And the war-fighting hopes of big nations were almost always beset by contradictions, particularly an unworkable schism between the pleasant tea-party (the bone china, not Boston, sort) morality of their home societies and the mercilessness demanded in battlefield combat. Torture, indiscriminate killing of civilians, and other inevitable calamities of violence were tolerated by those societies only when national survival was clearly at stake. In any less dire situation, they became politically and ethically toxic. "For the insurgents," Mack wrote, "the war is 'total,' while for the external power, it is necessarily 'limited.'" Mao Zedong, the father of modern guerrilla tactics and blessed (depending on how you looked at it) with an instinctive feel for his opponents' weaknesses, spotted another hitch. "Countries with legislative bodies," Mao wrote, "cannot take a war of attrition, either financially or, in the long run, psychologically."

Unwinnable wars—and it is vitally important that we stare that 21–1 score in the face, acknowledging that there is no silver bullet, no technological breakthrough, no robotic soldiers or DNA-altering high-tech gas that will fix this problem—now rest at the center of our military future. And even small wars and conflicts can produce effects much larger than we might initially suspect. If you look at American history, at, for instance, the American Revolution, the War of 1812, the Civil War, the occupation of the Philippines, the world wars, the wars in Korea and Vietnam, the interventions in Lebanon in 1983 and in Somalia in the early 1990s, and the 2003 invasion of Iraq—all of these conflicts shape-shifted in ways never anticipated when they were begun. And in our more complex order now, it's not only that such changes are inevitable, it's that sometimes they will produce new security challenges faster than the old ones are solved. Starting a war will very often simply create new, harder to treat headaches. Our old way of war is increasingly useless. It is senseless to aspire to periods of "peace on earth" during the lifetime of anyone reading this book unless we begin to change how, where, and why we do fight. Threats to our physical security are complex, new, and growing. They demand nothing less than a complete reinvention of our ideas of security. And that is where we will turn now.

PART II

. . .

Deep Security

CHAPTER SIX

Mashup

1. The Girl from Allegheny

Gertrude Stein was born in Allegheny, Pennsylvania, on February 3, 1874. Her father, Daniel, was a German Jewish immigrant who had made a fortune in the American railway boom of the nineteenth century but held, somewhere, the idea and hope of the kind of polish a feeling for European life might give his children. When Gertrude was a girl, he moved the family briefly back across the Atlantic before finally settling in Oakland, California, where Gertrude spent her teen years. It was a well-rounded, prosperous, comfortable beginning, one intended to produce a well-rounded, prosperous life with all the usual accoutrements of family, stability, and friends. In fact, however, it produced a woman who was to become one of the most important aesthetic arbiters of her day. Stein caught a taste for Europe early and realized quickly that she would never be at home in the United States. "America is my birthplace," she later observed, "but Paris is my home town." It wasn't only that the puritanical traditions of American life chafed against her modern sensibility and bohemian habits; it was also that Europe was where she was most likely to see what interested her most: a collision between old and new.

Stein returned to Europe in her twenties, settled in Paris, and quickly became a sort of den mother to the most successful artists and writers and dancers of her age. They were, she recognized, moving right along the fault line that riveted her, the one that separated the classical European way of life, with its balls, carriages, and Victorian sensibilities, from what she spotted around her: the dances of Nijinsky, the sentences of Joyce, the paintings of Braque. This new world obsessed her. She loved the speed of its trains, the way the Renault factories in Croissy worked around the clock, the hustle of immigrants on the Paris streets. Almost like a collector of great art, she began to collect great talent: Ernest Hemingway, F. Scott Fitzgerald, Pablo Picasso, and a dozen other great names of the revolution that became known as modernism. What made Stein so successful in this endeavor wasn't only her ambition or her intellect or the strength of her own talent (which was debatable). It was that her way of thinking and seeing, her curiosity about the collision of old and new, was perfectly tuned for a moment when Europe was, cataclysmically, struggling with that collision. She was a woman alive to the great theme of her day, the at once violent, at once beautiful movement from one way of living to another.

If there was a single moment when she felt a sense of the harmony between her instincts and her environment most clearly, it might have been on a Paris street in the sixth arrondissement one night shortly after the start of World War I. Stein and Picasso were walking home from a dinner, when a French military convoy rolled past them. But this convoy was different. It *looked* different: the sides of the trucks and the cabs had been splotched unevenly with different colors of paint. The two of them froze.

Stein wrote later, "I very well remember being with Picasso on the Boulevard Raspail when the first camouflaged truck passed. It was at night, we had heard of camouflage but we had not yet seen it and Picasso amazed looked at it and then cried out, yes it is we who made it, that is Cubism!"

This is quite a scene—the saturnine Stein, forty years old, and the diminutive thirty-three-year-old Spanish genius, exulting together in a fresh aesthetic surprise of the Great War. That war became for Stein the defining moment of her sense of aesthetics and history. For her, 1914 marked a pivot between radically different sensibilities. It wasn't simply that the war destroyed so many lives; it was also that it destroyed an older idea of order. "You are, all of you, a lost generation," Stein told Hemingway when he showed up in Paris after the war. It was that same confused geography she had in mind when marking out the way the war had been fought, the way it looked, and the landscape it left behind. "The composition of this war," Stein wrote, "was not a composition in which there was one man in the center surrounded by many others but a composition that had neither a beginning nor an end, a composition in which one corner was as important as another corner, in fact the composition of Cubism."

What Stein was sensing, marked out on those trucks or the paintings on the walls of her apartment, was, for its age, very much like what we are feeling now, a violent change in the way the world appears to work. In her case, the world really *looked* different. (If you've ever stared at a great Cubist painting, you know that the movement proposed a radically different way of seeing.) But there are important similarities between her historical moment and ours: a sense of new complexities, fresh interactions, and a speed that bedraggles old language and confuses old ideas. Statesmen of World War I lamented afterward that if only the negotiations in the days before the first mobilizations had *not* been conducted by telegraph, the war might have been avoided. The problem, they said, was that none of the kings or foreign ministers of Europe had accustomed themselves to the speed of information, to the quantity of it that became available when telegraphs replaced letters. And in their confusion, they felt they had to act and decide at the (then-blistering) speed of a telegraph machine. It destroyed their judgment.

Every important historical moment is marked by these sorts of shifts to new models of living, which expand in velocity and complexity well past what the current ways of thinking can handle. Our moment is no exception. And usually the source of the greatest historical disasters is that so few people at the time either recognize or understand the shift. Artists, with their tuned instincts for the new, often do. This is, at least partly, why their hearts sometimes seem to break as history collides with their lives. But for diplomats, politicians, or businessmen buried under piles of old ideas and biases, well, for them real comprehension is usually impossible. This is, we are about to see, what bewildered and derailed the best minds of the early part of the last century. And it's worth looking at how Stein spotted the distilled essence of her age, because in a moment we will turn to the distilled essence of our own.

2. Deep Security

In the first part of this book I tried to destroy, politely, the idea that our current thinking about international affairs is of much use. I didn't really need to tear down much of anything; those out-of-date ideas are collapsing under their own weight every day. When presidents pronounce wars won before they are, when central bankers are apologizing for what were once their very best ideas—at such moments it's easy enough to recall what Hayek said in his Nobel Prize speech about the dangers of too much certainty. What I have tried to present instead is a way to see how changes in the international order are now creating an ever more dynamic power physics. This constant process of shifting adjustment, of innovation, of surprise for both good and ill, is what I have called the sandpile effect. We've seen how this effect demolishes the idea that we can somehow manage the international system toward a period of peace as if balancing it on a teeter-totter. We have seen how it erodes our financial, intellectual, and physical security. The sandpile effect takes notions at the heart of contemporary foreign policy, ideas like soft power or that democracies won't fight one another, and shreds them. The fundamental impossibility of adapting our old diplomatic or financial habits to this new world is similar to the problem statesmen faced during World War I or that physicists confronted in the twentieth century when they found that Newton's physics had run out of answers.

Traditional Grand Strategy took strength from its static nature. It began with a vision of the world as we wanted it to be—all democratic or all French or all British (and subservient)—and then directed every fiber of national life toward achieving it. Old grand strategies looked like the Cold War détente balance between East and West or the Monroe Doctrine, which said that no foreign power should establish a foothold in the Western Hemisphere. These grand strategies assumed, as you'll recall from Morgenthau, the primacy of states. They relied on the idea of rational powers, threats that could be named and monitored, violence that came in the form of armies, and usually clear lines between economic, environmental, political, and military policy. In a sandpile world no such division is possible. In a world that is changing fast, we need a grand strategy that's capable of the sorts of rapid change the world itself produces, because much of what we have to confront will be things that have never occurred to us before.

Such a world demands a whole new way of composing a grand-strategic view. I call this new approach "deep security" because it is about mastering the forces at work deep inside our sandpile world. Deep security doesn't answer all of our questions about the future. Indeed, it's predicated on the idea that *we don't have all the answers* and, in fact, can't even anticipate many of the questions. What it is instead is a way of seeing, of thinking, and of acting that accepts growing complexity and ceaseless newness as givens—and, used properly, our best allies. Deep security creates a context in which all of the change we now need and are planning for can make sense, can be as adaptive and flexible as the world we inhabit. Instead of starting with a view of how we want the world to be and then jamming that view into place, we start more reasonably with a picture of how the world is. We leave behind, to recall Per Bak's old joke, the spherical cows and start to think and live among the more complex real ones all around us.

Deep security works because it comes from the essential, *lifesaving* difference between us and the grains of sand on Bak's piles. We're not helpless or passive; we can move. Our world shares the same dynamic as the pile, the same complex mysteries and laws. But even though the flows are the same, the objects are not. A stick thrown into a river will simply float downstream. If you're thrown into a river, you might not be as passive. This is a crucial—and hopeful—distinction. Bak's sandpile *logic* accurately reflects the dynamics of our world, but the sandpile *experiment* only touches on what is possible. We can and should and even must do certain things. Our actions, our policies, and our dreams can influence everything around us. This is, in the end, the saving virtue of what is otherwise a very dangerous power dynamic.

Perhaps the best way to think of deep security is as a kind of immune system, a reactive instinct for identifying dangers, adapting to deal with them, and then moving to control and contain the risk they present. Many of the most serious threats we face today, from financial crises to terrorism, resemble nothing so much as epidemics: they start small, spread fast, and often are bred at the intersection of things that look benign until combined (jet travel and fundamentalism, home mortgages and hedge funds). Dealing with epidemics requires an unusually clear-sighted way of thinking. Good epidemiologists are relentless about asking how and where such contagions begin, what they involve, why they are spreading. Public-health officials will tell you the only way to control an epidemic is with a carefully orchestrated approach that works along many lines at once. Deep security is a strategy that makes this possible. But it also enables us to achieve the dreams of national power and global stability we cherish. As we will see, the very things we need to do to keep the world healthy happen to be in our best interest. Someone who is sick cannot do much hard work, so getting this global immune system running is a first step for almost any challenge, from poverty to environmental damage, that can only be faced on a global scale.

Part of the reason we know that deep security works is that

many players in our world order are already using it to survive and thrive. Largely these are the sorts of revolutionary figures we encountered at the start of this book: Internet firms, terrorists, successful investors. Revolutionaries see big changes early because they are looking for signs that things are different, not for those "Oh, I've seen that before" markers of commonality between old and new. Most people on the Boulevard Raspail that night in 1914 would have seen the military convoy and thought "military convoy"; Stein and Picasso saw it and knew instantly what it was: a signpost of the future. Once mastered, this instinct for looking deeply is as useful for the Central Intelligence Agency (CIA) as for businesses facing a radical shift, governments trying to frame new treaties, or families and church groups trying to decide what this age demands of their consciences. The one thing it requires absolutely is a comfortable fluency with the disruptive energy that is remaking the world. But as we grow comfortable with this new and sometimes counterintuitive language, old problems will become clearer and we can turn to new questions with fresh energy. How do we do that? Well, we could do worse than by examining a similar shift that blew up at the start of the last century. And this is where Picasso and Stein return to our story.

3. Dazzle Paint

When Stein labeled the Great War as "Cubist" she was referring to a movement that had changed painting. Cubism reflected Picasso's hope, cadged from artists such as Matisse and Cézanne and shared with his good friend Georges Braque, that he could make pictures that held a multidimensional view of the world. By distorting what they were painting, Picasso and Braque hoped to make paintings as dynamic and alive as what they were painting. In this view, a picture of a horse might look more like a horse if it captured the energy of the animal galloping instead of recording it with hair-by-hair fidelity. The terrifying bulls (and sometimes terrifyingly bull-like women) in Picasso's canvases didn't really look like bulls (or women), but they held, perfectly, the spirit of angry animals.

It was precisely this visual habit, this new and fragmented way of seeing that influenced the French artist who invented camouflage, Lucien-Victor Guirand de Scévola. One day in 1915 Scévola (a modestly talented painter who was in the French Signal Corps) watched from the height of a telephone pole as a German battery shelled a French unit mercilessly. In the bloody landscape, his painter's eye caught a possibility: with the right application of texture and color, he thought, it might be possible to distort the image of the troops and machines enough to make them harder to see. As a test of his theory, he arranged for one unit to be covered with different colors of paint. Observed from a spotter plane, the soldiers were nearly invisible.

Scévola's Section de Camouflage began work on February 12, 1915. "In order to deform objects," he recalled, "I employed the means Cubists used to represent them—later this permitted me to hire for my camouflage section some painters who, because of their very special vision, had an aptitude for decomposing any kind of form whatsoever." A year later the British followed with a unit led by Norman Wilkinson, a landscape painter moonlighting as an admiral, who developed naval camouflage— disorienting "dazzle painting" that made it harder to line up ships for artillery or torpedo fire. Cubism thus begat camouflage, life reflecting art instead of the usual opposite arrangement. Braque liked to joke that this wasn't a first. After all, he said, soldiers arrayed in the last century's pale blue or off-white uniforms resembled nothing so much as an impressionist canvas — at least until someone started shooting at them.

In labeling the Great War a "Cubist War," Stein was trying to explain more than simply how the war looked. It was true that under the pressure of millions of armed men and the industrial power of five great nations, the landscape of Europe had been transformed into something that could be said to resemble a Cubist canvas, crisscrossed with rail lines, trenches, and runways and deformed throughout by bomb craters and burnt cities. It would never be possible to look at Europe in the same way after 1914, just as it was no longer possible to look at a vase or a guitar in the same way after the Cubists. But Stein was writing about more than the deforming of objects by color or firepower. She saw the idea of Cubism, the notion that no object should be seen simply, as a symbol of the age. Modernity, she felt, required chopped-up and different perspectives if it was to make any sense at all. Cubism argued that traditional formal painting was a lie, that it froze objects too simply. Those detailed, accurate canvases had a certain charm, to be sure, but what real figure was like that? They were "realistic" in the same way Morgenthau's "realism" was: they hid a great deal. Painting, Picasso and Braque believed, needed a new visual language if it was ever to hold the range of influences suddenly apparent in everything from design to our own personalities. This was what Stein was trying to say about life after World War I, that it could no longer be made sense of in simple terms, like some Romantic-era painting of a country house — still, placid, *fixed*. Only Cubism, that trick of treating a single object with multiple perspectives, could hope to make sense of the intricately ordained carnage of 1914–1918 and the world that emerged afterward.

Looking back now from a distance of more than a hundred years, we can easily spot this instinct for Cubist multiplicity everywhere in turn-of-the-century Europe. The 1900s renaissance in Vienna, which included men such as the painter Gustav Klimt and the composers Gustav Mahler and Richard Strauss, was puzzling through similar questions: how to represent the full object, how the forces of modernity demanded a different way of looking and listening. Klimt was one of Vienna's most successful society painters. At thirty-five he was making a fortune hammering out traditional images of the city's aristocracy. He began to find the work intolerable. The old way of painting simply wasn't getting at what he found interesting about his subjects. His revolutionary spirit got the best of him, and he invented a whole new approach, transforming the bankers' wives who sat for him into vessels for statements about everything from politics to lust. What else to make of his portrait of beautiful, rich Johanna Staude, whose porcelain-white face hovers like a perfectly rendered cameo in front of a background of lurid orange and above a coat whose explosive Technicolor depths hint at the real woman lurking behind that bleached facade? The jealous line of Viennese gossips — that Klimt painted two portraits of every woman, one clothed and one nude — went further in capturing the multiplex spirit of the age than they might have guessed. Like the Cubists, Klimt was trying to reach deeper than any classical image would ever allow. In the portrait of Staude that we know, she is dressed, but everything about the image screams a sort of humid emotional nakedness. Today we may take this for granted, but in Vienna at that time, the pictures were firebombs.

Vienna was also home to the man who became perhaps the most famous mechanic of this new instinct for complex depths,

Sigmund Freud, who was composing a theory of the human mind the same way Picasso might have sketched a table. Freud's psychological explorations were all about the notion of how fragmented and shattered our personalities might actually be, how hard and often painful it was to make any intellectual coherence from the shards of experience that shaped us. Another Viennese native, Ludwig Wittgenstein, chased after a similar problem in his philosophical writings. Wittgenstein, who wrote most of his masterpiece, the *Tractatus Logico-Philosophicus*, while a prisoner during the Great War, was obsessed by a desire to reconcile what he called the innumerable "atomic" elements of the new world into a whole. And what was Einstein's 1905 relativity paper if not an insistence on a science of seeing the world differently from different angles? "Each generation," Stein once wrote, "has its composition, people do not change from one generation to another but the composition that surrounds them changes." Stein had found in art a marker, a very colorful and even very romantic one, of that "composition." Each painting of Picasso, each symphony of Mahler, even every one of those epic Freudian interviews—all of them were like beautiful, fluent reports sent in from a distant field station in a war. These artists and scientists, with their deeper instinct for the vibrations of history and culture, were making maps of a new psychological country without quite knowing what they were doing. It was to be called the twentieth century.

But if a few people could label this new world precisely, most of the continent's great figures were oblivious. They were stuck—as many of our leaders are now—with old ideas. The result was tragedy. Take the canonical moment of early twentieth-century Europe, the Paris Peace Conference, which became a sort of *tableau vivant* of the unintended collision between men and the composition around them. The conference was called to negotiate the details of the end of World War I. It was meant to be a masterstroke of contemporary power, an object lesson in the symphonic grace of nations working together. Representatives from twenty-seven nations, including the heads of state of the most powerful countries on earth, met to order the world. They worked for six months and numbered among their advisers some of the greatest minds of the time: the German sociologist Max Weber, the British economist John Maynard Keynes, the American lawyer (and future secretary of state) John Foster Dulles. In they end they produced a catastrophe. The Treaty of Versailles was a lose-lose agreement that not only failed on its own terms but also drove Germany and Italy into a pit from which they could escape only through another, even more violent war. The treaty was an attempt to jam a seventeenth-century style of treaty making onto a world far too dynamic for such a narrow document.

Keynes, who resigned as economic adviser to the British delegation midway through the conference, was sensible to the tragedy unfolding around him. He would walk the streets of Paris at night in an insomniac trance, performing what can only be called a Freudian analysis of power, trying to untangle the knots of personality and history that were binding these great nations into a disastrous agreement. "Wilson," he mused at one moment about the American president, using the Freudian technique of matching myths to a man, was "a blind, deaf Don Quixote." Walter Lippmann, the American journalist, looked back in 1922 on the meetings he had attended at Versailles with a still darker view and an almost angry sentiment. "Of the great men who assembled in Paris to settle the affairs of mankind, how many were there who were able to see much of the Europe about them, rather than their commitments about Europe?" he wrote. "Could anyone have penetrated the mind of M Clemenceau, would he have found there images of Europe of 1919, or a great sediment of stereotyped ideas accumulated and hardened in a long and pugnacious existence? Did he see the Germany of 1919 or the German type as he had learned to see it since 1871?"

For men like Keynes or the British diplomat and writer Harold Nicolson, who sensed impending disaster at Versailles, the immensity of the errors was baffling. It was as if the postwar world had been slathered over with enough of Wilkinson's dazzle paint, to make judgment of the situation impossible. There is a desperate sadness in Nicolson's written remembrances of these years, *Peacemaking, 1919*. If only, he wrote, Georges Clemenceau, David Lloyd George, and Woodrow Wilson had been able to really *see* the Europe around them, the Cubist Europe that Stein and Picasso had seen pass by that night in the sixth arrondissement, the atomist continent Wittgenstein was recording from a POW camp, then great tragedy might have been avoided. One thinks, by way of example of this new-dazzles-old dissonance, of Wittgenstein concluding his dissertation defense in 1921 at Cambridge in front of legendary philosophers G. E. Moore and Bertrand Russell, patting the two men on the shoulders and offering as a kindly concluding remark, "Don't worry, I know you'll never understand." (At least they understood enough to make him professor.) This was the frustration of Keynes that screamed from every page of his Versailles masterpiece, *The Economic Consequences of the Peace,* as well as, twenty years later, as Europe teetered again toward war, the words that are the epigraph for the book you are reading now. It was that sinking sense of mismatch you could find in the head-shaking words of

Mahler after the debut of his Fifth Symphony: "Nobody understood it. I wish I could conduct the first performance fifty years after my death."

There is nothing more horrible than to walk that fault line between new and old, seeing what the future holds, screaming about it in your art or your writing, and finding only mute incomprehension or dismissal in your audience. "We make to ourselves pictures of facts," Wittgenstein declared in one of the early propositions of his *Tractatus*, a line that foreshadowed Louis Halle's 1950s observation about making policy based on the wrong image of the world. The lesson of Stein's time, the lesson that the artists and intellectuals around her saw so clearly, was that just as the twentieth century demanded new ways of representation in physics, in painting, and in writing, it laid a similar demand on statesmanship and economics. But the intellectual and spiritual leap this required was, for the greatest men of the age, simply too much. Passing our eyes back on that history, we can only wonder how they missed it. And, if we're honest, we have to ask ourselves what we are missing about our own time. Surely the twenty-first century, too, demands its own tools of statesmanship and finance. Fortunately, stashed around us, as it was in Stein's day in those paintings of Klimt or the physics of Einstein, is evidence of precisely what is happening, of a force for change that's basically invisible using old ways of seeing. It's a force we have to let collide with and even destroy our old ideas about how the world should be before we can hope to make any sense at all of our own time. As such, it's the first concept we need in establishing deep security. And, just as it did in Stein's time, appearing on the sides of trucks or in the paintings of rebels, the signs of its emergence are appearing in some places you might not think to look.

4. Swinger-Totter

Thirty years later, when his last name alone had become a syn-onym for brilliance and creativity in certain circles, the detail almost everyone recalled about Shigeru Miyamoto's job inter-view at the Nintendo Corporation was the hangers. The hang-ers became a shorthand among electronics engineers, Web page designers, and video-game addicts in the same way Lorenzo Ghiberti's doors on the Battistero di San Giovanni in Florence might have been a shorthand for sculptors, or Michael Jordan's midair hand-to-hand ball swap during the 1991 NBA finals was for basketball geeks. "The hangers!" they would say to them-selves, laughing. "Miyamoto!" they would exclaim.

The year was 1977, and Miyamoto was a fresh college gradu-ate with an all-but-useless degree in art from an obscure Japanese technical college. Nintendo was at the time one of Japan's lead-ing manufacturers of playing cards and children's toys, though the company had recently begun exploring (and failing miser-ably at) the new business of electronic arcade games. Miyamoto knew a bit about Nintendo because his father was a friend of the chairman, Hiroshi Yamauchi, but Shigeru had not been the sort of student you would have predicted for a *sarariman* job at Nin-tendo. It had taken him five years to loaf through college. He spent his spare time (and time that should not have been consid-ered spare) playing guitar and card games, stretching his high-school rebellion out an extra couple of years. Even after he had passed fifty and was a titan in his field, he still was marked by an energy that led people to call him "mischievous" or "childish."

Something about Miyamoto intrigued Yamauchi at that

first interview, so he asked him to come back for another chat. "Bring some of your work," he said. So Miyamoto did. He brought the hangers. People around the globe who have followed Miyamoto's career will tell you the story of the hangers, which had been wrapped and wound so that the hooks were shaped like the heads of animals to appeal to children and make the act of hanging clothes into a game, as a mark of his precocious genius. *Miyamoto!* they exclaim of a man whose inventiveness was about to deliver billions of dollars of profit to the unsuspecting Nintendo Corporation. *Miyamoto!* His name by itself stood for the charming twist on the everyday that those hangers represented, much like the simple plumber Miyamoto would later twist into the star of Super Mario Brothers, a video game that has earned nearly $20 billion—five times the amount of all six *Star Wars* films.

But in fact, of the projects Miyamoto presented in response to Yamauchi's order to "bring some work," the hangers were probably not the most important. That honor belonged to something so impractical, so absurd, and so expressive of exactly where Miyamoto's real genius lay that one hardly knew what to make of it: a combination swing and teeter-totter he had designed so that three kids could play together, one swinging away under the others, propelled by their up-and-down movements. The hangers weren't irrelevant. Miyamoto *was* interested in the refinement and tweaking of particular *existing* objects. This was what he did later in refining to perfection Nintendo's flop Donkey Kong, which became the biggest-selling arcade game in history. But there was something important, brilliant, and prescient about that weird-looking amalgam of a plank, seats, and a chair on chains. It captured what was truly inspirational about

Miyamoto, his instinct for strange, impractical, and (pardon the phrase) game-changing combinations. If you had known it at the time, you might have gotten the same tingle from that strange design that you would have felt looking at Picasso's earliest Cubism, because what Miyamoto had delivered held, in its own way, the spirit of our age as clearly as those Cubist-camouflaged trucks did in Stein and Picasso's time. Probably, though, you would have just thought: What could we even call such an unwieldy Frankentoy—a *swinger-totter?*

Yamauchi decided the guy was either a genius or an idiot. Miyamoto was twenty-five, ancient by Japanese standards for a starting employee. Nintendo gave him a desk in the planning department and put him to work trying to fix the dying video-game business. At which point Shigeru Miyamoto made history. (And made Yamauchi Japan's richest man.)

5. The Wife-o-Meter

For most of the first decade of the twenty-first century, the Sony Corporation in Tokyo dominated the business of console computer gaming. Every few years dominance passed from one firm to another with a lurid and expensive jolt. Nintendo, Miyamoto's company, had briefly commanded the sector in the mid-1990s, but it had long since been flattened by its Japanese rival. The business was lethal and very lucrative. Home video gaming, which had effectively been the province of hobbyists a couple of decades before, had grown to such a size that hit titles regularly generated more profit than hit movies. Over the course of its four- or five-year life span, a successful console such as Sony's

PlayStation 3 would deliver billions to the firm that developed it. Even for Sony, which had many lines of media and electronics businesses, a successful console game had a meaningful impact on profits. To lose dominance would be a disaster.

By 2006 console games were producing astonishing levels of realism. Whether you were playing a hand-to-hand combat simulation or a version of football or basketball, the seamless graphics that appeared on your television and the (invariably loud) surround sound gave you the sense of living inside the games, a long way from whatever living-room couch or dorm-room bed you were actually inhabiting. Sony and Microsoft (the cash-rich computer software company entered the console business in 2003) spent hundreds of millions of dollars to custom-build graphics processors capable of performing several trillion calculations per second. These chips were so expensive that Sony and Microsoft lost money on each console, even at prices approaching $600 a box; they planned to make up the difference by collecting royalties on games.

In anticipation of several additional generations of power computing and the arrival of high-definition television, Sony and Microsoft were investing tens of millions in new chips and hardware. All of this made it particularly surprising when, in mid-2007, a new gaming system that used much older graphics technology—technology a full two generations behind Sony's bleeding-edge PS3 and Microsoft's Xbox 360—came more or less from out of nowhere to dominate the console business, reducing Sony to a distant, gasping, and surprised second place and shaving billions of dollars from the firm's market value. What was perhaps not a surprise was that this system came from Miyamoto's lab in Kyoto.

*   *   *

Starting with Donkey Kong in 1981, Miyamoto had become the reference genius of the video-game business. He had developed some of the most popular arcade games in history and delivered billions of dollars in revenue to Nintendo. In 2001 he invented a device called the Nintendo DS, an electronic push-button game that was about the size of a pack of cards and that quickly became attached with near-ubiquity to the palms of Japanese and American teenagers. But, and this was significant because it showed just how widely Miyamoto's work could spread, the DS was also beloved by an impressive number of adults. In fact, the best-selling game on the DS was a program called Brain Age, which flashed images and puzzles on the small screen, all designed to help people keep their minds lubricated as they aged.

Miyamoto jokes that the secret to his genius is a "wife-o-meter," which measures how much his wife likes what he is making. The more willing his wife is to have his work in the house, Miyamoto thinks, the more he must be on to something. She never would have used one of the handheld pure-gaming devices that Nintendo's competitors were churning out for adolescent endorphin junkies. But the DS intrigued her, and that intrigued him. Miyamoto sees himself as an artist. And, like many artists, he wanted to touch on forces deep enough in society that his work would appeal to everyone — even his wife. Sony and Microsoft were obsessed with chip speeds and frame rates and displaying millions of colors. Miyamoto was interested in a different sort of power. "Too many powerful consoles can't coexist," he concluded. "It's like having only ferocious dinosaurs. They might fight and hasten their own extinction."

Sometime after the turn of the century, Miyamoto turned his attention to the console gaming business. As he considered all those dust-free rooms of engineers with their black plastic boxes stuffed full of powerful hardware, he concluded there was a flaw in their logic. Of course, faster graphics chips were important to hard-core gamers, but Miyamoto thought that was just a small slice of the world that could be using consoles. It was a slice that didn't, for example, include Mrs. Miyamoto.

More than anything, this rebellion against what his competitors were doing was an instinctive twitch for Miyamoto. For Nintendo, however, Miyamoto's twitches meant multibillion-dollar gambles. (In fact, much of his success came from the fact that he was surrounded at Nintendo by executives who were brilliant at ensuring his dreams *worked* in reality.) When the gaming press heard that Nintendo was cooking up something radical, they bombarded Miyamoto with questions. It must involve some superchip, they speculated. They asked, "How fast will the new Nintendo machine be? How many images can it render in a second, how much power does it use?" Miyamoto didn't answer. He knew the questions were irrelevant. "We're kind of in a strange period where power is the crux of whether or not something is going to be successful," Miyamoto told them. "That seems a little bit odd. If we rely solely on the power of console to dictate where we're going with games, I think that tends to suppress the creativity of designers." Many of those listening thought Miyamoto had finally lost his grip. The man who had so famously created those hangers had, they thought, just looped a noose around Nintendo's neck.

In fact, there *was* an innovative chip inside the new Nintendo system. But it hadn't come from some geek-stuffed gaming chip design house. It had come, instead, from inside an automobile air-bag system very similar to what you have in your car. The chip was a small silicon tab called an accelerometer, a breakthrough device that could measure the most minute changes in direction and speed. In your car the chip is programmed to notice the sorts of changes that would be associated with an accident—sudden jerks, wild skids, the instant snap of collision. When it senses these radical changes, it fires off the air bags in a carefully planned sequence. But the best of these chips, the most advanced, could measure smaller and more nuanced movements. This entranced Miyamoto. Would it be possible, he wondered, to combine one of these chips with the hand-held controller of a video-game system? This could transform computer games from a button-pushing exercise into real, uncontained physical activity.

It took Nintendo four years to get the accelerometer to work. Nintendo's software engineers, who wrote the first games for the machine, had to develop ways to translate human movement into virtual action. But once they had, it was frankly amazing what the devices could do. If you swung the new Nintendo controller like a tennis racket or a baseball bat, the accelerometer would record the movement, and a virtual figure on your screen would swing as well. You could hold two controllers in your hands and jab them back and forth as if you were boxing. You could lean back while holding the controller and "bowl" it right at the screen, as if you were flinging a ball down a bowling alley. You could shoot arrows with it, conduct a virtual symphony (as Miyamoto once did at a conference, wearing white tie and tails). What you could not really do was stay seated, as you would have with a traditional game. In order to get the accelerometer moving, you generally had to move yourself. Air bags, after all, don't fire off in parked cars very often.

As all this was under way, word of Miyamoto's thinking leaked out of Kyoto. He was mocked. Professional gaming commentators complained that the system's graphics were weak. The whole point of gaming was to continue blurring the distinction between reality and game. All those frustrated mothers who wondered why their sons spent hours playing virtual soccer but not a minute on a real soccer field were an expression of an unquestionable axiom of the video-game business: gamers were *couch potatoes*. When Nintendo announced the name of its new system—Wii—the cackles turned into guffaws. The experts at Sony and Microsoft reminded journalists that there was a reason their machines had sci-fi-sounding names like Xbox 360 or PS3. When Nintendo introduced Wii at a convention in the summer of 2005, the crowd offered only a stunned, perplexed silence. "It was," recalled Miyamoto's boss, Nintendo's CEO, Satoru Iwata, "as though the audience didn't know how to react."

Consumers did. Within weeks of its introduction, Wii became a hit. It rapidly overtook those expensive Sony and Microsoft boxes, eventually surpassing both in total sales. And because the Wii console wasn't based on ludicrously expensive technology, Nintendo was able to sell it for less than half the price of an Xbox and make money on each console. In homes in Japan, the United States, and Europe—those homes lucky enough to actually lay their hands on Wii, which generally had a waiting list of several months—owners cleared space in front of their TVs, pushed their couches out of the way instead of sitting on them, then jumped, crawled, and flailed around with their Wiimotes. Wii killed the idea that a video game was something you played without breaking a sweat.

As if to hammer this point home, Nintendo introduced an exercise version called the Wii Fit. If you didn't know better, if, say, you worked for Sony or Microsoft, you might have thought the Wii Fit was some sort of elaborate joke: an *exercise system* designed for fat, out-of-shape gamers who only let go of their remotes to open a bag of potato chips? What next, a dating service? In fact, the Wii Fit, which involved a small platform on which you could jump, twist, and bend, became an instant best seller. Large numbers of women starting buying Wii, a first in the thirty-year history of console games. Miyamoto had demolished the wall between real and virtual, eroded the idea that the world was split into "gamers" and "nongamers," and forced his competition to completely rethink the whole idea of a game, of what they were doing when they came to the office every day. And how had he done this? Well, this was why the Wii mattered for reasons important well beyond the world of tweens.

6. Danger Mouse

In technology circles there is a word for what Miyamoto made with Wii: a mashup. He had "mashed up" two seemingly unrelated things—an accelerometer and a video game—to create something new. And in our revolutionary age, the mashup is a sign of a different landscape of power, more or less what Cubism was one hundred years ago. If the Cubist revolution demanded that we look at one thing from multiple perspectives, mashup logic demands that we look at the world as multiple objects mixed in multiple—unpredictable—ways to create totally new objects or situations. Earl Gray, an American environmental scientist, calls this "the new math," an expression derived from experiments he's performed in which chemicals separately have no effect on the body but mixed together create a toxic, cancerous result. Gray calls these cases "zero plus zero equals something."

New-math combinations are all around us now. They are

being created deep inside systems of finance or warfare to produce surprise and newness at an accelerating pace. They torch many of our old ideas about how to conduct diplomacy, manage the global economy, or imagine our future. They are the reason financial executives can insist their firms are safe, only to see them blow up weeks later, as previously unlinked risks mash into each other. They explain how leaders in places such as the United States and Israel can launch wars only to find their best plans quickly undermined and destroyed. Understanding mashup logic is, we will see, the first step toward a new, deep security in which our ideas match the world around us.

The word "mashup" gets its hipster ring from its roots in 1990s dance music, when DJs were taking musical snippets called samples and combining them into music that was wholly different than the original source material. When DJ Cheekyboy mixed, say, music from Nirvana's "Smells Like Teen Spirit" with tracks by the South Los Angeles rappers N.W.A. into a new track called "Smells Like Compton," it was hard to say what exactly you were left with. Not the anguished grunge of Nirvana or the street-fighting crip hop of N.W.A. It was a musical swinger-totter. Same with tracks like Cabaret Voltaire's "Low Cool," which mixes techno beats and recorded street talk to produce something that is as much sociology as chill-out music. The most famous mashup in this spirit was a 2004 album by a Brooklyn DJ named Brian Burton, who goes by the *nom de spin* of Danger Mouse. Burton took the Beatles' *White Album* and mashed it into Jay-Z's *Black Album* to produce *The Gray Album*. The idea sounds hardly plausible: weave two megahit records, separated by decades on the fast-moving river of popular culture, into something coherent and interesting. Yet this is exactly what Danger Mouse did, to great effect. *Entertainment Weekly* called it the Best Album of 2004, ahead of some of the most expensively produced records of the year. Danger Mouse had done the mixing in his bedroom.

Mashups capture a sense of creativity that passes established borders, that combines a sort of deep, curious yearning—*how do I get my wife to like the video game I am making? how can I strike the Americans? how can I make a fortune?*—with a hands-on, practical tinkerer's spirit. But when these two are wedded, innovation becomes inevitable. Our world abounds in mashups. They are often harmless and delightful, as when the Spanish chef Ferran Adrià packs his kitchen with chemists, centrifuges, and other accoutrements of a research lab to produce "molecular cuisine" delicacies like passion-fruit caviar. But many mashups are life-changing. They emerge in the combination of data processing and biology to track genetic diseases, or of short messaging and epidemiology to control the spread of disease in Africa, or of financial markets and credits for carbon pollution. They are part of the reason, as we saw in our discussion of Gorbachev and the Cold War, that it's impossible to conclusively say one ideology, ours, has "won" some sort of global bakeoff. The ceaseless combining of ideas, which will be mixed and matched as people look for sensible ways to fit their hopes and faith and fears into a coherent political order, assures a future of new and different ideologies. In this way mashups have the weird effect of making the unimaginable not only possible but inevitable. Mash up authoritarian rule and capitalism, previously thought to be incompatible, and you get China. Mash up high petroleum prices and caudillo politics, and you get Venezuela. Nothing is permanent in any of these mashups; they may be gone tomorrow, mashed into some new combination. And unless we understand this mashup energy (and even learn to use it ourselves), a truly secure future will continue to elude us.

"I would warn against attempts to forecast novel technologies by the existence of building blocks already in place," the economist Brian Arthur has written. He's right. In an era of new math, simply guessing at the shape of a combination of existing blocks tells you almost nothing about what might be built. The great thing about our future—and the terrifying thing—is that we can't imagine what sums the new math will yield. This sense of so many possible combinations, of a limitless dimensionality, presents us with a staggering level of complexity. Opportunities for spectacular innovation explode around us. To call our current financial battles or terror battles "mashup wars" would not be too far wrong, any more than calling World War I a "Cubist war." You can almost imagine Miyamoto or Danger Mouse watching reports of the latest improvised explosive devices in Iraq—mashups of explosives, cell phones, and text messages—and feeling the same sinking shock Picasso must have felt on that Paris night when he said, "Yes, it is we who made it." Yet here is the hopeful truth: understood properly, used to make a new kind of security, mashup energy will also let us say of a world fifty years from now, prosperous and stable, "Yes, it is we who made it."

7. Risk Society

The revolution under way around us isn't something we can choose to be a part of or not. It is largely unavoidable. In this regard it is distinct from, say, the revolutions of the nineteenth century, in which the big challenge for revolutionaries like Marx was how to get people to care enough to act, to get involved. Today there's no choice. We're participants, like it or not. It's not as if we can wake up some morning and decide, "Okay, today's the day I'll start mashing up my life." Your life is already being mashed for you. The Internet, your derivative-laced retirement account, chemical compounds that sit in our food or our clothing—all of these are expressions of an unstoppable, infectious genius for combinations. We'll turn in a moment to refining our skills for living in such a world, but the new tools we'll need come from accepting that mashup energy changes the ecosystem around us and, as a result, changes us. Networks of innovation we cannot see enmesh us in connections through stock markets or gas prices or disease. The nature of these networks is often not apparent until, awkwardly, they shift and fracture the world we thought we understood. That was what happened on 9/11 and in the financial meltdown of the summer of 2008, when powerful-looking investment banks essentially destroyed themselves. And there will be a lot more of these strange sums in our future.

German sociologist Ulrich Beck has called what we're living in *Risikogesellschaft,* or "risk society," where we all share risks, where the richest Palm Beach socialite shares health or financial risks with the poorest of the planet's inhabitants. Indeed, what modernity manufactures better than anything else, Beck says, is new and incalculable risks that we all share and partake in, even if we're not aware of them. The result, he once wrote, is that "at the beginning of the twenty-first century, the human condition cannot be understood nationally or locally but only globally." The forces that shape our lives are a new-math collision of ideas that can and do come from anywhere.

The lesson of Miyamoto's success is about the sort of astonishing revolutions that become possible once we start to make our sums using the new math. What we are about to see is that laying the foundation for a sensible international order—one that fits 2009, not 1989—requires moving into areas where traditional thinkers about power are least comfortable, a whole way of thinking where old math rules are discarded. It involves accepting that the most important things cannot be predicted with any great accuracy. It involves radically refiguring the balance sheet of power in such a way that the aim isn't to hoard power but to give away as much of it as possible it can be mashed, mixed, and used in new and decent ways. It requires mastering the notion that the most powerful action is often inaction. It will involve pursuing deliberate failure and reimagining the kinds of violence we must use. It requires harder truth telling than our leaders are used to and experimentation right up to the very edge of collapse. It involves moments, even, of useful panic. But—and this is crucial—it also means understanding that mashing up is something we can do too. Our policies, dreams, and ideas can be combined to release new and unexpected power. It is this key difference between us and passive, helpless sand grains that will mark out our ability to have a secure future. It was unthinkable that Shigeru Miyamoto's old technology would upend a multibillion-dollar industry overnight. And it might be unthinkable too that we can grasp, from what seems a very dangerous and unstable world around us, a prosperous, stable, and better future. We can. And that is where we turn now.

CHAPTER SEVEN

The General and
the Billionaire

1. Spymaster

When Aharon Farkash was made the head of Israeli military intelligence in the winter of 2001, he was aware of one fact: of the thirteen previous occupants of his post, six had retired or been fired before finishing their complete terms. The abrupt dismissals were no reflection on the men's brilliance, combat machismo, or skills as commanders. Rather, it was that the job of heading military intelligence in Israel is perhaps the most difficult intelligence job in the world. The country is surrounded by enemies. It must oversee parts of the West Bank of the Jordan River and the Gaza Strip which are filled with groups committed to Israel's destruction. The country's foes are secretive, from cultures in which you go out killing with people you've known since childhood, mistrust anyone you haven't known for that long, and find easy financing and arms available from the running taps of nearby oil money. These enemies often feel, deeply, that they are doing the work of God.

Since the founding of Israel in 1948, the country has been in a constant state of alert, poised for instant war, the call for which has come more than once every decade. The nation's intelligence services, considered to be among the best in the world, have in fact amassed a history filled with missed signals and nearly fatal mistakes. The most famous of these was the 1973 Yom Kippur war, which came just twelve weeks after the Israeli general Moshe Dayan assured *Time* that "the next ten years will see Israel's borders frozen along their present lines, but there will be no major war."

Such errors were not artifacts of some distant past. In 2006 the country launched an offensive against Hizb'allah in southern Lebanon and found itself faced with a foe that, after six weeks of what were intended to be punishing attacks, emerged triumphant and with a bounty of Israeli tanks, transports, and even a missile-hit ship (the first time the Israeli navy had been hit by Hizb'allah, called in near real time on TV by Nasrallah, like the Babe gesturing toward the bleachers before a home run). These sorts of surprises, on offense or defense, were an unpleasant part of Israeli national life. Farkash once told me, "I was at a conference reviewing Israel's intelligence history and one of the speakers observed that of thirty important strategic moments in Israel's history, intelligence had failed in twenty-eight cases. The general sitting next to me leaned over and whispered: 'He is only saying that because he doesn't know the details of the other two.'"

Farkash's career had carried him through some of the most secretive parts of the Israel Defense Forces (IDF). Just prior to taking the top intelligence job, he spent three years overseeing the highly classified Unit 8200, which recruited the best Israeli scientists and engineers for intelligence and defense work. The nonclassified spin-offs from Unit 8200 had produced nearly sixty civilian high-tech companies worth billions, while the still-secret work of the group included breakthroughs that American intelligence officials described as "world-class" and, in some cases, "years ahead of the US." When Farkash finished his term in office—his *complete* term—in early 2006, before that disastrous Lebanon war, he had not only avoided the fate of those now-dismissed chiefs but had established a record of devastating clarity. One of Farkash's admirers in the Israeli policy establishment, a mutual friend of ours, pointed out that Farkash had "covered himself in accuracy" during his term as head of military intelligence. In the months before Operation Iraqi Freedom, the general had politely but urgently given his American counterparts a nearly pitch-perfect play-by-play of what would happen once U.S. forces arrived in the Tigris River valley. He was ignored.

2. "Where can I fail?"

Buddhist masters like to say that if you're trying to reach enlightenment, you must develop, in this order, "right view, right intention, and right action." If you're not seeing the world properly, you have no hope of any sort of breakthrough. The question I want to explore now is: what is right view when it comes to life in a revolutionary age? When the defining trait of life is those sandpile developments that, by definition, are new in our experience, how should we look at the world? Do we have anything to learn from people who are particularly successful in places where fast change and surprise are facts of daily life? These are vitally important questions if you're trying to train yourself to make sense of a world order that looks increasingly out of control. If you're running a corporation, planning for your kids' education, figuring out what countries to bomb and which to befriend—what should you be looking for? We'll turn later to the other Zen-master problems of how to *think* about such a world and how to *act* in it. But if we can't even master the art of *seeing*, then as Louis Halle said, we're not very likely to hit what we're aiming for.

Many of our problems today aren't the result of too little information. Instead, they come from the challenge of sorting through a huge (and growing) amount of data, all constantly changing, and much of it irrelevant or misleading. I had heard through friends in both the United States and Israel about Farkash not only because he was renowned for finishing his whole term but because he was known as one of the great instinctive spies of his generation. *Go see Farkash* was a refrain among the spies and analysts I most respected. He was someone who could see through that data haze into what was really essential. Farkash, I was told, had a way of talking about the world, a way that sometimes even he couldn't quite explain, that was profoundly different from that of most everyone else in his profession. You could joke that he was the Israeli Yoda, filled with barely scrutable insights, but his record spoke for itself. He seemed, my friends said, to have made the uncertainty of the world around him an intuitive part of his mind. This was, they said, what we should all aspire to be. He was the closest thing to a spy's Zen master that I was likely to find.

Shortly after leaving the Ministry of Defense, Farkash took up temporary residence at Israel's Institute for National Strategic Studies in Tel Aviv, where he operated from a small, sparsely furnished office on the second floor. He divided his time between academic pursuits and business, often with companies that had once been a part of his ambit at Unit 8200. One afternoon, as we sat over cups of bitter Israeli coffee, he began to tell me the story of his time as head of military intelligence. "After I got the job in March of 2002," he began, "I asked myself, 'Where can I fail?' I decided that there were two areas: Hizb'allah and Iran. But to deal with this I decided to make an effort to change the way we gathered intelligence, to shift our methods and the sorts of sources that we used."

By way of example, he said, in the 1980s the United States moved away from so-called internal sources of intelligence, the sort of dark black-bag operations reminiscent of a le Carré novel, and toward external sources, such as satellites and signals intelligence, which means listening to phone calls or reading e-mails. This change had many origins, from Jimmy Carter's discomfort with the ethics of a cloak-and-dagger world to Ronald Reagan's technology-heavy defense budgets. The result was to lock into place an approach that was profoundly outside-to-inside. As satellite spy photos got better and the ability to pick a single phone conversation out of the air evolved, spies in the United States and Israel thought they were getting a clearer picture of what was happening. So they spent more and more money on these sorts of systems, betting that they were moving toward a keener understanding of their enemies.

Farkash disagreed. In his opinion, such an approach had a lethal flaw: it led intelligence analysts to think that they understood more than they actually did. Sharper satellite photos did not, in fact, mean a sharper understanding of your enemy, any more than real-time stock market tickers meant a better understanding of the market. They were tools, not answers. "The problem," he explained, "is that in a dynamic environment it is the internal factors that often have the most impact." And those internal factors were invisible to satellites and rarely clearly stated in a phone call or a letter. "Sometimes there are things that seem like they don't affect you at all," he said, "but in fact they matter a great deal. You know that famous map of the U.S. from the cover of the *New Yorker*, where New York is giant and the rest of the country is very small? You can't look at the world like that map, from the perspective that you are the center of everything."

In essence, the leap Farkash was making was to accept that Israel would never be able to fully see the world around it with anything more than a very dim level of accuracy. There was, he thought, no sense in trying to develop a perfect picture of the enemy. Appealing as it sounded, it was impossible in practice, and it distracted you, possibly fatally, from what did matter, which was not what you could see but what you couldn't. In Israel's case, Farkash explained to me, the temptation had been to focus only on issues that seemed to be a direct threat and to try to describe them as perfectly as possible. This was a natural instinct—after all, with limited resources, it made sense to concentrate most on what appeared to be the greatest danger. But Farkash was convinced this was a mistake. It was often, he thought, things that didn't seem to be related to Israel or that the country had never seen before that led to the most perilous situations and unpleasant surprises. The strategic landscape Farkash faced, like Bak's sandpile, was changing every second. It became more complex as time passed.

"You have to constantly ask new questions," Farkash explained. "This is very difficult for a large organization like the CIA, but for a small organization like ours it is possible. When you ask different questions, you get different answers." Spending years staring at the same problem blinded you to other, more important targets. And you usually (remember those USSR analysts?) missed the answer to the question you had started with. If "right view" was the key to Zen enlightenment, this insight of Farkash's evoked another Zen insight: "The question is the answer." How you asked and what you asked mattered a lot. And the problem with the CIA or almost any bureaucracy, Farkash felt, whether it was IBM or the Department of the Treasury, is that people have the habit of asking the wrong questions, of looking in the wrong places and in the wrong way.

"Look at Assad," Farkash said, referring to the Syrian president, Bashar al-Assad. From Israel's perspective, looking at Assad's most urgent concerns, none of the top three seemed a direct danger: the survival of his perilously perched government, made up of Alawite tribesmen, who represent a fraction of the Syrian population; the stability of his economy, which was related to the ability of Syria to export labor to Lebanon; and the situation in Lebanon, which Syria regarded as a "little-sister state," to be ordered about and shaped as Syria pleased. Only when you got to the fourth item—Syria's thirty-year-old grudge with Israel about the Golan Heights—did Israel's security seem threatened. But Farkash bet that it was the balance of all of these factors—and the injection of problems he couldn't imagine at the time—that would determine if Syria would attack.

If, for instance, the Lebanese economy slowed down, Assad might attack as a distraction. In 2005, for instance, Hizb'allah stepped up attacks on Israel's northern frontier. Did this have a tie to some Lebanese grievance? No. It was coordinated by Syria and Iran as a reaction to growing pressure on Tehran and Damascus to stop nuclear weapons development. The longer Farkash looked, and the deeper his human intelligence led him inside Syria, the more convinced he became that these strange interconnections drove a lot of Syrian policy. "We couldn't just ask the question of 'what is the threat?'" he told me. You might be tempted to wait until you saw a buildup of tanks on your border before realizing an attack was imminent. You'd still be staring at those tanks when you were surprise-attacked by sea, bombed by unplanned airplanes, or attacked in some other way you had never dreamed of.

So, shortly after coming into office, Farkash started directing his spies to look at details that his predecessors had thought irrelevant or regarded as second-order concerns: Were people out shopping in Beirut (a sign of the Lebanese economy's health)? What was intellectual life like on the streets of Damascus? How were Iraqi refugees inside Syria settling in? What interested Farkash about such inquiries is that they were new and changing, very different from the "where are the Syrian tanks" questions he had been told he should ask. Sometimes he would deliberately put some stress on his enemies just to see what he could learn, and not just in Syria. A friend told me about Farkash's idea for blowing up meaningless crates going to Iran, for instance, or shuffling around safe houses, simply to see what would happen. Actions like this might appear to be irrelevant, but they allowed him to watch his enemies react. And—this was every bit as crucial—Farkash said what he liked best about this approach was that the questions stressed his system, too. They forced him and his team to look and think differently. Traditional intelligence briefings came in binders that marked out the military situation, the economic situation, and the political situation as if they shared only the loosest of connections. These sorts of briefings had been prepared for years. They were an old-style way of looking. And they were, almost uniformly, wrong.

3. Darwinian Killers

Starting in 2002, Farkash expanded his innovative approach to Israel's problem with terrorist attacks. And in the process he made a discovery that changed almost everything about how Israel (and later the United States) fought terrorists. Using some of the tools at his disposal, including still-classified technologies from Unit 8200, Farkash began asking different questions about terror attacks. Instead of the usual "Where will the next attack be?" he began asking "How long does it take to move $10,000 into Gaza?" and "What is the best way to smuggle bomb parts *into* Ramallah?" He became less interested in why terrorist attacks succeeded and curious instead about how others had failed. Farkash studied these failures in excruciating detail. This was a shift for Israeli intelligence. But Farkash figured that the terrorists devoted little time to their successes but obsessed about the failures. He thought he might try to do the same thing for a little while.

When Farkash stepped back from his surveys of these misfires, he discovered something surprising. Inside the terror webs he was watching, he saw two different processes at work. On one level — a surface level, the one you could see with the usual tools of spying — cells were carrying out the day-to-day business of violent fundamentalism: gathering money, recruiting bombers, and passing talking points to the mullahs in the mosques. But another process was also under way, and it was far more important and far harder to spot: at a deeper level the terror organizations were changing. In response to Israeli actions they would adapt. And it was this level, Farkash realized, that was the key to understanding a terror group. It involved very few people, a hot little core of change and innovation pulsing away inside the larger ball of a terror network. But the operators at that level were the smartest of Israel's enemies. The traditional way of attacking terrorism involved tearing down the houses of people who supported the groups, jailing huge masses of Arabs who had even the lightest connection to terror, trying to cut off routes into Israel. The goal was to "drain the swamp," as American anti-insurgent planners in Iraq liked to say, to remove the support for terror. It was all about attacking the outside of the terror web. Farkash knew this approach was failing; now he began to suspect it was actually backfiring, making Israel's enemies *more* dangerous. "Day by day, the tactics we were using," Farkash told me, "were forcing them to be more innovative." He paused, and added, as if slightly incredulous, *"We forced them to evolve."*

But his new questions had told him, at least, precisely where he should try to strike: at the level of the efficient engine for adaptation. Doing this required new tools. Farkash and his teams borrowed network-analysis software developed for phone systems and ecological food webs to discover where the adaptive "nodes" of a terror group were located. Farkash's algorithms could look at any network, whether a train system or a telephone exchange, and find the most devastating points an enemy could attack. (In fact, there was evidence that Al Qaeda was doing this as well. The July 2005 attacks on the London Underground occurred at three stations that a computerized network analysis might have identified as weak links in the system. London police, running their own simulation, found that the target combination was the second best among 320 million possibilities. It seemed unlikely that the bombers had made these choices randomly.)

Farkash found that while terror groups could involve hundreds of people, only a few had the skills that were used to help the groups change their communications patterns, an essential part of evolution under pressure. So he aimed right at them. And generally he began an effort to find and then isolate the terrorists who operated at this evolutionary level. What did this mean in practical terms? "I hate to say it," one of his colleagues explained when I asked, "and I am glad we don't have to decide who. But the answer is targeted killings." Targeted killing is just what it sounds like: taking out only the most essential pieces of a network instead of trying to wipe away the whole system. This was a complicated, expensive process. Israeli intelligence task forces coordinated teams of hundreds of people who would spend millions of dollars for a single kill. It also presented all sorts of moral questions for the Israeli military: for instance, how many innocent civilians was it acceptable to kill when trying to take out a keystone terrorist? (The Ministry of Defense asked a group of mathematicians to work on this problem. They submitted an answer—3.4 civilians per dead terrorist—but no one was happy with either the process or the coldness of such a figure.) The tactic, once it had been perfected, seemed to have astonishingly effective results. The groups were unable to grow and change. Terror attacks plummeted.

There was a lesson here. After all, hundreds of now-defunct Islamic terror groups were closed files in the offices of Israeli intelligence, having been run out of business. Some of them had looked like sure winners—well financed, stocked with angry young fundamentalists. What went wrong? If you asked yourself this question, as Farkash did in a moment of philosophical reflection, you found the answer was that they had failed to adapt. Hizb'allah, Hamas, the Palestine Liberation Organization (PLO)—these surviving groups were different. They did adjust and evolve. They grew stronger. If you could stop that evolution, he bet, they would die instantly. If you could understand and even *feel* how they grew and changed, then you could wipe them out very quickly. But first you had to be looking much deeper than traditional counterterror spies ever had.

*   *   *

In the old days, many problems in international affairs seemed as if they could be understood from the outside in. If you knew, say, how many tanks Russia had in East Germany, you probably thought you had a pretty good idea of Russia's intentions. Far-kash's argument was that this way of seeing was usually wrong and often deadly. It caused analysts to focus too much on what they could measure and not enough on what they could not. What he was proposing was a way of seeing that never lingered on a single variable. This week you might look at how many tanks Syria had, next week at the most popular program on Iranian television. The goal was to watch for change, to see how the society was moving and understand that the snap of instant change could come from many surprising places (Gorbachev's regime-shifting *nomenklatura*, for instance, or the combination of air-bag technology and games). From time to time this way of looking would yield a crucial insight—like the one about the "evolutionary heart" of terror groups—that you could act on. Then, the next day, you had to go back to this way of seeing all over again, looking for fresh insights. What you could never do was treat what you needed to know as something fixed, some-thing that could be managed the way you would run down a list of things to pack for a vacation: underwear, swim trunks, sunscreen. As the arms inspector David Kay explained to the journalist Bob Woodward about the flaws in America's hunt for weapons of mass destruction before and after the Iraq war, "You simply cannot find weapons of mass destruction using a list. You have to treat this like an intelligence operation. You go after people. You don't go after physical assets." He continued, "You treat it by going after the expertise, the security guards that would have been there, the movers, the generals that would have seen it, the Special Republican Guard." It was a suggestion right out of the Farkash playbook: look deep, focus on things that move and change, never ask the usual questions.

But if Farkash had mastered this instinct, if his Yoda-like prescriptions to his staff had yielded a relatively successful and surprise-free time in office for him, it remained a highly personal accomplishment. He was unable to inculcate it even into the "small" Israeli defense bureaucracy. Six months after he left office, Israel launched that disastrous 2006 air war against Hizb'allah. The strategy was classically old-school: pound the visible Hizb'allah to kill the invisible. Sure enough, Hizb'allah evolved exactly as Farkash would have predicted; it changed in midwar by finding new ways to communicate that Israel couldn't penetrate and by developing battlefield tactics the IDF hadn't trained for or even imagined. It wasn't that there was some problem with Israeli airpower or with the accurate spy-satellite and drone photos they possessed of every Hizb'allah redoubt and rocket site. Israel had started the war with what its commanders thought was an almost perfect picture of Hizb'allah. "This time, it will be the end," they said. It wasn't. What went wrong? The problem wasn't the Israeli planes or the exhausted and unprepared ground troops. Rather, it was a battle plan that aimed impatiently at Hizb'allah's surface, missing the deeper muscles that drove the group. Israel's defense establishment, Farkash confessed to me, was infected by a way of seeing the world so fundamentally flawed that it was possibly the greatest threat Israel faced. That's a conclusion that should make us wonder at least a little about our own habits of seeing as well—and about how we might change them.

4. The Guru of Sand Hill Road

Sometime in the summer of 1999, Michael Moritz, a Silicon Valley venture capitalist, received a call from one of the founders of a firm he had backed several years earlier, asking him to take a meeting with an upstart Internet company. The call was not unusual. In Silicon Valley, home to the most dynamic information technology firms in the world, business is still often conducted in a manner that reveals the deeply personal roots of the place: friends invest in other friends' companies, share technology and ideas, and work together even as they compete.

Moritz, who was then in his mid-forties, was a partner at Sequoia Capital, one of the Valley's oldest venture firms, and he had developed a reputation as a masterful talent spotter of Internet companies. The founder calling Moritz was ringing about another, smaller firm he had been impressed with. The firm was operating in an already crowded sector of the Internet business, providing online search services in the same way companies such as Inktomi, Ask Jeeves, and a dozen others did. But Moritz, who often looks at a dozen possible investments in a week and had already been keeping an eye on the firm, agreed to the meeting and found himself unusually impressed. So, even though the field was packed with competitors, Moritz decided to make a significant investment.

The decision, however, flew in the face of what was a lot of pretty well established wisdom about how to make money in Silicon Valley. To begin with, the search business was very crowded. The firms already in the game had billions to spend hiring the smartest engineers and puzzling out the fastest search algorithms. The list included not only such giants as Ask Jeeves and

Yahoo!, but also established media and technology companies such as Microsoft and America Online. The key to astronomical returns for venture-capital investors was usually getting into new businesses early, before giant and well-financed competitors arrived. Getting in late, backing a small firm that was essentially a wholesale provider of search services—this was exactly the sort of investment that several decades of experience suggested should be avoided. It wasn't so much that the management team of the new firm was inexperienced (both were still in school at Stanford) or that the name of the firm didn't make much sense to anyone; it was simply that the overwhelming lesson of history was clear. Nearly a dozen other investing firms in the Valley had reached a similar conclusion about the firm, deciding to pass on an investment. Why should Sequoia be different? But in the face of skepticism—and even a small bit of local derision when the $12.5-million investment was announced—Moritz persisted. Six years later Sequoia's stake in Google would be worth billions.

There was, as we are about to see, something special about Moritz. Silicon Valley, sort of like Israel (and our sandpile world), was a place that was filled with surprise and unanticipated danger (and opportunity to make a killing). No business was really safe from innovation: Yahoo! could think it owned search only to find itself trashed by Google; Motorola might think it had control of microchips for cell phones only to discover Intel eating its lunch. The Valley, the heart of so much American innovation, is a place where the revolutionary spirit of our age is particularly alive. But that also means the challenges of working there, of staying alive yourself, especially if you are an investor, are like the ones Farkash faced: rapid and surprising change that could come out of nowhere (a dorm room at Stanford) to remake the landscape. How you should look at such a world was as important a question for Moritz and his investors as it was for Farkash. What Farkash had figured out was that understanding a sandpile meant looking deeply into the pile, not simply relying on outside-to-inside satellite techniques. In Silicon Valley, Moritz was perfecting another important technique. How, against a landscape of thousands of start-up companies, tens of thousands of engineers, and billions of investment dollars, could you pick out the kid who was about to make history?

Investments like the one Moritz made in Google are myth-making. But they are, to be honest about it, very, very unusual. The thousandfold returns for early shareholders in firms like Netscape or Yahoo! were a sort of greed magnet that drew cash into venture capital in the 1990s. But the reality was that a decade or so later the returns on venture-capital-fund investments had barely outpaced the S&P 500—and with a great deal more risk. Most venture capitalists dump money into companies you have never heard of, working on products you'll never use, and run by entrepreneurs whose dreams far outstrip their reach. Eighty percent of venture-backed firms fail altogether; most of the rest return double or triple their money, which looks great but has to be offset against the millions lost on the bad ideas.

Yet in this environment of expensive, risky mediocrity, Moritz and one other venture capitalist, a former microchip salesman from Intel named John Doerr, who works on Sand Hill Road just down the street from Moritz, stood out. (The street's name, in one of those accidental tributes, captures perfectly the complex dynamics Per Bak would have spotted at work in the Silicon Valley.) Moritz had not only picked Google out of that pile of mostly forgettable failures, he'd also shaped investments in Yahoo!, Pay Pal, YouTube, and a long list of other successes. At one point companies Moritz and Sequoia had funded accounted for 10 percent of the total value of the Nasdaq. A list of the firms he had discovered, nurtured, and taken public from his office in Menlo Park ("I don't like any investment more than thirty minutes away," he once told me) looked like a day trader's dream portfolio. While you might think this was because Moritz and Doerr were gifted technological geniuses, übergeeks with cash, you would be wrong. Übergeeks, like Microsoft's cofounder Paul Allen, *had* gone into the venture business during that 1990s bubble. Almost as a rule, they had blown up spectacularly.

Moritz was probably the greatest technology investor of his generation, and what set him apart was this weird quirk: he didn't care so much about the technology. Any number of venture firms — maybe even most of them — were stuffed with Caltech and Stanford Ph.D.s who could easily outscience Moritz, a crisp Welshman who held degrees in literature from Oxford (he once wanted to be Norman Mailer) and in business from Wharton. It wasn't that Moritz didn't understand the technology, it wasn't even that he didn't think it incredibly exciting — he did. The difference was that he didn't place it at the center of his thinking. When he looked at the Valley or at a company, he looked differently. "What sector in technology investing are you excited about today?" he was once asked in an interview. "That's independent of where we choose to invest," he said.

This koan-like conclusion signaled a very different way of seeing. If you and I were starting a venture-capital firm today, we'd probably go out and hire a bunch of engineers who knew the technology and some finance guy who could work on the deals. Then we'd most likely lose a ton of money. Moritz's point — and it was a point that made him hundreds of millions of dollars over the years—was that success in a rapidly changing business like technology wasn't determined by gear or deal structure or even genius. Rather it was determined by the hard-to-predict, always-changing interaction between the context and the company. His job was to pay attention to both, to adjust the context as much as he could (which wasn't usually very much), and to be obsessive, even impolite, about adjusting the company as fast and as often as necessary. Moritz's special genius was to do this, not in reaction to the market but ahead of it. This process of trimming and sculpting his companies never ended. The lesson of the Valley was that the moment it stopped, companies were usually blind-sided by new competition (see Yahoo!) or bankrupted by a market that no longer wanted their products (see Atari). "A year in the world of technology," he once explained to me about that Google investment, "is an eternity. What might be perceived by others as a late entry into something isn't always quite like that." When he first made his investment in Google, he confessed, "No one understood what it would be, no one had the faintest clue." Google wasn't born great; it became great. And how this happened had everything to do with the way Moritz operated, and how he saw the fast-changing world around him.

As Moritz watched his competitors at work, making one expensive mistake after another, he became convinced that often it was the very expertise of other venture capitalists that killed them. They obsessed about the technology or about the transformative powers of the Internet itself. There was a double trap at work here. The first was a too-strong faith in technology, as if the fate of a firm rested on the quality of its ideas alone, not on the complex interaction of those ideas with the world; the second was the old scientist's habit of breaking problems into pieces to solve them. In the same way you might answer a hard math problem by solving it bit by bit, engineers–turned–venture capitalists tended to look at companies as a sum of their parts. It was a deadly instinct. Moritz was the first to admit that his own mistakes, and he had made plenty of them, usually came from these kinds of math errors, from thinking that the combination of team and idea would be enough. In fact, no amount of spreadsheet mechanics would have convinced you in advance that Google was a likely home-run investment. "Parts of the critical system," Per Bak once wrote about complex networks, "cannot be understood in isolation. Studying the individual grains under the microscope doesn't give a clue as to what is going on in the whole sandpile. Nothing in the individual grain suggests the emergent properties of the pile." Studying Google's tech in isolation told you very little about the firm's potential value. So you had to learn to look at everything at once.

If you weren't accustomed to his methods, of course, working for Moritz could be disorienting. He was constantly pushing his companies for quick pivots. No "plan" lasted longer than necessary. There was only ceaseless interaction and experimentation. What Moritz had discovered was that good companies were flexible, and he had learned to look for that. If you had a company that could shape-shift fast enough and a mind like Moritz's that could see what was needed, then you were in a very good position to avoid the mistakes of investors who stared obsessively at their cool geeky solutions wondering why the world didn't care. In fact, most of Sequoia Capital's biggest hits were companies that had started in their own offices, close enough to Moritz and his partners for them to ensure that they were being shaped in exactly the right way, like young trees putting down that first, all-important root base. YouTube, a company that returned hundreds of times its initial investment for Sequoia when it was sold to Google, spent a third of its entire life as an independent company just down the hall from Moritz. You can imagine that working for a company he had funded could be exhausting. Even if you were the CEO of a firm you had dreamed up yourself and built from scratch, you often couldn't see what Moritz saw; you were wandering sleepless, worrying about your technology or your employees or some imagined idea of how your firm would destroy Microsoft. Moritz, however, was seeing beyond all of that, and, if you listened to him, he was probably going to make you very, very rich.

Watching Moritz think through an investment was like watching one of those Evelyn Wood–trained speed-readers who could take in an entire page at a time instead of slogging through a book word by word. He devoured information, sucked up more data about an entrepreneur in an hour than a psychologist might do in a month of private sessions. Moritz's genius was that he wasn't cutting companies up as he looked at them but placing them in context. The forces shaping a technology market, consumer demands, changes in software design, shifts in microchip pricing, the up-and-down emotions of a founder—he was watching all of these for signs of change. His point was that you might have a dream of what you wanted to do—index the Web, help people talk as they traveled—but unless you constantly refined that dream, constantly updated it, your chances for success were limited. For this reason, one of the critical features of the tech business is the constant revising of products, operating systems, and software. There is no right, final "view" of the world. Rather, the correct image is more of a manic movie: World 1.0, 2.0, 3.0—and so on into history.

Moritz knew there were lots of mysterious, nonengineering pieces to keeping this treadmill of fresh innovation and change alive. Take, for instance, the personality of tech entrepreneurs themselves. Moritz cultivated a skill few engineers cared about: the ability to empathize with company founders. It was crucial to see their dreams exactly as they did, he believed. Even if they were deluded, you had to know how and where to adjust their imagination. And sometimes—usually in the case of the most brilliant ones—they were onto something. "The thing I am terrified of is losing that empathy," Moritz said to me one afternoon as we sat in his office on Sand Hill Road. "The best investments we have missed recently came because the founders came in here and we blew them off because we didn't understand them. We couldn't empathize," he told me. "That is a fatal mistake." And, he reflected, "If I were running American foreign policy, I would want to focus on empathizing."

5. The Smoking-Pile-of-Rubble Problem

When Mike Moritz says he's not driven purely by technology or when Farkash talks about using Syria's Lebanon strategy to understand Israel's risks, they're telling us something priceless about how we can get that "right view" that the Zen monks are so fond of. They are reflecting the sense that in a fast-changing world, what really matters is often hidden in corners where the usual "experts" in their professions don't—or can't—easily look. And they are giving us some guidance about how we *should* examine problems. "Intelligence is not a blend of deduction, insight, and inference from the body of evidence as a whole," one famous Cold War–era CIA paper explained. "It is a sequence of judgments on discrete units of evidence." But intelligence, then and particularly now, is *exactly* a blend of deduction, insight, and inference. It's this skill that marks the greatest successes of the age, from men like Warren Buffett (who negotiates billion-dollar deals in an afternoon if they feel right) to Steve Jobs (who attacks improbable markets with radically different technology and design). Yet the old habit of discrete, piece-by-piece thinking remains, in financial markets ("Ah, those mortgages will never affect our insurance business") as often as in foreign policy. But in a world where everything is connected, advance signs of change, of turbulence, are likely to appear only when we look in unexpected places.

Farkash was right when he lamented that an agency like the CIA can't quite grasp this. It's true of almost any large organization. In a postmortem examination of how the CIA missed signals of Iraq's plans to invade Kuwait in 1990, for example, the agency concluded it had simply been trying to solve the wrong math problem. "The bottom-line judgment that Iraq was unlikely to initiate warfare in the near term, issued repeatedly in the year before the assault on Kuwait," one study concluded, "was based on the assumption that Iraq needed several years to recover from the military and economic devastation of its long war with Iran." This old-style analysis reduced Saddam's intentions to a single variable—had the Iraqi army recovered?—that would be watched and studied and obsessed over, even as it became less and less relevant. American officials were similarly astonished when, one morning in 1998, they discovered that India had tested a nuclear weapon. Everything they had been looking at—the assurances of the Indian government, the booming technology entrepreneurs, basic relations with Pakistan—suggested that a test was unlikely. The three-letter acronym of the agency that let the Americans know that India's bomb had detonated was not CIA, it was CNN. Narrow-gazing not only leads to these kinds of misfires, it also fatally constrains the ability to imagine *good* ideas or policies. The chance for real brilliance or flair is usually best seen out of the corner of the eye.

John Doerr, the only other venture-capital investor with a record to match Moritz's, liked to joke that educating a young venture capitalist was like training a fighter pilot: it cost millions of dollars and often produced little more than a smoking pile of rubble. But the reality, rarely discussed outside Silicon Valley, was even grimmer. Doerr's firm had spent tens of millions of dollars trying to teach the younger partners to fly. It never produced anyone to match Doerr; Moritz's firm had the same experience. "It's very difficult to figure out from somebody's background whether they will be successful in the venture-capital business," Moritz once mused. "I can think of numerous examples of people with glittering résumés and burnished credentials who you would have thought would thrive in the venture business, and they flame out. I can think of people with very unlikely backgrounds who have flourished in the venture business. We've given up on trying to predict who will and won't do well in the venture business."

The big problem in training those young venture capitalists was that it was hard to get them to see like Moritz, to take in everything at once instead of fixating on pieces of companies as if they were linear math problems. Engineers, for instance, failed as investors because too often they fell in love with MIPS and bandwidths; the MBAs swooned over "cram-downs" or "ratchets" or other geeky cash tricks. This was lethal. In places like Silicon Valley or Israel, the greatest threats and opportunities were so new that there were no experts. The only way to spot dangers (and opportunities) was to break out of narrow ways of seeing. It meant not simply changing how you ran your firm or collected intelligence but also—and this is the tough part—undoing a couple of millennia of Western intellectual habits, notions that went all the way back to Aristotle's idea that you could understand something only if you could break it apart and examine all the pieces. This way of seeing bankrupted some of Moritz's most brilliant-looking competitors during the dot-com collapse of 2001. It was what sent Israel into Lebanon with its hopes pinned on air power in 2006 and sent America into Iraq with a war plan that anticipated an end to violence within two months. And it allowed radical deregulation of financial and commodities markets under the assumption that if we knew how all the parts worked, there was no danger in their sum. Acting without seeing the whole environment was suicidal. But acting with such a view? Well, that led to great fortunes and real security. And that is why the first step toward our own deep security — whether for our country, our business, or our families — is teaching ourselves to see differently.

6. The Tiger in the Forest

For much of the last decade, the experimental psychologist Richard Nisbett has devoted a large part of his research to the question of how our cultural backgrounds condition the way we think. Nisbett dates his curiosity about the subject to a debate he had with a Chinese graduate student in the early 1990s, when he discovered that there were fundamental differences in the most basic elements of how the two of them thought. "The Chinese believe in constant change," his student told him, by way of possible explanation. "Westerners live in a simpler, more deterministic world. They think they can control events because they know the rules that govern the behavior of objects."

Until that moment, Nisbett later wrote, "I had been a life-long universalist concerning the nature of human thought." That is, Nisbett (like most other psychologists) believed that everyone basically thought and reasoned in the same way; any differences were due to the quirks of our education, families, or experiences. There was no shortage of literature, dating back even before Freud, documenting the ways in which overambitious parents, painful economic status, or personal appearance affected the way we thought and behaved. In fact, the entire discipline of modern psychology was to some extent based on unearthing and then deciphering these secret codes of our personalities. But the more Nisbett thought about what his graduate student had said, the more curious he became. Culture, he figured, had to make some sort of difference. But explanations about how it might do that, he found, were surprisingly underdeveloped.

If such explanations were hard to come by, evidence of cultural differences, once you started to look for them, were everywhere. Colleagues of Nisbett, for instance, once conducted a study in which they observed American and Japanese mothers playing with their children and found that everything from the way the two groups fed the children to how they talked to them was distinct. American mothers used nouns ("Look at the doggie," they might say) twice as often as the Japanese, who instead emphasized relationships ("I give this to you; now you give it back to me"). When they tested children from different cultures, they discovered that the East Asian children were picking up new verbs nearly twice as quickly as nouns—and far faster than American or French children of the same age, who were busy learning noun after noun. The question that soon obsessed Nisbett was whether these early cultural twists in education played out in later life. Did they, for example, offer insight into old truisms about Asians being more family-centered or Americans being more rebellious?

So, starting in 1993, Nisbett began a series of experiments that offered some of the first reliable data on how culture shapes thinking. It was controversial work. After all, suggesting that culture shaped thinking seemed awfully close to making other uncomfortable suggestions about how culture might limit intelligence or individual potential. The research could quickly lead, critics feared, into ideas like "Asians can't handle democracy." So Nisbett stuck tightly to quantitative science, and most of his papers—and those of the researchers who joined his work—were carefully written to avoid stretching the conclusions about what they found in the lab very far outside it. But what they did find, particularly in experiments about how people see, offered one of the clearest explanations about why we often make the errors of the type Louis Halle warned against and that Farkash and Moritz somehow instinctively avoided.

7. Change Blind

In late 2004 Nisbett and two graduate students, Hannah Faye Chua and Julie Boland, set out to recruit a group of fifty graduate students from around the University of Michigan campus in Ann Arbor. Half of the students had been raised and educated in the United States; the other half, though now students at UM, had been raised in China. On the day of the experiment, the students arrived at Nisbett's lab and filled out a short questionnaire about their personal histories. Then Chua led them to an awkward-looking lab setup on a table which included a computer screen at one end and a chin rest at the other. On a desk nearby was a head-mounted device that would track the students' eye movements. After strapping on the device, the research subjects placed their chin on the small plastic rest, and the lights in the lab were turned off. A picture of a small cross was beamed onto the screen in front of them. Then, one by one, at thirty-second intervals, a series of pictures appeared on the screen. The pictures all had a similar visual motif, an image of a large object in what Nisbett called a "realistic complex background": a tiger in a forest, for instance, or a horse in a field of flowers. The research subjects were shown thirty-six images for about three seconds each. After each image, the screen returned to the white background with a cross, and the students were asked to refocus on the cross. When a new image appeared a few seconds later, the eye-tracker silently recorded where they looked and for how long. Then the screen went to white again and the process was repeated.

When the students had finished, Chua sorted the eye-movement data and found a pattern so clear that her first instinct probably should have been to wonder if there was a mistake somewhere. While observing the images flashed in front of them, American students immediately looked at the foreground objects—the horse or the tiger, for example. And once they spotted that image, they spent the bulk of the time before the screen went white again looking right at it. The Chinese, by contrast, usually looked at the environment around the main object first, probing that "realistic complex background" of forest or field. They did look at the focal object, but for far less time than the Americans did. "There was no time point at which the Chinese were fixating [on] the objects significantly more than the backgrounds," Nisbett wrote later. This was, to a Western point of view, a bit weird. It was as if someone took out his wallet to show you pictures of his kids and you started complimenting the furniture in the snapshot.

It was too simple to say that the Americans stared at the main object to the exclusion of everything else, but when the researchers later tested the students to see what they recalled, this was more or less the pattern that emerged. The Americans had a better ability to recall specific objects they had seen: horse, car, dolphin. The Chinese often forgot what object had been in a given scene but recalled the backgrounds in detail. In fact, simply by changing the backgrounds, Nisbett and his colleagues could fool the Chinese into saying they had not seen a particular object before. You could flash a picture of a brown horse in a field, a stream, or a forest, but if you put the same brown horse in a street scene later on and asked the Chinese students if they had ever seen it, they usually answered no. What was going on? Nisbett hazarded this guess: "East Asians live in relatively complex social networks with prescribed role relations. Attention to context is, therefore, important for effective functioning. In contrast, Westerners live in less constraining social worlds that stress independence and allow them to pay less attention to context." That was partly true—and you can see why, in a world where context matters so much, Western-style seeing might be a liability. But there was something much more profound occurring as well, something vitally important for our own thinking about the world.

Have you ever seen a Chinese landscape painting? If you have seen one done in the traditional style, it was probably what Chinese call a *shanshui* painting, literally a "mountain and water" image, with looming peaks, hazy clouds, and an ocean that stretches across most of the painting. People or animals usually feature in a *shanshui* landscape only as tiny brushstrokes, almost accidental ticks of ink dwarfed by the mountains or rivers around them. This is an expression of the idea in Chinese philosophy and art that the environment is far more powerful than any individual. It is never stable and, in its sudden changes from one state to another, more important than the desires of any of us. (No matter how much we want to have a picnic on a rainy day, for instance, there's not much we can do.) In other words, *context* is everything—an idea right out of Moritz's or Farkash's (or Gertrude Stein's) thinking. The most cherished Chinese nature paintings take their power not from photorealistic accuracy but rather from their ability to capture and hold the unfathomable and terrifying tension of a natural environment shifting, colliding, and evolving around the much smaller humans. Great Chinese paintings are inked context-snapshots that are designed specifically to be a little intimidating.

This emphasis on everything around us instead of a "me-first" view of life reveals a quirk in the Asian way of seeing, one that also showed up in Nisbett's study if we look at it in the right way. Western science saw the world as something that could be understood and dominated. But ancient Chinese thinking was obsessed instead with the mysterious, impenetrable part of nature. The foundation text of Chinese philosophy, after all, is called *The I-Ching or Book of Changes*—the very title emphasizing that we live in an environment of constant motion. The most famous oscillation, of course, is between yin and yang, but those mountain-and-water paintings also contain a balance between the stability and hardness of mountain stone and the softness of running water. With this view of the world, one that takes constant change as a given, it's easy to see why you might want to keep your eyes moving. More than anything, what you want to know is *when* change is going to begin. In Chinese philosophy this sense is known as a mastery of *incipience,* and the skill is often praised as the highest form of wisdom. Those Chinese graduate students dancing their eyes around the background of Nisbett's images were furiously trying to gather information about what surrounded the central object because they believed, at a level so deep it was programmed into their eye movements, that the environment contained clues to what was about to happen. If you stared at a single spot in the world around you, that incipient sensibility would be dulled to the point of uselessness.

The Americans, by contrast, spent their time looking at the focal object, which, they clearly thought, was surely the essential element. Think of a famous Western painting, and you will probably recall something like a warship pounding over waves or Venus rising in the center of a Botticelli landscape. Western culture's cult of individual power, the self-determination of man, is one of its fundamental features. But it limits what we see when we look at the world. That tiger in Nisbett's image, for instance, took up about 25 percent of the space on the screen, but it captured 80 percent or more of the Western students' attention. We think the focal object is the most important part of any image in front of us. We *stare.* And in so doing we miss crucial details *around* the object. In another study, Nisbett reversed the trick he had played on the Chinese students. Would American students notice a change in the environment if the focal object remained the same? If, say, the horse stayed the same but the field around it went from spring flowers to fall colors? Most of the subjects missed the shift. When it came to the environment, Americans were almost completely "change blind."

8. The Lingering Gaze

This important insight reveals something a little uncomfortable and awkward about our habits. After all, it's not particularly difficult to see that ignoring 75 percent of the picture of a fast-changing world could lead to some pretty suicidal decisions. When you focus on an object ("Saddam" or "bank bailouts") to the exclusion of the swirling, furious energy of the environment around that object (clan rivalries, say, or the real-economy demands of homeowners), you force yourself into a very limited understanding of the world. It's like trying to watch a football game by fixating on the thirty-five-yard line. Look, for instance, at the way the Pentagon has strategized for decades, using what is called "threat-based" planning: picking a particular danger and then budgeting, training, and organizing to step into the conflict just in time to save the day. Such views are appealing. They are easy to explain, they make the process of preparation simple to map out, and they offer compelling stories for Congress and the public. But they are disastrous in practice. In peacetime they exhaust the military as it runs ragged trying to prepare for conflicts that never occur. When the military is called into action, it is almost always used in ways (think Afghanistan, Somalia, Iraqi reconstruction) that this threat-based thinking never envisioned.

A better approach would be to build an adjustable military, one that understands it can't know what it will face and is constantly prepared for the widest possible range of contingencies. It might be wiser, as one RAND Corporation paper suggested, to think of the Pentagon as a sort of investment portfolio that is constantly, boldly rebalanced to reflect the demands of the market for violence — and that prizes real and easy liquidity over long-term fixed positions. This idea of an "adaptive national defense" has been pushed by a few intellectuals, but usually it goes nowhere. That is part of the reason the historian Martin van Creveld, taking a thousand-year look at nations with functional and dysfunctional defenses, comes to the conclusion that "already, today, the most powerful armed forces are largely irrelevant to modern war. Indeed, their relevance stands in inverse proportion to their modernity." We have military planning that stares instead of shifts. Little wonder it is often surprised. Pick up a copy of the latest *National Security Strategy of the United States,* for instance, and you will find nothing about empathy or about enhancing our ability to feel the environment or about financial panic, or global disease. There is ten times as much in it about remaking the world as about remaking our own institutions. And it focuses maniacally, like those ogling, slow-moving eyes of the American graduate students, on a single object: terrorism. Who knows what we may be missing?

One of the studies Nisbett liked to mention was by Masako Watanabe, a Japanese historian who examined the differences between the way Japanese and Western teachers taught history. The Americans, she found, tended to begin with the outcome of a historical event. This approach condensed history into something resembling a cake recipe—specific sequential steps of the sort you might remember from high school tests: "List the five reasons the Germans lost World War I." When Watanabe observed Japanese teachers, though, she saw something different. They began not with the outcome but with the context, sort of like a Chinese painter framing an image with mountains and oceans. The teachers pressed students to picture themselves in the shoes of the participants, to understand how they felt, to think of the options and pressures they confronted. In this approach to the world, history isn't baked like a cake—three teaspoons revolution and one cup religious strife—but rather emerges from the complex interactions of subjects and environment. The Japanese teachers thought that if the goal was really to understand history, they were better off grading students by their ability to "show empathy with the historical figures." And maybe the way history is taught in Japan is a reminder, in a way. Perhaps it carries an indirect message too: that the country once was a source of terrible disaster when empathy was replaced with a blind, fanatical, and mercilessly focused ambition.

Empathy. Recall that it was the one thing Moritz most feared losing, the key element Farkash tried to cultivate in his spies and war planners. It was their way of saying that in a world of constant change, you need to try to connect with the environment around you any way you can: by sweeping your eyes, by opening your mind to uncomfortable ideas, even by trying to sympathize with historically noxious figures. Only then could you improve your chances of not missing the signs that something, something important, was about to change.

The virtue of this kind of constant probing and ceaseless updating of your worldview was once captured by the American political scientist and psychologist Philip Tetlock, who teaches at Berkeley. For more than a decade, starting in the late 1980s, Tetlock ran studies on what he later called the "fox and hedgehog difference" in types of predictions. The name came from the famous assertion by the British philosopher Isaiah Berlin that there were two kinds of thinkers in the world: hedgehogs, who know one big thing, and foxes, who dart from idea to idea. "Plato, Lucretius, Pascal, Hegel, Dostoevsky, Nietzsche, Ibsen and Proust are, in varying degrees, hedgehogs," Berlin wrote. "Herodotus, Aristotle, Montaigne, Erasmus, Molière, Goethe, Pushkin, Balzac and Joyce are foxes." Tetlock and his team interviewed hundreds of "experts" on subjects such as economics, international relations, and politics and asked them to make predictions about the short-term future (the next five years). Then they divided the subjects of the study into a number of categories: optimists and pessimists, left and right political orientation, foxes and hedgehogs. After some time had passed, Tetlock's team reviewed the prediction sheets to see who was most often right; they found that the only really reliable predictor was the one that divided foxes and hedgehogs. "Low scorers look like hedgehogs," Tetlock wrote later; they were "thinkers who know 'one big thing' and aggressively extend the explanatory reach of that one big thing into new domains." High scorers, he said, looked more like foxes: they were skeptical of easy historical analogy, they tended to be more probabilistic in their thinking, and they were comfortable updating their models.

It wasn't, Tetlock explained, that the foxes knew any more or less about the subject. After all, they were experts too. It was how they acquired and updated their knowledge that seemed to matter. The more wide-ranging their curiosity—the more they looked at the world like those Chinese students—the more accurate they tended to be. "We normally expect knowledge to promote accuracy, so if it was surprising to discover how quickly we reached a point of diminishing returns," Tetlock wrote, "it should be downright disturbing to discover that knowledge handicaps so large a fraction of forecasters." The problem, he suspected, was that hedgehog personalities were generally very eager, *too* eager, for closure. They stuck with one big idea precisely because they wanted to know it completely, to have the sensation of reaching a total and final understanding, as if they had finished the Saturday *New York Times* crossword in pen. But that instinct for a final sigh of knowing was, in a fast-changing and unpredictable world, deadly. Sometimes the stubbornness of these hedgehogs did mean they made correct predictions; they were often right when calling big changes. But overall, they were measurably inferior to fast-updating foxes. And the cost was stark: "When hedgehogs were wrong," Tetlock concluded wryly in his award-winning book *Expert Political Judgment*, "they were very, very wrong." The list of misfires he found included predictions of "the disintegration of nation states that are still with us (Canada, Nigeria, India, Pakistan, Iran, Iraq, etc.)" as well as a few nuclear wars, the end of political parties, and early calls of economic collapse—in 1988.

Changing how we see isn't easy. All of us have a little hedgehog in us, that desire to see and understand something completely, once and for all. It's not only that the habits Nisbett and his team studied are pretty much hardwired into our brains; it's also that it is exhausting to constantly change our point of view and options and attitudes. It's nice to feel certain, even if the certainty is that Canada will collapse. But the point is that the world is changing constantly—ever faster, frankly. So mismatching our slow way of seeing with the way of the world is predictably disastrous. Picking up the habit of looking constantly for new ideas and *empathizing* with our enemies is a bit counterintuitive and uncomfortable, but it is a really valuable kind of insurance against self-delusion. It is strange to try to understand the mind-set of a Pakistani scientist, the dreams of a rogue trader, the fears of someone helplessly trapped in poverty, or to sit side by side with a Hizb'allah leader and really try to see the way he does for a time. But it might also have felt peculiar to explain that the most successful Israeli general endured because he could feel the way a Gaza Strip mullah did, or that a venture capitalist owed his riches in part to an ability to climb into the head of a dorm-dwelling twenty-three-year-old geek. What Farkash and Moritz and those Chinese grad students and the foxlike experts are telling us is that the more we paper over complexities with simple old ideas and the less we try to take in the whole picture, the greater the risk we're running.

Per Bak once found himself puzzling over how to keep track of his sandpiles as they grew ever larger. It was impossible, he figured, to separate any one grain from another, to study the pile in pieces, or even to leave it alone for a while, hoping the math would somehow settle down. It never did. "In the beginning, when the pile is flat," he wrote, "a local description in terms of individual grains is appropriate. But in the critical state where the interactions tie far-away parts of the system together, only a holistic description in terms of one sandpile will do." Everything is connected. And that makes simple analysis very, very dangerous. The implications are clear if you are trying to make foreign policy or manage a global financial or ecological program. You can't ever let your gaze settle or fixate on a single image of the world. You can't—as the United States did—go into a turbulent place like Iraq (made more turbulent by America's arrival) and not update your plan for three years. You can't pressure a constantly changing nation like China in the same way for a decade without, at the most basic level of philosophy and strategy, rejiggering how and why you are pressing for change. Trying to confront nuclear proliferation with policies that are three decades old is similarly absurd. We'll see later on how to act more as Farkash and Moritz might have acted on all of these problems, but here it is enough to observe that any time you hear a crisis response from our leaders that seems to focus on just one object—"bail out the banks" or "kill Osama"—you should feel nervous. Of course, this also means we can't demand such simple, one-shot policies from our leaders either. We need to accept that the best policies will look like something out of one of Moritz's constantly updating software companies.

But—and this is where Moritz and Farkash show a bit of genius in their work—even though an interconnected world may make analysis harder, it doesn't make it impossible. If you can master the skill of looking deeply, it can deliver everything you may have dreamed of. "We must free ourselves from seeing things as they are!" Bak wrote once. His point wasn't that we should ignore things as they are but that what mattered most was looking in such a way that we could see what they might become: sandpiles, our children, physics itself, the global order. Everything Bak knew about the history of science told him that only then could the real work of invention begin.

CHAPTER EIGHT

The Management Secrets of Hizb'allah

1. Balance of Terror

In the summer of 1960, a Harvard professor named Henry Alfred Kissinger completed work on a book about American foreign policy called *The Necessity for Choice*. Kissinger was thirty-seven (the book was dedicated *To My Parents*) and was known as a rising academic star in Cambridge, one of those teachers so popular he caused students to redirect their ambitions or change their majors. The book was a sequel to Kissinger's 1957 *Nuclear Weapons and Foreign Policy*, which had begun to build a reputation for him in Washington that matched the one he had in Cambridge: brilliant, driven, and with complete fluency in how history might be a guide to the future. *The Necessity for Choice*, the jacket copy told the potential buyer, "is a book which every concerned American should read, if he wants to understand the facts behind the newspaper headlines, and to be informed as to possible solutions — even if imperfect." Shortly after John Kennedy was elected president in the fall of 1960, his aide (and Kissinger's colleague at Harvard) Arthur Schlesinger, Jr., slipped the senator an early copy.

The essential idea of *The Necessity for Choice,* the problem "behind the headlines" that interested Kissinger, was an uncomfortable one. Americans, he explained, needed to ask if a nuclear attack by the Soviet Union could be deterred. There was good reason, he argued, to worry that the answer was no. The United States had the wrong sorts of missiles, it wasn't prepared to absorb an attack and then deliver a devastating revenge strike, the country's allies were too vulnerable, it was bungling negotiations on everything from arms control to relations with newly independent nations, and Americans were possibly less psychologically secure than the Russians. (Here Kissinger had in mind the Soviet pillaging of Hungary as the United States stood by, deterred, he wrote, "by our unwillingness to pay the price of victory.") The idea that America faced a "gap" in its deterrence ability, one that could be measured in missing missiles and then made up over time like some sort of factory production shortfall, Kissinger argued, was absurd. "There can be no gap in deterrence," he wrote. "Deterrence is either effective or it is not. There is no margin for error. Mistakes are likely to be irremediable. If the gains from aggression appear to outweigh the penalties even once, deterrence will fail." This was terrifying, particularly given that the likely price of failure was nuclear war or endless Soviet blackmail.

The ideas in *The Necessity for Choice* were a rough sketch of what Kissinger and others later polished into détente, a policy in which American Minuteman missiles and Soviet SS missiles marked out a binary bargain that would either secure the survival of mankind or result in its near-destruction. This cold balance had at least the merit that it reduced international power to its most elementary calculus, a question that almost defined international politics: how do you stop another state from attacking you?

You can see, already, the limits to this question in our revolutionary age. The logic that guided international affairs for centuries was that *threats* of violence could buy safety. This "my dog is bigger than your dog" theory of politics and military affairs led to arms races like the one that made Kissinger so nervous in the 1960s. But that logic can't even begin to contain the dangers of an age of surprise. There's no way to deter terrorists eager to die for their cause or diseases that start at the intersection of man and animal and spread by airplane. Financial panics in markets dominated by instruments it takes a Ph.D. even to discuss are unpredictable *and* undeterrable. You cannot deter the changes in the global economy wrought by a rising China, the pressures of Hindu nationalism in India, water shortages in Mexico, or the hot-blood appeal of a charismatic dictator. In some respects, these sorts of undeterrable wildfire scenarios aren't new. (Think of the Great Plague.) But what *is* new is that such threats spread more quickly and widely than ever, mashing up into new dangers when we try to regulate or control them.

Physicists call such perplexities, parts of a complex system that can't be modeled, ironed out, or removed, "irreducible unknowns." Often they're not only irreducible but *novel:* never seen before. Traditional approaches to stability rely on observations, on historical lessons, on a record of experiment. This is how we build bridges, airplanes, political systems, and even our own lives—we use models of what's worked in the past. But when you're constantly confronted by the unthinkable? When those irreducible unknowns produce "once-in-a-hundred-years" events every few months? Well, that marks out the next transition we need to make in pursuit of deep security.

2. The Snapped Ruler

Learning to *think* in deep-security terms means largely abandoning our idea that we can deter the threats we face and, instead, pressing to make our societies more resilient so we can absorb whatever strikes us. Resilience will be the defining concept of twenty-first-century security, as crucial for your fast-changing job as it is for the nation. We can think of resilience as a measure of how much disturbance a system can absorb before it breaks down so fundamentally that it can't easily return to the way it once was. Think of a plastic ruler. How far can you bend it before it snaps? Or an ecosystem: how many trees can you slice from a forest before animals that live there start dying? Resilience is a broad concept: How many fights can you have with your spouse before your marriage collapses? How much religious fervor can a country like Pakistan contain while still maintaining the characteristics of a democracy? What about a terror attack, which then triggers a bond market sell-off, which triggers a depression, which triggers riots? Once a system tumbles off a ledge and goes catastrophically bad, it is very hard to return it to its earlier state; usually it is impossible. Scientists call this "hysteresis," which comes from the Greek word *hysterein*, which means "to be late"—as in, once a system cascades like this it is too late to do anything about it. What happened to the U.S. investment banking business in the summer of 2008 was a cascade of this sort. None of those firms, packed with money though they were, had nearly enough resilience to bend under the force of the sudden—if self-inflicted—financial shock they received. The snapped ruler remains snapped forever.

Yet to a degree that's almost unimaginable until you've seen it in action, real resilience manages time and again to rescue triumph from what initially looked like disaster. Remember Farkash finding that terrorists who survive do so because they can adapt under pressure? They thrive because they evolve in the face of the unexpected. The best resilient systems are like this. They don't just bend and snap back. They manage to get stronger because of the stress. They capture the good from avalanches of change without letting the bad wipe them out. Today we're not nearly as resilient as we need to be. In fact, one could say we now confront a "resilience gap," not unlike the missile gap Kissinger and a generation of Cold Warriors worried about. The awful truth for them was that you could deter your enemy or you couldn't. There is no gray for us either. The border between normality and hysteresis is invisible until (ask Gorbachev or the unemployed bankers from Lehman Brothers) we are on the wrong side of it. We now must master resilience just as Kissinger and his generation once mastered deterrence.

3. Accidental Extinctions

Let us say for a moment that you and your family live on a lake. The fish in the lake represent your sole source of food and income. You know, by instinct if nothing else, that it's possible to overfish your lake. If you had one bonanza year in which you pulled out as many fish as possible, it would probably be your last year of fishing. Still, it's your living, so you want to catch as many fish as you can, just not too many. This danger of overharvesting is one of the most intuitive in wildlife management, and it makes a great deal of sense for any scarce resource. (If you relied only on rainwater for your house, your showers would be a lot shorter.) Needless to say, you'd be very careful about how you fished on your lake.

Let us also imagine you are familiar with the work of the Russian ecologist F. I. Baranov, who in 1918 developed the first mathematical model to describe the exhaustion problem, known as the "catch equation." The equation was one of those powerful ideas that led to a revolution in thinking. In particular, it encouraged a group of American ecologists to perfect a concept that seems ideally fitted to your small corner of the world. Their idea was called "maximum sustainable yield (MSY)," and it reduced the problem of wildlife management to an equation. The idea of MSY was that if you made a careful survey of your lake, recording how many nutrients were available, how fast your fish bred, how many fish you had to begin with, and a handful of other variables, you could calculate the natural "replacement rate" of the lake. As the Canadian ecologist P. A. Larkin described it, "Any species each year produces a harvestable surplus, and if you take that much, and no more, you can go on getting it forever and ever." That surplus, if you could find it, would send your kids to college.

MSY was widely implemented in the 1950s and 1960s, a period when species protection was taking hold in thinking about natural systems. It made so much sense that it was quickly applied to everything from halibut in the Pacific to salmon in Chile. It served as the basis of international treaties and limits on recreational fishing—those "three fish and you're out" rules that are still in place to this day. MSY seemed to offer a sensible compromise between commerce and conservation. One scholar later observed that with MSY the years after World War II were a "golden age" of sorts for American lakes and rivers: "The mid-fifties were a fine time to be a fisheries biologist because you could be so single-minded about your job. The object was to get out there and get the harvest of the maximum sustained yield." So, knowing all this, you might head home and do the same with your own lake, carefully measuring the replacement rate and then fishing right at that limit, never passing the specified abundance that you had measured.

At which point, very likely and completely surprising since you were, after all, *following the rules*, instead of thriving, the fish in your lake would start to die in massive numbers.

The failure of MSY, which became obvious when mass extinctions started blipping up in what were supposed to be the best-run ecosystems on earth, was a disaster for ecological science. MSY looked perfect on paper, and it had won the approval of hard-line ecologists and the endorsement of fishermen. So when MSY started killing the very animals it was intended to protect, it was like watching the world's best-designed airplane go down in flames. Repeatedly. In a way, MSY was easy to understand (perhaps, scientists said later, *too* easy). In this view the lake was a fish factory: nutrients came in, fish came out. The idea that some sort of nonlinear collapse could occur made no sense. The scientists went back over their models; they fine-tuned the inputs, recalibrated the data, and got, in the end, yet more extinctions. "The consequences for theory and management were enormous," C. S. Holling soberly recalled several decades after the MSY crisis had stunned both environmentalists and fishing firms into a perplexed silence.

Holling had been among the first to identify the lethal mistake lingering in the heart of MSY theory. In an influential 1973 paper, "Resilience and Stability of Ecological Systems," he explained it this way: "If we are dealing with a system profoundly affected by changes external to it, and continually confronted by the unexpected, the constancy of its behavior becomes less important than the persistence of relationships." In parts of the world where there isn't a lot of change, Holling was saying, it's perfectly fine to keep track of the things you *can* measure: the number of books in a library, say, or the amount of food you need to get through a day. But in places where there is daily, often explosive readjustment, such measurements are worse than useless. Lakes may look stable, but in fact they operate with a level of deep, hidden complexity. The stability of a lake ecosystem can't possibly be reduced to a few variables. What matters isn't something you can score quickly but rather the strange mesh of interactions that make a lake resilient or not, the vibrancy that protects against exactly the sorts of extinction cascades MSY managers were trying to avoid—but accidentally triggering. What you can easily measure in these systems matters much less than what you cannot: How strong are the relationships between different parts of the lake ecosystem? How fast can it adjust to shocks? How far can you bend the food chain in the lake before it breaks? In short, how resilient is it?

Holling's radical idea was that the MSY extinctions were caused by forces entirely *outside* the system, factors no scientist had even thought to study or include in their models because they appeared so frankly unrelated to the problem at hand. For example, when Holling looked closely at a lake ecosystem (in fact he looked at hundreds of them in the course of his career), he found that increasing fish harvests to maximum sustainable yield may have brought more fishermen (confident that the spot had not been overfished), and they left behind more trash than before, which blocked drainage channels, which in turn wiped out a floating moss needed to feed other fish, which were the staple diet of the "target" fish. No one had thought to ask: *How much foot traffic can the lake handle?* "The effective and responsible effort to provide a maximum sustained yield," Holling explained, "might paradoxically increase the chance for extinctions." Over the years, however, MSY became *more* popular rather than less. What seduced ecosystem managers was the sense that they were doing something that felt scientific. The equations of MSY made sense on paper—even though they were often deadly in practice.

Yet Holling knew there was an alternative. After all, he had seen plenty of systems in nature that were able to snap back with astonishing speed from shocks like forest fires or earthquakes. This sort of lifesaving resilience under extreme stress was an expression of what the physicist Murray Gell-Mann, who studied the phenomenon, has called "complex adaptation." In Gell-Mann's view, "simple adaptation" resembles the on-off of a household thermostat trying to maintain a particular temperature: "It's too cold, it's too cold, it's too hot, it's just right, it's too cold." These kinds of on-off systems have almost no flexibility, which makes them very efficient and, at moments when they are faced with something new or confusing, mind-blowingly dangerous. Deterrence logic, for example: "If you threaten me too much, I will attack you" can bend no further than the amount of time it takes to launch a counterstrike to avenge yourself—about three minutes from sensing what might or might not be the radar signature of a missile to launching a retaliatory strike. Slightly better than these on-off switches is what Gell-Mann labeled "expert adaptation," which leans on a preprepared model, usually based on what's worked before, to figure out how best to tackle a serious problem. This was Simon Levin's biological-risks panel in action, dealing out solutions to the nightmares they could think of. But the limit here is obvious: you can never push such adaptation beyond the frontier of your imagination or your own history. *Complex* adaptive systems, however, are the ones Gell-Mann admired most. They are like our immune system. They don't just react, they learn. Simply adaptive ants, for instance, exhaust one food supply before moving on to another one. When they run out of food altogether, they die. Complex adaptive ants are capable of switching between high- and low-nutrition foods as circumstances dictate, allowing their habitats to refresh. You can probably guess which type of ant survives best in harsh settings.

When I said earlier that being resilient was a way both to protect ourselves (by reducing the chances that we'll snap under an attack) *and* to capture those benefits of mashup innovation, complex learning adaptation was what I had in mind. Resilience allows us, even at our most extreme moments of terror (in fact, precisely because we are at such a moment), to keep learning, to change. It is a kind of battlefield courage, the ability to innovate under fire because we've prepared in the right way and because we've developed the strength to keep moving even when we're slapped by the unexpected. But resilience has to be built into our system in advance, like a strong immune response before flu season. In practice this means widening how we interact with the world—the better to learn new skills and make new connections—instead of narrowing to the fewest possible essential threats or plans or policies. "A management approach based on resilience would emphasize the need to keep options open," Holling wrote in one paper, using language that fits neatly into a view of our own future security. "Flowing from this would be not the presumption of sufficient knowledge, but the recognition of our ignorance; not the assumption that future events are expected, but that they will be unexpected." What might matter most for us in the face of a scary biothreat future might not be the preparation of anti-bioweapon vaccines, so much as investment in a durable, efficient, and broad-reaching national healthcare system. A high national savings rate, instead of policies that encourage high levels of personal debt, might be more important than the regulation of specific financial instruments. Resilience pushes these fundamental concerns right to the front lines of protection. If the goal of resilience began to guide our policies and leaders, it would change a massive national spending program from a mere short-term economic boost into — done properly — a lifesaving security investment.

When Holling, Levin, and other scientists began digging deeper into ecosystems, they discovered something else. Complex environments, whether they are stock markets or nations, are stuffed with influences that run on different clocks. Scientists say that these systems have a "broad timescale." The lives of bugs in a forest, for example, are measured in hours; those of fish in weeks; trees in centuries; rocks in millennia. And sometimes it's hard to pin down when utility begins and ends: dead trees can continue to play a role in a forest's ecology for decades, providing nutrition and shelter for animals even as nitrogen leaches from their dead branches into the ground, fertilizing new generations of plants. A classic Ecology 101 error was to go into an ecosystem and pull out all the dead trees, thinking they were irrelevant. (This was what overeager German naturalists had done to their forests in the 1800s, "cleaning up" dead trees and accidentally deforesting huge parts of the country before they figured out that the rotting trees mattered as much as the living ones.)

* * *

Levin and Holling found that what was most likely to cause big shifts in a system wasn't changes in fast variables—like how many fish you were catching every day—but rather shifts in the slow ones. In fact, even though it didn't always appear so, fast variables such as the movement of sand grains on a dune or the population of fish in a lake were often "slaved" to slower variables like changes in temperature or sea level. For example, the Yale University ecologist Lisa Curran, in her groundbreaking studies of forests in Borneo, discovered that the most destructive influence on local ecosystems wasn't overharvesting of trees but the way in which deforestation combined with El Niño, a slow-variable weather phenomenon that operates on a timescale of centuries. Mixed up with local modernization, El Niño changed from being a source of healthy twice-a-century fertilization into "a destructive regional phenomenon, triggering droughts and wildfires with increasing frequency." This logic is broadly true for all complex systems, whether natural ones or the sorts we now confront in dealing with financial markets, terror cells, or drug runners: the things that linger longest often have the most profound impact on the system—yet they tend to be the things we ignore, precisely because they do move and change so slowly.

Holling has said that resilience may be the hardest quirk to figure out about complex systems. You could run around our world forever, chasing the fast variables, trying to address the surface concerns of security and stability—attacking missiles, trying to kill terrorists and regulate diseases. Unless you were in touch with those underlying slow forces, you would fail. If you were in touch with them, however, you could survive almost anything. You could learn to *use* the chaos, to become a complex adaptive system yourself. Then most apparently dangerous attacks would, in the end, be like small, controlled burns in a forest, clearing away just enough underbrush to make you invulnerable to a larger fire. Yes, individual trees or fish or, for that matter, people might perish. But as a whole, you would live to tell the tale. This was the logic of economist Raghuram Rajan, who argued in 2004 that a Fed policy of constantly fighting for economic growth was limiting the ability of the financial system to develop tools to deal with crisis and slowdown. "Perhaps Chairman Greenspan should be faulted for allowing only two mild recessions during his tenure," he wrote. "And perhaps we can sleep better at night if we pray, 'Lord, if there be shocks, let them be varied and preferably moderate ones, so we can stress test our systems.'"

This is deep security. And it shows up in some rather unexpected places.

4. The Management Secrets of Hizb'allah

We are coming up the road toward Sidon, and the traffic has slowed. There is a spot on the coastal highway here, south of town, where the asphalt chokes down to about ten feet wide, a narrow, rutted channel that runs, at the moment, between two giant Israeli bomb craters. This stretch of road is repaired from time to time, but it seems to be one of those little corners of the world where efficiency is destined to be undone by history. Whenever Israel begins dropping bombs on Lebanon— something that happens with more regularity than either the Lebanese or the Israelis might like—this mile-long section of ruined beachside highway is on the target list.

We are all a bit tired. The day has been hot, and while we've managed good cheer through the dust and the sad little villages that dot the land between the United Nations buffer zone and the Israeli border, there is something wearing about the landscape, a dejected collage of cratered hillsides and thin, snaking rivulets of dry rivers, footpaths, and tank traps. We move on and off the shoulder of the road as we skirt the craters. Looking ahead, I see the back of my Hizb'allah driver's head, slightly coated in sweat.

In the rear of the car we have the windows down as a sort of bargain between the boiling air and the road dust outside, the kind of negotiation that, without air-conditioning, is determined by your relative preference for perspiration over coughing fits. One of my Hizb'allah hosts and I are arguing about a subject you find yourself debating only in the Arab world. Wearied by traffic and coming down off a high of Lebanese coffee, we have been reduced to shorthand conversation. "Ted Turner," he says, looking at me with the intensity of a chess whiz hitting a checkmate. "Jew."

By this point I've been reduced as well to economic expression. "No," I reply. "Ted Turner. Episcopalian." Honestly, I have no idea where Ted Turner prays, but I know it won't have much impact on the outcome of this dialogue, which ostensibly involves CNN's coverage of the Middle East. CNN has been a constant bugaboo for Hizb'allah. Why couldn't they get airtime, they wanted to know? Why did attacks on Israel get so much more coverage than attacks on Lebanon? In response, Hizb'allah had started Al Manar, its own TV station, in the years before Al Jazeera. While Al Jazeera, the Qatari channel with a global reach, had pretensions of objectivity, Al Manar, designed to be an inspiring Islamic antidote to Turner's channel, had none. Al Manar's programming included videos, set to Islamic rap music, showing Hizb'allah fighters snaking through the same towns we had just left behind, en route to night raids. Though Turner redeemed himself in the eyes of Hizb'allah from time to time with a slap at Israel, Hassan's answer to me as we crept back toward Beirut on that steamy late afternoon pretty much summed up his final judgment on Western media and the Arab world: "Ted Turner," he shot back with a patient and knowing nod designed to end debate. "Jew."

Such narrow-mindedness (after all, a quick look at the Internet would have answered the question) might blind you to the fact that Hizb'allah is arguably the best-run Islamic militant group in the world, so efficient and well designed that it has not only survived nearly thirty years of Israeli and international pressure but has also developed some of the most powerful and successful tactics for fighting its enemies. "This is by far the greatest guerrilla group in the world," Israeli Brigadier General Guy Zur confessed after his tank brigade had been pounded by Hizb'allah in southern Lebanon.

I had spent part of the morning jammed into the back of a navy blue BMW blasting around the tiny roads of a linked set of towns less than a half mile from the watchtowers of Israeli border sentries. And it was clear that Hizb'allah, "great" or not, was masterfully run. We were always in the grip of their net of watchers, planners, and fighters, even when it seemed we were not. As we shot through the streets at seventy or eighty miles an hour, people stepped back into doorways or pressed themselves out of the way under arches. Men stood behind columns with radio wires running discreetly up their jacket arms or walkie-talkies in hand. When our position was too close to Israel, where there was a chance the tower sentries would open up with high-powered rifles that could hit a target a mile away, our driver would stop hard and turn. Warning shots usually came through the car's engine block or, if the Israelis were feeling less charitable, the front windshield.

But the sense of a great and intimate conspiracy was sort of reassuring. Every three or four minutes we would pass someone who seemed to know we were headed his way and who would either give us a sign to keep driving or step out and wave a hand quietly at the ground to stop the car, then come to the window to share a few words with the driver, who would then pull us into reverse and drive back toward where we had come from, quicker this time—the same movie of heads ducking in and out of windows and shopping women stepping into doorways, but played faster. Everyone was someone's cousin or brother, even the Lebanese regular army officers we sometimes stopped to chat with. They were supposed to be part of the effort to collect weapons from Hizb'allah, but the usual conversation was something like "I'll see you at your mother's for dinner next week?"

Beyond the video-game driving or the intricacy of the Hizb'allah network or even the proud ambition of my guide ("This is where we will invade Israel," he explained as we passed a few narrow hillside paths), something else made it impossible to miss the evidence of how deeply Hizb'allah was woven into the fabric of southern Lebanon. "We built this house," our driver would say from time to time as we drove. "And this house." The houses were, I knew, the work of Hizb'allah's Campaign for Reconstruction Institution, a charitable arm of the militant group that had built hundreds of homes in southern Lebanon, trying to keep up with the Israelis' pace of bombing them flat. The campaign often failed by that measure, but they were doing something far more valuable: the houses, every one of them, put Hizb'allah in touch with the most important slow variable in this chaotic environment, the one that Levin or Holling would have quickly told you was most likely to determine the future.

Begun as a Lebanese Shia opposition group in 1982, Hizb'allah established itself by mixing the Lebanese national distaste for external interference with the political and religious spirit of the Iranian revolution. At the time Lebanon was overrun: Americans, Israelis, Syrians, and a mosaic of peacekeeping forces and Arab-world military adventurers were all jockeying for influence and power. And though the Party of God (or "the Party of Allah," as Hizb'allah can be translated) was ensnared by the domestic violence of Lebanon's civil war, it was the attacks against outside powers that brought out the group's particular talents. Hizb'allah's first military innovation was the so-called linked suicide bombing, in which several targets are hit at nearly the same time, a tactic now familiar to Americans since 9/11, which originated on October 23, 1982, when Hizb'allah bombers hit the U.S. marine compound at the Beirut Airport and the French Foreign Legion camp in central Beirut minutes apart. The group is probably best remembered in the United States for the 1985 hijacking of a TWA flight from Athens to Rome, but it also played a role in the kidnappings that plagued Beirut during the Lebanese civil war.

In the late 1980s, after it had forced the United States out of Lebanon, Hizb'allah turned its attention to Israel, which held a ten-mile-wide buffer strip in southern Lebanon, just wide enough, Jerusalem officials hoped, to stop rocket attacks. From time to time Israel would launch dramatic raids or probes aimed at the Hizb'allah leadership, but the Israel Defense Forces and their partners in the South Lebanese Army never upset the group's operations for long. It was a slow, grinding sort of struggle. At times the back-and-forth strikes almost appeared to be a carefully managed, if unusually violent and creative, chess match. After Israel assassinated the Hizb'allah founder Abbas al-Musawi in 1992, for instance, Hizb'allah retaliated by suicide-bombing the Israeli embassy and then a synagogue in Buenos Aires — demonstrating a willingness and ability to strike overseas if need be. Eventually, Israel decided the price was too high and, in the spring of 2000, exhausted by the political strain, withdrew its forces, in one night, from Lebanon. Hizb'allah had done what Egypt, Syria, and Jordan had failed to do for forty years. It had beaten the Israelis.

As a condition of its survival during the years of its fight against Israel, Hizb'allah had become a machine for innovation, as much terror lab as terror group. Backed by Iranian cash and training — some Israelis insisted Hizb'allah was little more than the unofficial "fourth division" of the Iranian army — the group was constantly developing new ways to communicate, attack, or train. They were among the first to develop improvised explosive devices of the sort that later made Iraqi roads into a nightmare for the Americans, then the Brits and other U.S. allies. They perfected camouflage techniques that made remotely fired mines along roadsides indistinguishable from rocks or trash. Hizb'allah ran a world-class smuggling network, acquiring arms while UN "truce" officials watched helplessly. (Among other things, they smuggled decryption chips inside PlayStations.) Hizb'allah found ways to quickly assemble and use Soviet Katyusha rockets, which caused little damage in Israel but tremendous frustration; then they stockpiled 10,000 of them. They also loaded up on state-of-the-art antitank missiles. "We knew they had the best antitank missiles in the world," General Halutsi Rudoy of the IDF said after one in ten of his tanks was hit in the 2006 war.

"But we were surprised by the amount, which at times seemed endless."

Calling Hizb'allah's feeling for innovation a "passion" was perhaps a bit strong, but the group had a vigor that seemed to transcend the mere brutal demands of survival. You might, for instance, chalk up their obsession with learning to night-fight to raw survival instinct—a reaction to the Israel Defense Forces' historical preference for attacking on a black night with a new moon. But they did much more than train under the Lebanese stars. They built their own telephone network to keep it secure from Israeli penetration; they devised a clever surveillance camera system and installed it surreptitiously at Beirut Airport so they could keep track of planes coming and going. In 2004 and 2005 they conducted test flights of small, home-built unmanned aerial vehicles, cheap versions of the multimillion-dollar drones that Israel and the United States used for overhead monitoring and, occasionally, for sending missiles into bedrooms or offices or front seats of terrorists' cars. This was more than an instinct for survival. It was a will to invent, loaded into the Hizb'allah genetic code. The group didn't simply react, they learned and even anticipated. It was Gell-Mann's complex adaptation at work. And they empathized: "We understand Israelis," a Hizb'allah fighter told me. "You look at me and you need to know I am already dead. I am just here now temporarily. If I die, it does not matter. Israelis are not like that. They fear death."

Shortly after the Israeli withdrawal of 2000, Hizb'allah turned to its dream of political legitimacy. In the spring of 2001, the Party of God offered a slate of fifty-eight candidates for the national parliament. But when only nine won, Hizb'allah found itself forced into some soul-searching. Lebanon, it seemed, wasn't quite ready for an Islamic state. So, like some company that had launched a failed product (say, New Coke), the group had to answer the question "What is our core competency?" And while they didn't abandon their dream of one day becoming a political force, they began looking for ways to do in other places what they had done so well at home: kill Israelis.

The natural, convenient location for such an effort was inside Israel, where Hizb'allah trainers and supplies began appearing among various Palestinian militant groups. When word got around the streets of Gaza or Ramallah that Hizb'allah had come to help the Palestinians, it was an electric jolt to the balance of Palestinian militant power. Hizb'allah showing up was like Google arriving in a town and opening an office: the most innovative, ambitious, and curious young minds all wanted to join. Established groups such as Hamas watched as their best bomb makers and planners were drawn into Hizb'allah's orbit. The turf war, Israeli intelligence later discovered, was resolved only by the stern mullahs in Tehran, who ruled that Hizb'allah could instruct the Palestinians but must back off the franchise strategy. It was too effective.

All of which might have made you wonder, as you sat in the back of a car making high-speed squirts through the towns of the Litani River valley—land that seemed destined to pass back and forth between Israel and Lebanon in perpetuity, land that wore its exhaustion like a blanket of dust—why Hizb'allah was building houses. If their core competency was devising cutting-edge ways to kill Jews, if their political future would likely be measured out for them in the streets of Beirut or the mosques of Tehran or the palaces of Damascus, then why were Hizb'allah forces throwing up slab-sided houses one after another here? For that matter, why were they building schools and running hospitals? Why was it that when people in southern Lebanon had a problem with plumbing or noisy neighbors or a child who wasn't interested in the Koran, their first call was to Hizb'allah?

The answer was that by living in the places where Lebanese Shia most needed help and support, Hizb'allah had become inseparable from daily life—and deeply connected to the slow variables in Lebanon. They drew no distinction between plumbing and making bombs; often the same fighters did both jobs. They had gone deep, and this gave them everything from information to gratitude to quiet spaces where they could engineer their latest terror gadgets or bounce back from Israeli poundings. As much as Hizb'allah owed its survival to roadside bombs, they probably owed just as much to unclogged toilets and primary schools. What had kept the group alive for more than two decades, under intense pressure both within and outside of Lebanon, was this obsession with innovation and an instinct for slow-variable resilience.

This created a dangerous problem for Israel, a problem whose lethal irony Farkash had pointed out: direct attacks on Hizb'allah made the militants *more* resilient, not less. Small perturbations in natural systems—and, on the Hizb'allah timetable, most of Israel's actions were small perturbations—are usually the best way to build resilience. Swallowing antibiotics at the first sign of a cold, in the same fashion, destroys your chance to build a healthy immune system. At some point you need to get a little sick so that in the long term you become a lot healthier. In Lebanon every bombed house was replaced by one built via the reconstruction fund; every destroyed school meant a chance to build a madrassa that would produce future Hizb'allah fighters. The group wasn't some magical self-creating force. It would have evaporated quickly if it hadn't been for the strong support of Iran. But *how* they used that support was what mattered. They could have spent all the money on munitions and fake documents. But Hizb'allah's greatest survival secret had nothing to do with cracking Israeli codes or smuggling missiles or building up a leadership hierarchy. It was in creating a system that allowed them to shift and learn and change—and that did all of those things even better when they were under attack.

"I don't see how they are resilient," an Israeli officer said to me one day after the 2006 war. "We destroyed most of their buildings and communications. And every time we tried to kill them they just ran away."

Exactly.

5. The Department of Resilience

Construction of a resilient society need not be complex. The aim is simple enough: to withstand the surprises that await us; to absorb the worst nightmares and walk away with the core attributes of our freedom intact. The best way to do this is not to chase our enemies around the globe (making them angrier and cleverer) or to invest only, as we do now, in what are essentially resistance strategies. Resistance is very different from resilience. It is an attempt to prepare for every possible contingency, which is of course impossible and exhausting. As we check off a near-infinite list of boxes—harden nuclear reactors; develop road-monitoring systems; toughen border security—resistance also leaves us in a state of unnerving psychological weakness. It forces us into a reactive mode, waiting to be hit. It drains us, and when resistance policies fail, they leave us more afraid, insecure, and vulnerable. How is it, we wonder, that our expensive and extensive resistance systems can't protect us? The fact is they never had a chance. When the U.S. Department of Homeland Security describes its mission as "deterrence, prevention, and preemption of, and defense against, aggression," it fails, item by item, to touch the true nature of resilience. As we've seen, much of what we face can't be deterred or prevented. Often it can't be predicted, which makes much of the mission of Homeland Security the stuff of fantasy. Of course, there's nothing wrong with wanting to harden our nuclear reactors; in fact, certain defensive efforts make a great deal of sense. Hizb'allah isn't just unclogging toilets, after all. But an obsession with building walls blinds us to the chance that someone might tunnel under such bulwarks.

It might be best to rechristen Homeland Security as the Department of Resilience (a twin to the Department of Defense). The recognition that we need a major commitment to fostering real resilience would in turn elevate ideas like national health care, construction of a better transport infrastructure, and investment in education to a new level of importance. Universal health coverage makes sense not only because it is decent but because building a medical system that touches everyone in the country prepares us to better deal with the unknown. Resilience acknowledges that we can't possibly anticipate or prevent all future dangers any more than you can look at your beautiful newborn child and be certain that it will never catch a cold or break a leg.

Resilience expands the virtue of slow-variable policies beyond their traditional domains. Such efforts are valuable for what they accomplish in and of themselves, and they are also a way to bind Americans into a compact of responsibility and a network of personal relationships sealed by working hand in hand. Government alone can't ever construct a system fast and flexible enough for our modern world. So we should begin with what can be done with our own hands. We should start with the sorts of questions we *can* control and answer, reaching for the places where the slow variables of our own society are within easy grasp: how do we consume? educate our children? run our businesses? invest our money? In the end government can't make us fully resilient. It's a process that has to include—and ideally *start with*—each of us at home.

6. Holling on the Euphrates

Resilience isn't just a passive virtue, it's also something we have to be able to incorporate into the way we act in the world, whether it is regulating financial markets that change faster than we can think or, as we've often done in the Middle East, stepping into unstable landscapes of ethnic and religious fury. You might recall that earlier I mentioned something about Holling's work on what he called "maladaptive systems," which were doomed because they couldn't change or adjust fast enough in the face of surprise. Well, that can happen to policies, too. If they are based on bad information or old ideas, they may snap when confronted with the real world. Ecologists call this situation "lock-in," which captures the way in which inflexibility and mistakes become a prison of sorts as time goes on. Probably nowhere have our own maladaptive policy twitches been on clearer display in recent years than in the U.S. war in Iraq. The war was begun with a set of highly inflexible policies based on flawed assumptions—and then updated and changed far too late. The American failure to adapt in Iraq was primarily a postwar error, but lock-in started well before the conflict even began, with a whole set of war-thinking habits that were dangerously hardened by overconfidence and by an "input soldiers, output democracy" set of ideas. It's not that there was no advance planning for postwar Iraq. In fact, parts of the Pentagon and State Department had been planning for such an eventuality for a couple of years before the first shots were fired. But the worries of those policy groups about managing a postwar order were largely steamrollered, replaced with a system that was incapable of the speedy refiguring that life in a war zone would inevitably require. And in that error there are tremendous lessons for the future.

The first flaw we can learn from was the notion that the war in Iraq would have a clean, fast end—a way of thinking and seeing that ensured no plans stretched out to nearly the time that would be required. This in-and-out sensibility was captured in what is perhaps the single most famous line of the Bush presidency, from his speech of September 14, 2001, at the National Cathedral, in which he said, "This conflict has begun on the timing and terms of others. It will end in a way, and at an hour, of our choosing." This poetic idea contained a very fundamental misapprehension, not only about 9/11 but about the world in general: there's no final whistle in international politics. As we've seen, sandpile energy never stops, because complexity is always expanding. There is rarely an end to conflicts or crises now. They simply change shape, but rarely toward a *simpler* landscape of the sort Bush and his aides hoped for. Remember Simon Levin's observation that complexities tend to accumulate? That insight clearly didn't inform the thinking of men like Deputy Secretary of Defense Paul Wolfowitz, who told Congress in February 2003 that "it's hard to conceive that it would take more forces to provide stability in post-Saddam Iraq than it would take to conduct the war itself." And the White House's best guess of the number of troops that would still be on the ground in Iraq in the fall of 2003 was 30,000 to 40,000. (When General Eric Shinseki suggested that something on the order of several hundred thousand troops would be needed, he paid for the insight with his job.)

To assume that an invasion could be run with a clear time limit was to ignore the nature of a complex world order (to say nothing of the history of Iraq itself). You didn't need to look at Holling's dead lake ecosystems to learn this. Frankly, it was a lesson that should have been clear from American experiences in places like Somalia, Bosnia, Kosovo—and even Afghanistan in the 1980s, where walking away from the mob of Islamic warriors that the United States had once funded there allowed them to grow, evolve, and change into the Taliban and Al Qaeda. Insurgent groups or military crises or financial panics aren't like those singing electric bears at Disneyland that snap off as soon as you walk out of the room. Complex global problems keep growling, looking for ways to survive, and—if you're not careful—may eventually come hunting for you. This is crucial to keep in mind as we combat shape-changing dangers as different from each other as bank failures and Iran. Disrupting life in a place like Iraq or Afghanistan only makes obsessive maintenance more important. At a fast glance, the flawed American in-and-out view looks a lot like maximum sustainable yield: it assumed easy-to-map interactions, a bet that the "ecosystem" of Iraq would settle into something stable that could be left to run itself, and a sense that the most important variables could be predicted and managed like fish food. Dangerous externalities, from guerrillas' grudges to enthusiastic disruption from Iran, were footnoted.

This last idea, that Iraq would snap back to stability after the war, was exactly the sort of error that adaptive strategic thinking might have caught before it was too late. The United States assumed, for instance, that most of Iraq's major institutions, from its ministries, like health and education, to telephones and electricity, would continue to work well after the initial shock of the war had passed. No one planned for the possibility that they would collapse. In reality, however, the speed and violence of the occupation left such a vacuum that the Iraqi government system folded in on itself, essential infrastructure was looted and gutted, and the United States found itself facing a rapidly decaying country where security was impossible and life for ordinary Iraqis became more dangerous with each passing day. One of the accidental ironies of the Iraq war was that much of the valuable infrastructure American fighters had obsessed about protecting by using high-tech precision weapons during combat was then trashed by the Iraqis themselves in the weeks after the war as U.S. soldiers helplessly watched. Combat had gone very well, but the postwar the United States had planned for was built on that Nisbett error of focusing exclusively on an easy-to-spot object (Saddam) and ignoring a host of serious dangers lurking in the surrounding context.

As a 2008 RAND report concluded, "Despite a predilection for questioning virtually all operational military assumptions from several directions, and despite the existence of alternative analyses within the government, those charged with planning for Iraq assumed that one particular scenario would play out and did not plan for other possible contingencies." Indeed, American leaders were so fixed on their invasion plan that they didn't let the truth stand in their way. Confidently misleading the public about what intelligence they had was yet another sign—recognized only too late—that those running the war had not only ignored the context but weren't even paying attention to the whole of the central image.

In fact, one of the more dangerous ideas about postwar Iraq reads like something out of a C. S. Holling case study: thinking that a single variable—political reform—would determine the future of the country. The idea was that after U.S. forces booted out and de-Baathified the Iraqi army, security would come from a strong constitution and an open democracy. In postwar reports and in the biographies of men such as Tommy Franks and George Tenet, you find a confident sense that safety for Iraqis would emerge naturally once the country had new rules. So the United States spent billions constructing a "green zone" under the illusion that creating a safe haven for an acting parliament would somehow bring the country into an easy order. But this was ridiculous, as soldiers on the ground began insisting almost immediately. Sure, a constitution and a parliament mattered, but without basic security they would be worse than pointless. There would be no certainty about *anything* in Iraq, least of all a political order, without security. As Holling and a group of other scholars had observed about wildlife settings, "In contrast to an efficiency-driven, command-and-control approach, management that accepts uncertainty and seeks to build resilience can sustain social-ecological systems, especially during periods of transformation following disturbance." This, in a nutshell, should have been Iraq. It took the White House more than three years to change its policy.

How might Holling have fought the postwar in Iraq? How would he have prepared? Well, he'd have delivered an adaptive management approach that didn't lock in simple ideas. His plan probably would have involved building up a huge reserve of skills and people and tools—everything from translators to health and security experts. He'd have been more focused on how many Arabic speakers he had who understood Iraq than on how many smart bombs were available. He would have made sure we delivered more toys to Iraqi children than we did soldiers to their communities (and made sure those soldiers knew how Iraqi kids played and learned). He would have restocked libraries and made sure any homes destroyed by the fighting were rebuilt and were twice as nice as they'd been beforehand—that old Hizb'allah reconstruction trick. He'd also have been ready to move fast: no postwar vacuum for him—after all, you never knew which particular grievance (water shortages, no electricity, a mosque bombing) could avalanche into a disaster. He would have put stability above everything and not relied on the idea that a paper constitution could ever control the full dynamism of a just-invaded nation.

In his analysis of what works best in managing chaotic ecosystems, Holling looked at places such as the Mae Nam Ping basin in Thailand and the Kristianstads Vattenrike in Sweden, where adaptive management had worked to save species or stop ecosystem collapse. Among the elements common to successfully resilient systems was an ability to constantly reconceptualize problems, to generate a diversity of ideas, to communicate with everyone from fishermen to truckers, and to encourage novelty and even small-scale revolts or crises and recoveries instead of waiting for a big, unanticipated collapse. Holling would have invaded Iraq with technicians, with ideas, and with a far better sense of the landscape than the United States had. He would have engaged Iraq from top to bottom instead of relying on a few elites to help reorder the country. He would have amassed his bank of translators, cultural experts, engineers, and other skilled operatives well in advance so they could begin building relationship networks that would hold up under pressure. In fact, this would have been so urgent that he would have postponed an invasion until he felt he could manage much of what lay ahead, which he would have characterized in one word: uncertainty. That Wolfowitz line about needing fewer troops *after* the war than during? Holling would have labeled that as exactly what it was: a marker of a very maladaptive system at work.

There's one final point we need to come to terms with. It's very tempting for us to look in the mirror and remark that we live in systems that are already very resilient or to think that the policies we choose are resilient or adaptive enough. Certainly this is true in a relative sense. We're much better off than that creaking centralized system Gorbachev was trying to repair; our ability to change and adjust in Iraq shows that we have some flexibility. But we should bear this in mind: we are now tied to one another in ways we can't see, through webs of finance or disease or information, and—here's the dangerous paradox—the more closely we're bound, the less resilient we all become. Studies of food webs or trade networks, electrical systems and stock markets, find that as they become more densely linked they also become *less* resilient; networks, after all, propagate and even amplify disturbances. Worse, the more efficient these networks are, the faster they spread those dangers. Interconnections such as the ties between brokers and banks or between the health of every passenger on a long-distance airplane flight are vehicles for sharing risk, for triggering hysteresis. In a simple linear system, say one bank and one farm, you can map out the effects of a crisis as if you were plotting the route of falling dominoes. But in a networked society, lit up by revolutionary change, such easy prediction is a fantasy. Drop a shock into a network and you get, the strategist Edward Smith has written, "the chain reaction that is set off when a single ping-pong ball is tossed onto a table covered with mouse traps upon which other ping-pong balls are balanced—an almost explosive reaction whose direction and end-state cannot be predicted."

The more closely we are bound together, the weaker we may become. Simon Levin, in his worried essay "Ecology for Bankers," included two charts: one of the financial system as it is, which looked like a giant dense hair ball, and the other of the way regulators see the same system of interconnections, which looked like a child's Lego project. His point was that we can't hope to manage or control systems that are tens of thousands of times more complex than our conceptions of them. So we have to find ways to build resilience into the system itself instead of imposing it slapdash from the outside at times of crisis, as if we were trying to repair an already buckling bridge. "Older models of systemic shocks in the financial system may no longer fully capture the possible channels of propagation and feedback arising from major disturbances," Levin and other colleagues observed in a report for the Federal Reserve. "Nor can existing models account entirely for the increasing complexity of the financial system."

He could have been writing about any aspect of our lives in which unmappable interconnections bring speed, convenience, and—in direct proportion to how speedy and convenient they are—danger. How much does resilience matter to a deeply secure future? Think of each new relation or connection in our world as an unsprung ping-pong-ball trap. Every day now we are bound more closely. We are less resilient at this moment than when you started reading this book, and we shall be less resilient still when you finish. But those same connections, dangerous as they may be, also offer the best possible way to transmit changes for radical decency. This table full of unsprung traps that seems to fatally imperil us is, understood properly, about to be the key to our salvation.

CHAPTER NINE

The Limits of Persuasion

1. Warrior Geek

One morning in August 1982, a British mathematician named James Moffat was sitting in his office in the Ministry of Defence (MoD) in London when he received an urgent message. Moffat was then one of the MoD's senior scientists. "Staff mathematician" was perhaps not the most macho title in the British military establishment, but the link between science and warfare, one that emerged long before the Royal Navy ruled the seas, assured at least that it was among the most influential. The urgent message was in tune with other code-red dispatches flying around Whitehall that morning. Argentina had, rather improbably, just invaded the Falkland Islands.

The British were desperate to stem the flow of Argentine soldiers and weapons now streaming through the lone airfield on the islands, at Stanley, as if it were a duty-free store. This wasn't an easy task. The Falklands are a twenty-hour flight from London. The only plane that had a hope of getting all the way to Stanley was a Vulcan bomber, which would have to be refueled in flight several times, and even the refuelers themselves would probably have to be refueled in midflight. The Vulcans, designed to carry nuclear bombs, would need to be rerigged. But before any of this could be arranged, Moffat had to answer a math problem for his commanders: "How many bombs do we need?"

Moffat returned to his office and, this being a few years before the advent of online information, ordered up a map of the Stanley airfield from archives in the basement of his building. Then he poked around a bit and found the name of the firm (a British firm, fortunately) that had built the runway there. They gave him a detailed description of the runway's structure so that he could calculate how to bomb it with utmost efficiency. Moffat then set out to determine the number of craters he needed to make on the runway and, importantly, the number of bombs the planes would have to drop to guarantee that many holes. Tossing bombs onto a runway is a bit like throwing darts, and he wanted to calculate the most probable distribution of hits. Moffat worked through the math, wrote up a report, and, almost as an afterthought, tucked in a copy of the map and the hand-marked plastic strips he had used to chart the possible craters. Within hours, Prime Minister Margaret Thatcher was herself laying the strips on the map, counting the blast holes Moffat had predicted, and, finally, ordering Vulcan planes into the air. The operation was code-named Black Buck. Just days after Moffat received his first call, the bombs had landed, and, as Moffat's math had suggested, one had hit the runway hard enough to knock it out.

The immediate effect, of course, was to stop flights in and out of Stanley. But the Brits noticed something else happening: the Argentine air force began shifting the disposition of its planes, readjusting them nervously, like a teenager rearranging his hair before a date. Mirage fighters, which had been prepared to mount an aerial defense against the British, were moved to Buenos Aires. Other planes, intended to attack the British navy, were moved into a defensive position. "Black Buck not only reached and bombed the targets," a British military study later concluded, "but in doing so it showed the Argentines that the RAF had the potential to hit Argentina." The effect of this information was electric: it convinced many of the generals in Buenos Aires, almost immediately, that they were fighting a lost cause, and it triggered political shifts inside the government. In short, the impact of that one blast radiated far beyond the tarmac. It wasn't simply that Moffat had managed to take out the Stanley airport; he had indirectly taken out a large chunk of the entire Argentine air force. This was good fodder, finally, for stories to swap with the fighter jocks around the office. But Moffat knew he had stumbled onto something deeper. He had discovered, almost by accident, a profound and even strange theory of action and reaction in global power, one that touched on everything from why nations collapse to how we might control the forces that now seem the wildest in the international system.

Remember one of Bak's laws, that small things can have huge impacts? We've seen that this law is a fearsome force for unknitting some of our most cherished ideas about how the world works. We've watched how it unraveled brilliant men as different as Gorbachev and Greenspan. We've seen how our enemies use small events to trigger big changes in our lives (think of 9/11) and how the new math of our age can also produce powerful sums when we mix harmless things like mortgages and securities trading. This constant surprise, and the demand it makes for an "always-on" defense, is one of the reasons we need a deep-security immune system instead of an old-style Grand Strategy.

But how to engineer such a system? If the dangers we face seem able to hit us where we are least prepared, is there some way we might do the same to them? Are there ways we can learn to hit at the joints of the problems we face, to use indirect techniques? Particularly since our direct approaches—whether confronting nations, terrorists, or crises like nuclear proliferation or financial panic—often seem to make the problems worse. Can we make cascading avalanches work *for* us? Moffat's one-bomb victory had been such a case: small input, dramatic output. The problem fascinated Moffat for twenty years after that Argentine raid. It led to the question that would shape his career: what can we learn from the idea that one bomb, exactly placed, is as powerful as an entire air force?

An awful lot, it turns out.

2. The Limits of Persuasion

There's a dangerous directness buried in the way we now confront the complex problems of a new-math world. When we want to change something, we stab right for it, whether it is the Chinese policy on currency or Iranian plans to develop nuclear weapons. Faced with a financial crisis in banks, for instance, we worry about banks instead of, say, homeowners. Our approach to diplomacy and other policies reflects this natural instinct for directness. Largely, of course, this habit is a holdover from a view of power from a time when the map of a continent *could* be debated, imagined, and inked out directly by two men in a room in Dresden. You can see this instinct at work when a secretary of state wings around the world to *persuade* enemies into agreements or when an American president caucuses with leaders of disenfranchised nations as he edges them (he thinks) ever closer to a deal. Such moments are great theater. They reflect a lot of our biases about how the world ought to work: that big global issues should be resolved as swiftly and directly as possible, that the shortest distance between us and the world we want is a straight line, that charismatic leaders make history. But, like a lot of what we face today, these old-style approaches are failing and — too often — backfiring.

Part of the reason a direct, head-to-head approach fails is that today we often can't find or name the threats we face. You'll never corral most terrorists in a room long enough to negotiate with or persuade them. The new-spun mashup risks of modernity, everything from greedy hedge funds to accidental bioreleases, can barely be understood, let alone confronted, in one place at one time. And often, the minute we try to attack or pin them down, the threats morph into something unrecognizable and even harder to name or confront. Frustrated intelligence analysts call these "self-negating prophecies": as soon as you figure out what your enemy is doing and move to stop him, he simply shifts to something else.

One way to understand this is to recognize that many of the dangers we confront aren't easy-to-target objects like tank battalions or even individuals, like Nasrallah or Osama bin Laden, so much as they are systems or networks. A group like Hizb'allah is best seen as an interconnected web of ideology, technology, and nationalism. Press on the system directly at one part — say, by bombing missile sites — and it simply adjusts elsewhere. Our enemies are masters of this sort of indirectness. They know instinctively what we now have to learn, that the right force, applied in exactly the right place, can deliver an impact no amount of force delivered in the wrong place ever can. The first two transitions to a deep-security view were learning to look holistically instead of narrowly and then learning to focus on our own resilience instead of trying to attack everything that looks scary (and making them more dangerous in the process). The third change, which we'll turn to now, is to augment our instinct for direct action with a new sense of the incredible power of an indirect approach.

3. The Halt Problem

A year or two after the Vietnam War ended, a few American air force officers began asking themselves an uncomfortable question: "If we had to fight Vietnam over again, what would we do differently?" This sort of retrospective analysis is useful in any context. *If we had to react to 9/11 again, what would we do differently? If we had to think about the nature of our global financial markets all over again, how would we change what we did and did not do?* Such postmortems are rare in real life—time moves too fast. But something about the way Vietnam turned out was so searing that the military, particularly the generation of officers who had flown in Vietnam, wanted to see what had gone wrong. The pressure for new ideas, one study later remarked, came largely "from wartime experiences of young U.S. Air Force officers who were appalled by the frequently mindless and ineffective use of air-power in Vietnam. When their turn to lead came, they were determined to do better." To some degree, the numbers of Vietnam spoke for themselves: the United States had dropped more ordnance on the Vietnamese than they had dropped in all of World War II and had still failed. We already knew that so-called strategic bombing didn't work. The fire-bombing of German cities starting in 1942 had the effect of unifying the German population instead of, as predicted, turning them against Hitler. The Vietnam campaigns were supposed to take those lessons into account. But somewhere in the blur of politics and war, the strikes settled into the blunt math of sorties flown, bombs dropped, body counts. It was proof, if any were needed, that you couldn't beat an insurgency with B-52s.

Looking at the problem with fresh eyes after the war, a few of those frustrated officers suggested a radical idea: what if the right way to win an air war was by dropping *fewer* bombs? This was, to be honest, the sort of idea designed to get you retired pretty quickly from the military. So before they started pushing the notion in the halls of the Pentagon, they quietly arranged to test it in newly adopted computer simulations and war games. The results were eye-opening. Take, for instance, the standard land-war puzzle of the Cold War: a fast-moving Soviet army pouring into Western Europe through the Fulda Gap. Could any amount of power stop the probe at fifty miles inside Western Europe? One hundred miles? This was a challenge so familiar to strategists—they still worry about it today in Korea—that it had its own name, "the halt problem." The usual answer came from the pages of Carl von Clausewitz's strategic classic *On War.* Clausewitz's logic said to aim for your enemy's *schwerpunkt,* his point of greatest weakness. This was the military equivalent of trying to blow up a wall by battering one spot over and over. If the Soviets would stop once you had killed a certain percentage of their soldiers—and three centuries of attrition warfare suggested this was the case—then the faster you could get to that number the better. (The *schwerpunkt,* in case you needed any reminder of the Newtonian view at work here, was also often called the enemy's "center of gravity.") Yet simulations of the Cold War halt problem showed that this battering approach took too long. It was like trying to stop a flood with a bucket. The best case had the Soviets well across Germany before they even stopped for breath—and that would happen only after NATO fired off tactical nuclear weapons. The necessary bloodbath would make previous wars look like skirmishes.

This failure of traditional approaches opened the door to alternative ideas like the ones those rebel officers had been cooking up. And, as they began to try their ideas out in simulations, they found the "fewer bombs" approaches worked surprisingly well. Say you brought the fury of concentrated fire just to the front line of the advancing soldiers, trying to pull them down as you might peel a potato. This "leading edge" strategy was particularly disruptive as the Soviets tried to reinforce losses all across the front. Or what if you used technology to blind the Soviets instead of killing them? What about aiming to disrupt the army's nervous system, putting most of your firepower on their fuel depots, supply trains, and command centers? The simulations showed these direct attacks would stop an offensive far faster, maybe within fifty or one hundred miles. These approaches to the halt problem became known as "effects-based operations" because they achieved their goals through mental and physical effects. You could win, not by killing some magic number of enemy soldiers but by immobilizing the enemy's brain. Such an approach took a bit of stomach. It meant directing limited military resources, at a moment of intense peril, *away* from a big mass target. It meant accepting that the most brutal response might not be the one that involved the most explosives. This was deeply counterintuitive, in much the way Niels Bohr had described quantum ideas. The standard dismissive joke among old-line "ready-fire-aim" artillery officers was that it was like trying to call a bully's mom even as he was slugging you in the face.

The Cold War, fortunately, never produced a test. (In any event, it was hard to imagine the United States responding to a Soviet attack with anything less than a full blitz.) But by the 1990s, many of the rebellious war planners who had championed effects-based fighting had risen in the Pentagon. They inserted their indirect tactics into plans for the first Iraq war, in which they moved to isolate and disable infrastructure rather than aiming to slaughter clueless masses of Iraqi recruits. The plan worked brilliantly. (Norman Schwarzkopf, the commanding general in that war, called this one of his biggest gambles—not least because a brigade of "pave Iraq" artillery officers had been pressing that bodies-equals-victory approach.) Effects-based planners then tried their tactics in Belgrade, raining thin foil strips on the city's electrical system in the opening hours of that war, for instance, blinding and darkening the city instead of leveling it. Milosevic's country was understood not as a simple target but as a system. And by leaning on the most vulnerable part of that system, the United States was able to exert pressure that no number of direct attacks could achieve. This was like aiming for the tires of a getaway car instead of aiming for the harder-to-hit driver. That such an approach to warfare killed fewer people was, of course, a fine dividend in a media age, when the PR battlefield can be as perilous and crucial as the real one.

In the second Iraq war and in Afghanistan, the fighting was run along these same effects-based lines; in fact, the tactics worked almost *too* well. They remade the landscape so quickly that the U.S. forces were left without enough time (and without plans) to manage a radically different postwar order. Resident Iraqi combatants and Afghan insurgents, however, caught on right away. After all, the alternative for them was destruction. They swapped military uniforms for civilian garb, changed their habits and became harder to isolate, and dispersed into places where they became essentially invisible. Then the enemy started using effects-based operations of their own: roadside bombs, strategic kidnapping—the sorts of small but disruptive jabs that rattled both American commanders on the ground and nervous politicians back home. It was Moffat in reverse, one roadside bomb stopping a multimillion-dollar convoy, freezing a superpower. Effects did work. Now it was simply a race to see who could master them.

4. Unknown Generals

Effects-based operations have a completeness direct attacks never can, because they treat targets as systems and reach far deeper and wider for leverage and information. For this reason they are useful as a way to think not only about military operations but also about diplomatic puzzles or any complex situation, whether it is global warming or Pakistan's management of its nuclear weapons. Effects are less *replacement* for direct negotiations or conflict than enhancement. They operate everywhere, from an adversary's skies to the hearts of the people. They are as helpful in managing state-to-state conflicts as in dealing with new-era threats that linger in networks or markets or laboratories. To be honest, effects do make planning far more complex, not least because of what war fighters think of as the echo chamber of effects battles: it's hard to predict exactly what effect the effects will have in practice and what other effects they in turn will cause. This sounds like a very knotty way to fight—and it is. But the benefit of such an approach is that it forces you to touch as many parts of the system as you can, constantly hunting for signs of unexpected and dangerous echoes bouncing back at you. And in fast-changing systems, as Mike Moritz would remind us, that's a *huge* advantage. It's the logic of deep security as immune system again; after all, our immune system never switches off. It attacks disease directly but also draws on all sorts of resources, from the vitamins in our bloodstream to our state of mind, to bring disease under control. In the global body politic, real power isn't always loaded into obvious implements like armies or bombers. Milosevic's electricity, for instance, was far more important than his army. One way to think of this is in terms of the most modern cancer drugs: instead of attacking tumors directly (an approach that tends to kill healthy cells at a dangerous rate), these drugs aim for the blood supply leading to the tumor. Better to strangle a tumor than ineffectively chop or cut at it. This is the sort of medicine we now need.

One way to make this contrast between direct and indirect is to return to Richard Nisbett's lab at the University of Michigan, where he conducted those eye-movement studies with American and Chinese students. Let's imagine for a moment how the American students might have conducted a war if asked. We can probably assume they'd bring their same ogling instincts to war fighting. They'd stare right at what seemed to matter most and then hit at it hard. They would direct 90 percent of their force to where their eyes were 90 percent of the time: the center of the picture. This was the same sensibility that animated Clausewitz's "battering ram" battle tactics. This approach reflected not only his own experience of European combat, with its history of head-to-head fights, but also something much more profound:

the basic idea that outcomes are usually determined by direct collision, whether it be armies (think of the trench-to-trench staredowns of World War I) or ideas (the yea-nay debates of Congress or university students). As the French scholar François Jullien observed in his masterful study of Western and Eastern ways of thinking, *Detour and Access,* this idea is an extension of some of the deepest concepts of our culture, rooted in the Socratic notion that batting ideas back and forth, slamming them together like Athenian and Spartan armies, would yield the fastest route to truth. You can find this instinct at work not only in those "let's talk it out" Camp David summits but also in television courtroom dramas, political debates, and even the quotidian discussions around your kitchen table about when the teenager should be allowed to drive or where you should go on vacation. Direct confrontation with problems is more than a habit of Western culture; in many ways, it is a defining trait.

But what would happen if, for a moment, you looked at the world as those Chinese students in Nisbett's lab did? What if you asked them to plan a war? Recall that they believed the environment mattered more than the central image. This was why their eyes constantly moved from place to place, taking in the *context* of an image. Such a view produces a very different logic of action, one that sees us and our aims as only one part of a larger system (whether it is the Middle East or global financial markets) instead of as the center. If you can understand and master the environment around your enemy, you can indirectly manipulate him, which is far more effective—and inescapable—than trying to persuade or confront him directly. It would be like making it rain on the day someone has a picnic planned instead of trying to talk or argue her out of it. Manipulation of the environment in this way is faster, in a sense, and more reliable than persuasion — a fact as true for dealing with Iran as for picnickers or tumors. But this demands making contact with and using the whole system. "Sometimes the river is running east, sometimes it is running west," a Chinese aphorism goes. An effects-based manipulation strategy means knowing which way the river is running, then forcing your opponent to battle upstream. Sun Zi, the Chinese military strategist believed to have lived twenty-five hundred years ago, locked up this instinct in his writing, which was obsessed with avoiding direct collision. In this, he was as much a product of his indirect culture as Clausewitz was of his direct one. Much of ancient Chinese philosophy suggested that truth emerged not through debate but rather through study, reflection, meditation, and, at long last, insight delivered like lightning. Collisions, whether of ideas or armies, were seen as wasteful and inelegant.

The question for Sun Zi was how you might make the outcome of a battle inevitable *and* avoid collision. It was far better, in this view, to attack your enemy's strategy instead of his troops. If you could immobilize him at the level of his neural cortex, he would collapse. If you could force him to go east when the river was running west, then nature would exhaust him far more efficiently than you ever could. Hundreds of years before any substantial discussion of "effects-based" strategies could be heard within the Pentagon's inner ring, Sun Zi was articulating a way of war in which the ideal wasn't simply fewer collisions but none at all. "For a man who is expert at using his troops," Sun Zi wrote, "the course of a battle may be likened to making round stones roll down from the highest summit." Chinese writers would praise masters of this gravitational skill by saying they had found a way to "open a ten-ton door with a one-ounce key." American generals, meanwhile, would be requisitioning ever-bigger battering rams.

What we must do now is start to extend this logic to all the problematic, indirect fights ahead of us: stemming financial panic, stopping the spread of nuclear weapons, or any other number of shape-shifting dangers. How can we surround, contain, and choke all those perils that can't be confronted directly? Well, we must master this idea of using the environment—of shaping and designing it for our use. The question isn't, for example, "How do we handle Russia's belligerent plans?" but "How do we create an environment that gives us the leverage we need to manipulate Moscow?"

This is a leap, to be sure. But the very success of such a strategy is why you might find the Chinese reminding you that "the greatest generals who ever lived, we don't even know their names." As Jullien explains, they're unknown to us because they never had to fight a single battle. Their sense of the terrain, of their environment, allowed them to create effects so profound and irresistible that they mooted the need for actual combat. They challenged that old line about diplomacy being "the art of the possible" with the idea that it should be the science of the inevitable. In this sense, Chinese often find the Western Odyssean narrative of the lone idealist battling an implacable environment baffling, as perplexing as a boat trying to run east in a west-running river. "One who is courageous and filled with derring-do will be killed," Lao Zi, the Chinese philosopher, once wrote. "One who is courageous and not daring will live." Chinese heroes were heroic because they got what they wanted *and* lived.

Chinese hero warriors are not like Pericles or Patton, marked largely by brilliance in bloody combat. Instead, they are recalled as sagelike. They do as little as possible. They prefer dominating instinct to titanic strength. They manipulate foes into positions from which there is no sensible release. And to do this they are ceaselessly generating options, as Holling's ideal ecosystem managers might, creating new ways to think, clever ways to act. Looking back at our own policy failures in places like Rwanda or Myanmar or the credit-swap markets, we must ask the question that obsessed those rebellious post-Vietnam pilots: "What should we have done differently?" One of the first things you realize when you do ask is that there were often no good answers at the time because there were no options. Our engagement with the world was so narrow that we neglected the tools of manipulation we'd need: people to call and rely on, government forces trained and suited for the challenges they faced. The question for Rwanda, for example, isn't only what you would have done differently as a massacre began to unfold there in 1994; it is also what you should have done five or ten years earlier to establish a context of influence so that you wouldn't have to rely only on a persuasive phone call to convince madmen to stop killing. Indian and Pakistani nuclear proliferation offered a similar reminder that earlier, and far more aggressive, shaping of the environment would have been far better than waiting to react to an Indian bomb test. Relationships and tools that can be used to manipulate a crisis have to be prepared years — sometimes decades — in advance. This reflects Holling's belief that in a changing ecosystem the persistence of relationships matters more than anything else. That's a reason that reacquiring the habits of international cooperation in everything from food aid to nuclear energy is so essential. It lets us begin to rebuild the webs of contacts, influence, and leverage to shape the environment around problems that we'll never be able to attack directly.

It's important, of course, not to reduce Chinese thought to a cliché. (In fact, to stereotype Chinese strategic thought as shaped only by peaceful, do-little Taoist perspectives is dangerous. Read MacArthur.) There's plenty of Chinese literature about trapping and killing your opponents. China, in its 3,500-year history, has not been a country filled only with polite, tea-drinking, Go-playing scholar-generals, blithely surrounding one another in bloodless checkmates. And, in fact, that's the point. The unimaginably murderous violence of ancient Chinese life—particularly in the Spring and Autumn Period and then the Warring States Period, 2,500 years ago—produced a philosophy obsessed with avoiding collision, with using effects instead of arms. The dream of an indirect victory was to eschew wasteful, costly engagements. To Western eyes, the work of Confucius or Mencius sometimes seems to say weirdly little about abstract ideas like justice or virtue and a great deal about the demands of pure survival. But some of the most successful deep-security accomplishments of our own age come from exactly this sort of approach, views that by necessity accept that our world is a system to be manipulated and not a *schwerpunkt* to be hammered. You can feel the puzzling, paradoxical potential of such a way of living by taking a moment to contemplate this one thought of Sun Zi, which does take a moment to sink in: "He who does not engage in battle is likely to defeat the enemy."

5. Poison Control

One morning in the summer of 2008, an American computer programmer named Dan Kaminsky was poking around the very deepest parts of the Internet as he sat in bed at home in Seattle. Kaminsky was already a legend of sorts among computer hackers, the geeky subculture of serious gearheads who spent much of their lives with their brains plugged into the network of fiber optics, servers, and PCs that has exploded around the world over the past twenty years. Kaminsky was twenty-nine and well regarded both by the "white-hat" hackers—the good guys who used their knowledge of networks to make them stronger—and by the "black hats," who spent time looking for holes in the Internet for less socially redeeming (though often very profitable) reasons.

To the degree that Kaminsky had an expertise, it was in a part of the infrastructure of the Net known as Domain Name Services, or DNS, which is one of the crucial behind-the-scenes technologies that keeps the Internet running. Kaminsky is pretty much right out of central casting for such a role: nerdy, given to silly jokes, enthusiastic beyond belief about technical details that are incomprehensible to all but a handful of people. But he also has an undeniable charm, one that has made him a hit keynote speaker at the big hacker conventions. DNS servers (servers are special computers on the network that "serve" data from one machine to another) hold master lists of the names of every location on the Net. You might think of them as giant real-time telephone books, since part of what they do is look up addresses and then match a request you've put into your computer with the machine on the Internet that you are looking for. When you type www.joshuaramo.com into your Web browser, it's a DNS lookup machine that finds the much more complicated numerical address and then does the business of helping the data get to your machine. If something went wrong with DNS, the implications for the Web would be immense, as if telephone numbers no longer matched the people you were trying to dial.

That morning Kaminsky had spotted a quirk in the way the system worked that, he immediately realized, could be fatal. The flaw had to do with the way those lists of names and addresses were maintained—in particular, a kink in the way the lists were saved and updated (called "caching" in computer-speak) that would allow a crafty hacker to redirect your request away from the address you wanted to anywhere they chose. If you were trying to access your bank account, for instance, this DNS hack could direct you instead to another Web site that looked exactly like your bank's (as far as you could tell) but was really a shill that would steal your account information, password, and other details. This was called "cache poisoning," and it would have made stealing personal information incredibly easy; in most cases users would have little idea what had happened until it was far too late. Worse, Kaminsky realized this hole had been built into the system as a *feature*—in other words, someone had designed the most fundamental part of the Internet with a giant, unintentionally open door. "It's really good," he later said of the hole. "Which in our business means it's very, very bad." Almost every computer in the foundation layer of the Internet probably had the same DNS flaw. If you tried to fix them one by one it would take an infinite amount of time, and you'd end up alerting the very hackers you were trying to keep from discovering the flaw in the first place. A stunned Kaminsky called his girlfriend, also a programmer, and in a combination of sheepishness and pride confessed, "Honey, I broke the Internet."

Kaminsky knew he was racing against time. His first reaction was to check that he was right. To do this he made a few discreet calls to some of the architects of the Web, most of whom knew him by reputation as a very good security analyst. Within hours they confirmed that the cache-poisoning threat was real. That left them all staring at the same dilemma: Kaminsky had uncovered a giant weakness, but the moment they announced it or even discussed it, they would be putting up a sort of "attack here" sign. If hackers discovered the flaw, they might be able to close down large portions of the Internet, a catastrophe people knew was possible but never thought would actually happen. So Kaminsky and his colleagues were faced with a very scary problem. A direct approach to the cache-poisoning dilemma—announcing it and posting a fix—would have been like group suicide. So they began hunting, furiously, for an indirect way out.

As Kaminsky thought about it, he realized that the best solution would be one that spread quickly and quietly. And here the systems nature of the Internet, the way in which every node is connected to every other node—the very thing that made the DNS hole so terrifying—was his greatest ally. If he didn't plug most of the big holes in DNS at once, then the networked nature of the problem meant hackers might slip through the unprotected parts of the system before he finished the job. But if he could get the Net's most important players to switch right away—and to trust he wasn't leading them down a blind alley—then the pace of repair might be fast enough to beat the hackers.

To begin with, Kaminsky and some of the key Web architects organized a secret emergency meeting. Because most of these white-hat hackers and engineers had worked together for years—a reminder of the importance Holling attached to the persistence of relationships in chaotic settings—all of them agreed to come (several from overseas) even under such strange conditions. The gathering was held in an anonymous conference room at Microsoft in Redmond, near where Kaminsky lived. Each member of the core group then began contacting selected friends who worked at the largest phone companies, network providers, and server software firms. They agreed early on not to speak directly about the problem via e-mail unless it was heavily encrypted and to avoid cell phones, whose signals might be intercepted.

The solution they came up with was known as a "spontaneous patch," and the plan was brilliant—as long as it could be kept quiet. Working together in secret, a group of programmers intimately familiar with the DNS rules would rewrite a chunk of code that would fill the DNS hole on most of the machines on the Internet. Their program had to be sneaky enough to work without revealing the location of the flaw to hackers, who would immediately start attacking machines that hadn't been vaccinated yet. Kaminsky knew the secret would get out sooner or later—in fact, he even decided that he'd divulge it himself at some point to make sure computer-systems managers understood what had almost happened—but it was vital that this take place *after* the spine of the Internet had been repaired.

After weeks of work by a group of engineers secreted away from their colleagues, the patch was ready. And on the morning of July 8, 2008, representatives for the largest information technology companies—firms like Microsoft, Oracle, EarthLink, and Google—slipped the patch into their computers. This was a huge leap of faith for systems administrators, but here Kaminsky relied on the fact that he had worked in tech departments at Fortune 500 companies for a decade. He assembled an all-star collection of programmers who hammered systems operators with an urgent message: "If we don't all hang together, we hang apart." Pentagon programmers, home-brewed web admins, heads of IT at some of the largest companies on earth—they all made the leap, and without any top-down order. By the first evening, *50 percent* of the Net's servers were repaired. Two weeks later it was 85 percent, and no hacker had found the hole—and this was done without urgent government intervention or big new laws. Kaminsky's lone PR concession was an explanatory online video featuring his niece. "I wanted people not to panic," he said. "And I figured, how can you possibly panic when a nine-year-old-girl is saying don't panic?" Given the Web-ending stakes, that patch launch day was, he said, as terrifying as it was gratifying. In a matter of weeks he had gone from diagnosing a potentially lethal flaw to finding a way to fix it. In short, a bunch of guys in a room, working indirectly, secretly, and urgently, had managed to do what no large corporation or government would have been able to do: they had saved the Internet from itself.

As we've seen, so many of the problems we face today are networked, meaning that simply acting will change the parameters of what we're confronting. As soon as we announce plans to restructure Iraq, the game on the ground changes. Pounding Hizb'allah, as we've seen, only makes them more resilient. Seeing the world as a system is something our enemies do well: if you look at the clever way Iran has wired the Middle East with alliances, loyal terror groups, and financial links, you won't be surprised to learn that President Mahmoud Ahmadinejad holds a Ph.D. in traffic engineering. If and when Israel attacks Iran, it can expect a cascade of indirect hits from all these sources, not just Iran itself.

When the very nature of acting changes the landscape or alters the flow of ideas or money or weapons, we have to find different and systemic ways of making change. This runs contrary to a lot of our habits. Recall how much our diplomacy leans on direct, public negotiations. That *directness* is an essential part of how we see and think, as we saw in Clausewitz. But a Kaminsky–Sun Zi way of acting not only works in our world of complex systems but, in some cases, offers a profound sort of security that will let us, finally, begin to feel we've got a grip on some rather insoluble-looking problems.

6. Rice Pulling in Gaza

To see how this approach might work, let's return for a moment to that Hall of Fame insoluble problem: the "Middle East peace agreement." It has been meant, for sixty years now, to be the proof of diplomatic brilliance in action, as if, simply by working hard enough, the scales of Arab and Israeli interests could be conclusively balanced. (Former Middle East peace negotiators joke that it's the only job with lifetime employment.) But what if we were to imagine peace not as something to be architected and dropped onto an unstable sandpile base but as something to be shaped by indirect effects, as Sun Zi might encourage? What if we put Kaminsky in charge?

The 2007 attempt at Middle East peace, the 1990s Oslo accords, and a dozen other now-forgotten efforts—all looked more or less like something the U.S. government would have dreamed up if they had been asked to tackle the DNS flaw. They started with an explicit announcement of the goal: to resolve the Israel-Palestine dispute once and for all, a so-called final settlement. Officials imagined a very particular narrative (like those American history teachers of Nisbett's) and then tried to persuade a group of unlikely, angry, and clever participants to stick to the script. Predictably, it was like waking up one morning and telling your entire family that they'd be heading in for unnecessary root canals during the day. Everyone would begin to adjust their lives and schedules to avoid the appointment. Long-forgotten baseball games or school reports would suddenly come to mind. So, too, with these "master plan" Middle East peace strategies. The announcement of each step simply created pressure that promised to undo the whole. Plans to give money to the Palestinians, for instance, only seeded new interest groups that fought over how best to take the proceeds (and the power attached to them). Trying to table a formal agreement drove each side—intensely aware of domestic politics—into more deeply entrenched positions. And the essential hope of such an agreement—*finality*—terrified many of the participants. If this was really *it*, really the last best deal, then they had best struggle as hard as they could for what they wanted.

What would Kaminsky do? What kind of effects and indirect tactics might we use? To begin, imagine a Middle East peace process with no big-name negotiators who felt it important to be visible and active, to announce the anticipated five-act performance of peacemaking. (Recall the feature Sun Zi prized most in his generals: anonymity.) Theatrical Camp David persuasion sessions would be retired. Few explicit cash infusions. No dreamed-of signing ceremonies. Instead, an effects approach would begin its patient work in the cognitive domain. It would take stability as its ultimate goal and treat the two sides as part of a dynamic system demanding constant vigilance, since a slip into chaos was possible at any moment. Destabilizing, finger-pointing debates by those in the White House or the European Union about how Palestinians and Israelis govern themselves would be muted at all costs, since even the slightest pressure could start a cascade of recriminations and violence. (As happened in Gaza, where angry Palestinians elected a Hamas-led government in 2006 despite—or because of—explicit American encouragement to do the opposite. "I don't know anyone who wasn't caught off guard," said Secretary of State Rice, who should have known better.) This approach to Middle East peace would trust that a sensible and durable arrangement would emerge from stability, for without stability no such agreement could be durable. Effects diplomacy would map the environment with hundreds of small policy efforts: creating dozens of new NGOs, empowering teachers, improving policing. The aim might be to change as little as possible in some areas and instead to encourage education, small business, and moderate religious figures—classic slow variables. Such a policy might even encourage small upheavals as a way to avoid bigger ones down the road, like those controlled burns that make forests resilient. The process could be managed by a small, secret group in a special peace "war room," not by a big name angling for a Nobel Prize. Patience, not persuasion, would be the virtue. The deadline would not be the end of a president's term or the run-up to an election—in fact, there would be no deadline at all. One day Palestinians and Israelis might awaken to a different landscape without quite realizing how it had emerged.

In sum, this would be systems-style leverage: avoid direct conflict, use the forces already at play, manipulate so quietly as to be unnoticed, know that no effort truly ends. Treat Middle East peace not as something to be hammered together but—to use Hayek's idea for economies—as a garden to be tended. In the annals of Chinese philosophy, there is a famous gardening story that captures exactly the problems we make for ourselves with our direct and impatient instincts: "There was a man from Song who tugged at the ends of his rice plants because he was worried they were not growing fast enough. Having done so he went home, not realizing what he had done. 'I am worn out today,' he told his family. 'I have been helping the rice grow.' His son rushed out to look, and there the plants were, shriveled up."

Middle East peace will most likely come well after we've stopped tugging.

Of course, direct conflict has to remain a part of our lives. There are plenty of situations in which a hard, violent option is the best one. This is why it's best to think of effects not as a replacement for action, but as an extension. You can imagine such approaches being tried in areas as different as financial regulation and negotiations with Iran, approaches that would take their strength from being clever, constantly engaged, and as flexible as the world itself. This could be done not only in places where we have real and enduring conflicts, but also in places where we're not quite sure where we stand yet. It's hard to know, for instance, if China will ultimately be a friend or foe to the United States. But at the moment, most U.S.-Chinese discussions are shaped by the American desire for direct, noisy, public collision at the *schwerpunkt* of disagreement: human rights, currency reform, environment. But what about being more like Sun Zi? Why not try an indirect approach, engaging China on many fronts at once, trying to shape the international environment as a way to shape China? What about working with China in dozens of areas more assiduously, instead of concentrating 90 percent of our effort on issues we disagree on. Why not look at U.S.-Chinese relations as a mesh to be shaped and managed instead of a series of diplomatic battles that look like nothing so much as trench warfare? As hard as it is to understand (recall Bohr on quantum mechanics), directly confronting China on these points has the same likelihood of success as most other direct confrontations in the sandpile world. There's plenty in Chinese policy that is urgently in need of change; in many cases China's leaders are the first to admit it. But foreign pressure often makes it harder, not easier, to trigger these shifts, since they can't be seen to be made as a result of demands from the West. It may well be that the best way to ensure development of human rights in China is to work quietly and around the margins.

We should not delude ourselves about what we now face. Having spent a couple of decades running around with the idea that we can directly convince the world to agree with us, we now confront a real shortage of leverage. This is a profound gap in our grand strategic immune system. We now need to construct everything from new treaties to new relationships as sources of indirect leverage. In areas such as nuclear proliferation or finance we have virtually no useful tools. And we need to learn an instinct for indirectness, one that, for instance, would have had us respond to 9/11 not only with direct attacks but also with even larger, more intense indirect efforts such as schools, hospitals, and other social initiatives. There will be many moments in the future where we will be surprised, confused, and terrified. Our usual reaction—to hit back or cower—needs to be augmented with an instinct for generosity and decency. This is a lot to ask. But direct attacks alone, as we've seen, fail over and over. Our deep-security immune system needs to work as efficiently indirectly as directly. The lesson of Kaminsky and Sun Zi should be starkly clear now. There's a reason that effects thinking has dominated Chinese strategy for centuries and our own immune systems for far longer than that: it works.

CHAPTER TEN

Riding the Earthquake

1. Superbug

The South African town of Tugela Ferry sits about 130 miles north of the city of Durban on the Indian Ocean coast. It feels dropped, almost accidentally, along the clay-red two-lane road that leads through the town and onto the vast Drakensberg plain. This is Zulu country, and you can see how the jolting physical beauty, the contrast of ochre cliffs and green hills, must have struck the British soldiers who fought here during the 1800s and waxed poetic about a land so deeply moving. Tugela Ferry itself, however, now wears the unmissable rags of severe poverty. The long-distance buses run into Durban Park in the center of town, improbably close to the mazes of indigo-clad women selling handmade clothes and food. You catch, at moments with them, glimpses of a rough joy that belies a difficult life, but mostly what you catch here is the rough life. Tugela Ferry is the urban center for 250,000 people, but it's the barest sort of center: a few stores, a modest hospital. Like the rest of this part of South Africa, the area around Tugela Ferry has one of the highest rates of HIV infection in the world. More than

40 percent of the population here has AIDS; in some nearby villages, where that rate can be even higher, you can feel you are driving through a quiet, sad, impending graveyard of stick-thin men and women.

Tony Moll, a tall and cheerful British doctor, is the Chief Medical Officer at the Church of Scotland Hospital, serving a region of 600 square miles. A dozen nurses in outlying clinics support Moll, but the serious cases quickly filter into the main hospital, where he and his team see them during workdays that are rarely shorter than twelve hours. Moll's house is on the campus of the hospital, a five-minute walk from the admitting rooms. He came to Tugela Ferry in the 1980s, just as AIDS was beginning to massacre much of the population of southern Africa. The Tugela Ferry hospital, like most hospitals in Kwa-Zulu Natal, simply couldn't handle or treat the flood of patients sick with the disease. Moll's job became one of managing their slow, inevitable decline.

Moll is an energetic, optimistic, and inventive man—as you'd have to be to practice medicine in Africa for decades. He did the best with what little he had, and when I first got to know him in 2001, he already had a reputation as a sort of superhero of triage. He had pioneered one of the best programs in the world for managing the pain of dying AIDS patients. He had helped develop nutrition strategies for his poor patients and assisted in aggressive disease prevention campaigns—everything from poster blitzes to roving minibus tours. It was all weak medicine. But starting in 2004, he began to see the first hints of real good news. That year the South African government finally agreed to let doctors prescribe antiretroviral drugs (known as ARVs), the miracle pills that promised to roll back AIDS symptoms. Though global pharma companies were still pricing the best of these drugs above the reach of South Africans, Moll began prescribing the basic ARVs he could get his hands on (he bought the first ones with his own money) and enjoying the *this is what I got into medicine for* experiences that AIDS doctors in the United States had enjoyed a decade earlier. Patients who had been wheeled into the hospital crippled by infection, covered with tiny cancers, or twitching with AIDS-related nerve corrosion, each with eye-blinkingly high loads of HIV in their blood, progressed to better health. Their immune systems began to snap back. In some cases, they were sent home with viral loads that were barely detectable.

Better still, Moll found, the patients seemed to stick with the complicated ARV treatment. This was the crucial accomplishment. One of the most persistent arguments against providing ARVs to people in places like Tugela Ferry had been that the effort was a waste. African AIDS patients were too poor to care for themselves, critics said, too illiterate to manage the cocktail of medications, and too ill with opportunistic diseases to respond to treatment. Moll's thriving AIDS patients were discrediting that view. You couldn't yet say the AIDS crisis was ending or even turning. After all, as late as 2008 South African AIDS patients were still dying at a rate of about one every minute. And there was little sign that infection rates were slowing. But the daily life of Moll's practice offered a sense of progress. In fact, his patients were doing so well that a team from Yale University arrived in Tugela Ferry to track their progress. So it was particularly jarring when, one day in the winter of 2005, many of those same patients, without warning or explanation, started dying.

To Moll and his nurses, the deaths made no sense. All of the patients had been relatively healthy. Most had recovered from their dangerous AIDS-related illnesses. Stranger still, whatever was killing them looked, at first glance, very much like drug-resistant tuberculosis—but that was impossible. To begin with, none of the dead patients had a history of regular TB. (In fact, the ones in the Yale study had been admitted precisely for that reason.) So there was no way they could be developing that particular form of the disease—as if a man had developed ovarian cancer, something simply beyond the possible biological explanations. On top of that, even though the disease looked like TB, with its night sweats, tight lungs, and rib-breaking coughs, Moll's patients failed to respond to the usual foolproof TB treatments.

Moll, right before the deaths began, in what he admits was a stroke of pure luck, had taken sputum samples from all of the patients in his hospital and sent them to the regional testing center in Durban. He now rang the center to see if they had any answers. When they got back to him, the news was chilling. Moll's patients *did* have TB, but there was a reason it had fooled the doctors: the type of TB in Tugela Ferry had never been seen before—and it was so virulent that it had beaten six different anti-TB drugs, the complete armory of medications available in South Africa. Tugela Ferry, the lab results suggested, was the center of an outbreak of a superbug.

Moll felt his stomach drop. He could barely concentrate on the last part of the call. His first thought, he told me later, was about the way TB spreads. Unlike blood-borne HIV, which is rarely passed from patient to health-care worker, TB spreads through the air. In that respect it is like the lethal African terror-virus Ebola, which kills 80 percent of the people it infects. TB was known to linger in the air of an unventilated room for hours. A single cough could infect a doctor or nurse. Two of Moll's staff were already dead. What he was hearing on the phone might be a death sentence for many others, including himself.

As Moll and his colleagues raced to isolate their patients—and themselves—they reviewed the situation. Something very dangerous was tearing through the jigsaw-tight TB wards in their hospital and in the scattered houses of Tugela Ferry. Within weeks the World Health Organization (WHO) called an emergency meeting in South Africa to discuss the strain, which they named XDR-TB, for "extensively drug-resistant TB." Soon after his call Moll sat down to calculate the impact of the disease and discovered that XDR-TB patients were dying, on average, just sixteen days after they arrived in the hospital. There was no time to stabilize and treat them. And in one respect XDR made Ebola look mild: it killed 98 percent of the people who got it.

2. Physician's Paradox

Tuberculosis was first described by Robert Koch in 1882, and it's one of the most common diseases on earth, infecting about a third of the people in the world. In most cases the disease remains dormant, constantly fighting a losing battle with the immune system. But in places like South Africa, which has millions of people whose immune systems are weakened by poverty, hunger, or HIV, TB thrives.

An effective treatment for TB, called rifampicin, had been used for nearly fifty years and was available in South Africa. The treatment course lasted six months and cost about twenty dollars. But there was a problem: rifampicin or the other first-line TB medications were almost too good at their job. They cleared up the most brutal symptoms relatively quickly, and always before molecules carrying the disease had been washed away. And since the treatment's side effects included nausea and exhaustion, the temptation to stop early was hard to resist. As many as 60 percent of TB patients in South Africa did stop early. Yet even though they felt better, they were still carrying millions of supertough holdout bacteria in their bloodstreams. These bacteria, now strengthened against the effects of rifampicin and similar medications, formed the basis of a new epidemic, known as multidrug-resistant TB (MDR-TB). If you quit that initial TB treatment early, you were at risk. If you were unlucky enough to get MDR-TB, it required a treatment that lasted a year and a half, cost the South African government $20,000, and involved hospitalization and daily injections for the first four months. The side effects of treatment included deafness, dizziness, and bursts of excruciating and unpredictable pain. This was awful enough that some patients said they would rather risk dying than finish the treatment. So, having quit the first-line TB drugs, they "defaulted" off the second-line drugs as well, which opened the door for another, apparently untreatable version of the disease. This was the plague that struck Tugela Ferry.

Because, by chance, that Yale study was under way at the time of the outbreak, the XDR-TB incident provided a microscopic look at one of the paradoxes of the story of TB and AIDS in Africa. In Tugela Ferry, you'll recall, Moll was proving that his very sick, very poor South Africans would stay on antiretroviral treatment for HIV. But many of those same patients were defaulting *off* the TB medication, which was surprising. The South African government and international organizations had spent hundreds of millions of dollars on TB education. Every health-care professional in the country had lumbered through a half-dozen mandatory seminars about the disease and its treatment. Yet in 2005, the year of the XDR outbreak in Tugela Ferry, as many South Africans would die of ordinary TB as were cured of it.

Unlike TB treatment, which lasted only six months, ARV treatment was a lifetime project. The pills also had unpleasant side effects, in some cases much worse than the TB medication's. And AIDS patients had a much less developed infrastructure of support and monitoring. But—and here's where we need to pay attention—even as they stopped taking TB drugs, the patients stayed on ARVs. The split seemed nonsensical. It was like discovering that all the children in a school were failing arithmetic but easily picking up calculus. Somehow an expensive, Ph.D.-engineered policy to fight TB seemed unable to control the disease. In fact, it had turned a manageably dangerous disease into a sort of airborne disaster-in-waiting. So why were South Africans sticking with the complex ARV treatment and giving up on the easy TB course? On the surface, the problems looked identical: sick poor people, a regimen of pills they needed to take. But there was one small, nearly imperceptible difference between the way the two diseases were treated, and it turned out to be the difference between a revolutionary health-care program that was saving patients and one that, to be frank, was doing something unthinkable: murdering them.

3. The Instability Virus

You may recall that earlier I said that radical newness is contagious. This is one of the reasons it is so useful to think about Grand Strategy as if it were an immune system. Doing so prepares us for all of those flu-like features of an unstable age and protects us well enough that we can thrive and grow amid real change. Contagion, of course, is a common trait of any revolutionary era. In 1848, for example, changes in the urban composition of

Europe and the nature of industrial labor (think Dickens) conspired to catalyze economic shifts that triggered continental
political revolutions (think Marx). But today this whole process
happens much, much faster and across a much wider network.
As we've seen over and over again, all sorts of links conspire to
accelerate the propagation of problems. What I'd like to turn to
now is the secret Moll's ARV patients had unwittingly discovered: how to propagate solutions.

We've seen how revolutionary seeing and thinking and acting works better in places like Silicon Valley or the Bekka Valley.
This is why Mike Moritz outperformed his investing peers, why
Aharon Farkash lasted longer in his job than most Israeli intelligence generals. But what if you could watch a test of two different
schools of thought, side by side, in action? This was exactly, by a
quirk of fate, what was happening in Tugela Ferry when XDR-
TB emerged. On the one hand you had a huge, centralized, old-
school approach to TB. On the other, an approach to HIV that
was ad hoc in many ways. In the case of HIV, success; in the case
of TB, a now-familiar problem: a policy that not only fails (doesn't
stop TB) but makes the problem more dangerous than the one you
started with (creates a superbug). And in the deadly space between
those two results, we'll find an essential difference between the
way our governments and most employers do work and the way
they ought to work. It's the last essential piece of a deep-security
way of living. And you'll be amazed at what it can produce.

4. Distributing Intelligence

First let's talk about what exactly had occurred in that TB-versus-
HIV treatment contest. From a standing start you might have

said that dying TB-infected South Africans had more "power" to deal with TB than with HIV. Look at all the resources that had been invested in saving them: more than twenty years of government support, tens of millions of dollars in investment, thousands of specially trained nurses and doctors, even a carefully developed idiot-proof program to monitor how they took and stayed on drugs such as rifampicin. (Clearly lacking the mnemonic verve of the Pentagon folks who dreamed up cool-sounding HARMS and LBADS, public-health planners simply called the program DOTS, for directly observed treatment, short course.) Health-care workers *watched* as patients swallowed pills for two months — and then often defaulted anyhow.

Against this were arrayed the often ad hoc resources of the antiretroviral initiative: a few mimeographed pages about how the drugs worked, a compliance program that asked relatives to keep an eye on patients, and a handful of overwhelmed doctors like Moll. So why was the expensive program failing? The answer was that TB treatment in South Africa was failing, not despite the huge amounts of money and time invested, but because of the way in which such huge amounts of money and time were being invested. The very importance and cost of the TB program meant it was run with great care and intensity by the South African government. Patients getting TB treatment were closely supervised by nurses — who often treated them like inert subjects in a study. Doctors told patients what to do by reading off specially developed checklists. Even that business of watching patients take pills carried a message: we don't trust you. Often no one shared with the patients any details about how the drugs worked or how they interacted with the disease. That information was left in the hands of health-care professionals. After all, it was hard to imagine what an impoverished and half-literate dying

South African really needed to know about how a TB drug functioned in her body.

Antiretrovirals, by contrast, were handled differently. As a patient, before you ever received a pill you had to agree to sit through an education program with a friend or family member who guaranteed in writing that you'd stay on the drugs. You had to attend support-group meetings, disclose the disease to any sex partners, and return immediately to the hospital if you developed certain symptoms. The pill prep classes included discussions of biology, explanations of the human immune system, and lessons about how the drugs interacted with each other and with what you ate and drank. This program of disease literacy had been pioneered, not only by public-health Ph.D.s, but also by unemployed rural women and infected South African city dwellers, usually patients themselves, partly because they didn't trust the drug companies or the doctors. They wanted to know what they were putting into their bodies. But they were also betting that their fellow infected citizens were smart enough to manage the disease and that most—the vast majority of whom had never completed high school—could be taught science and that such knowledge would serve not just as context but as motivation. ARV treatment literacy let patients manage far more of their own care than any outside expert would have guessed possible. And this changed the whole dynamic. ARV patients stuck with their pills.

The gap between the success of the ARV program and the failure of the TB program revealed a lesson that applies almost everywhere in our world now: the moment you hand power over to other people, you get an explosion of curiosity, innovation, and effort. This is a law as true for commodity markets (where it works to disastrous effect when we don't watch it carefully) as for disease treatment. And the universality of this law, for good or ill, is what makes it so curious and useful. It's not wrong to think of what's going on in our world as a race between forces that are unthinkably amazing and those that are unthinkably horrifying. For example, the very same technology that uses genetics to cure heart disease can create lethal biological weapons. As we move to build a really secure world, it's time for us to begin investing—heavily—in putting more runners for the force of good on the track. Moll's HIV patients are a reminder that, given encouragement and opportunity, people will run faster than we would ever have imagined.

When you spread power instead of hoarding it, you discover benefits that you couldn't have imagined in advance—and that sometimes run contrary to what you might have expected. Military historians have studied the bewildering efficiency of armies that swarm like bees or ants, highly decentralized groups that bend, adjust, and attack based on a far better sense of local conditions than any central commander could ever have. This form of warfare flew in the face of centuries of command-and-control warfare theory, but it was what made German U-boats so effective, even though they were often out of touch with their bases for days at a time. It's what made Mongol horse swarms so lethally efficient, and it has marked winning revolutionaries as different as Mao Zedong and Emiliano Zapata. Making this sort of decentralized approach work was the job of tech geeks who populate the ranks of groups like Al Qaeda and Hizb'allah. "Hizb'allah uses a swarming approach to deal with Israeli commando raids in southern Lebanon," RAND scholars John Arquilla and David Ronfeldt wrote in a landmark paper; "This approach is based on a general instruction to Hizb'allah's widely distributed units to converge—like antibodies, it seems—on

any intruders in a given area. No central leadership is required."
Swarming is, of course, the classic immune-system response. It's
what happens when your blood clots after you slice your finger
cutting cucumbers, and it's what's going on in your sinuses when
you sneeze.

This kind of self-organization, the ability to pull off an "all
hands on deck" reaction, exists in many of the most efficient
and resilient systems in our world. This has been a marked feature of life in an information age, when e-mails, telephone calls,
and text messages have diminished the effects of geography, put
people in closer direct contact, and, in the process, removed the
need for much central command and control. Take, for example,
what economists call "peer production," which is the previously
unimagined economic twitch for sharing work that has built
Wikipedia, file-sharing systems like BitTorrent (which now
accounts for at least 50 percent of all Internet traffic), or "open
source" operating systems like Ubuntu and Linux. "Peers" can be
producing anything from decisions to software, but what matters is that these efforts are largely bottom-up, which, strangely,
makes them more efficient rather than less. *A bunch of chaotic
hackers doing as good a job as* Encyclopaedia Britannica? Well, as
Nature magazine discovered when it compared the accuracy of
Wikipedia and *Britannica,* yes.

Once users step into active engagement, the dynamics of
the system shift forever: users stop being consumers and become
participants. This pushes the opportunity for innovation to the
edges of a network, where users reside, instead of leaving it in
the hands of some slow-moving, committee-oriented, centralized manufacturing center. This was, for instance, how the
whole mountain-biking craze got started, as Eric von Hippel
has written in his masterful study *Democratizing Innovation.* A

few trail-riding gearheads intent on customizing their own bikes began developing better, more suitable bikes from old-style street bicycle frames — swapping tips and information with each other as they went and accelerating the creation of a new sport. Von Hippel calls this "user innovation," and it resulted in both faster change and products that better suited the way bikers aspired to ride. It cut, in essence, the distance between "hope" and "product" to nearly zero.

Peer producers behave in ways that traditional economics says is absurd, just as public-health experts might have laughed at the idea that illiterate women could manage a complex medical training program. For instance, peer producers will work long hours for no financial reward, only for the sheer pleasure of making a better piece of software or a cooler mountain bike brake. They will renounce the right to own or profit from what they invent. Two hundred thousand people working together to create and edit Wikipedia and then giving it away for free (in fact, working so hard precisely because it *is* free) is something no standard approach to economics can explain — just as no standard health-care approach explains the effectiveness of those lifesaving techniques to fight AIDS. It's proof that once you give power away all sorts of unplanned efficiencies — boosts that are invisible to our standard way of seeing — emerge.

Peer production solves one of the great troublesome stumbling blocks to progress: that a few people usually control the most-vital information. Instead it creates an open system, one not so different from the one South African patients created when they started mimeographing their own home-made ARV guidelines. And there's a bonus here — what economists call a "return to scale" — that is like a dividend you get only when lots of people work together. The more users a centralized system has, the closer it comes to exhaustion. (Think of a mother with five preadolescent kids or an overloaded telephone switchboard operator.) But the more users a decentralized system has, the more efficient it becomes, since work can be spread around or picked up by whoever can do it best and fastest. The average time between vandalism of a Wikipedia page and its repair is now less than five minutes. The average time to fix an error in that version of the *Encyclopaedia Britannica* you have on your shelves is, well, never. It's already set in print. (And even if you bought a new edition, you'd have to wait years between versions.)

There's another impressively useful trait of these systems that's vitally important: they are much, much more efficient because often they manage to put excess capacity to work that would otherwise be wasted—the underutilized engineering skills of bikers, for instance, or the drawing and teaching skills of AIDS patients. The classic example of this phenomenon was a 2000 NASA project called Clickworkers, which let random users log in to a Web site and mark out craters and channels on photos of the surface of Mars. This was the sort of geographic work that was usually done by experienced grad students. But thousands of volunteer workers, often clicking for just a few minutes at a time during a coffee break, were as accurate as and far faster (and cheaper) than a few grad students. NASA said it wanted to answer two questions: Would the public lend a hand to help science, and would the results be as good as a traditional approach. The answer was yes on both counts.

Think of how much excess capacity lingers in our global system, from unused ideas to misallocated savings to underemployed academics or researchers in countries where information is blocked or embargoed. (Frankly, think of how much unused capacity lingers in your life or mine; we'll turn to this in a moment.) There is more potential power for action in our world system now than ever before in history—and also more need for action. What Jean Monnet, one of the most masterful strategists of the last century, wrote in 1951 is true today: "World peace cannot be safeguarded without the making of efforts proportionate to the dangers which threaten it." The more peers we can bring online for the business of saving the world, the easier the effort will be, and, in a sense, the stronger we'll each be. As the Yale law professor Yochai Benkler wrote in "Coase's Penguin," an essay that set out the virtues of this fresh economics in 2002: "The advantages of peer production are, then, improved identification and allocation of human creativity. These advantages appear to have become salient, because human creativity itself has become salient." As we've seen, our future is a race between good innovation and bad innovation. That's a sprint that will be decided purely by our ability to create. It's a shift so profound that it evokes the ideas of the American philosopher John David Garcia, who once said that we should reject the notion that increasing human happiness is the most important goal for society. Far better, he said, to increase human creativity. Happiness will follow.

We owe everything to human creativity. Everything that lasts, that changes our lives, that emerges from what was once unimaginable has its roots in that initial spark of innovation. What we need now is a way to spread the capacity for peer production of our own future. We need a global order in which those "irrational" forces of invention and surprise, forces that don't fit foreign-policy models—any more than free labor fits economics—can be used to improve the parts of the world in which we can't seem to make progress. In short, we need a global version of that distributed ARV approach. Sure, it may seem irrational that uneducated dying Africans could save themselves. But in practice they do just fine. Our standard models don't know how to make sense of these kinds of productivity miracles—which is why those models will never be able to save us.

As I sat with Moll in Tugela Ferry one afternoon in 2006, talking about XDR-TB, I was reminded of a friend of mine, who was building robots long before that was cool (assuming, of course, that it *has* actually become cool). In the early 1990s my friend was trying, and failing, to build a machine that would vacuum floors without human input. This problem occupied her for years, and it was interesting because solving it would open up all sorts of other possibilities, such as how you might robot-clear a minefield. The challenge was how to teach the robots about the millions of different rooms they would need to vacuum. Old-style artificial intelligence suggested this would involve finding a way to jam a map of every room in every house into the machine—the checklist approach. You'd need to be able to observe every room, the way those doctors observed every TB patient. It was impossible. But then my friend had a breakthrough: what if the robot could learn the map of the room by itself, without any preprogramming? It could do this by scooting around and gently bumping into walls, chairs, and sofas. Such a machine would be kind of stupid, actually. It would require only the barest amount of intelligence. But even in that state it would work in a way that the smartest centralized system never could. Once she and her engineers made this leap, they were able to develop a self-directed vacuum cleaner, the Roomba, which became a huge commercial success. The lesson of Roomba was that a slow-thinking, wall-bumping, but *empowered* vacuum cleaner was smarter than a room full of Ph.D.s. If only those

South African health officials had understood this, a great tragedy might have been avoided. And, of course, suppressing the devastation of AIDS in Africa has major foreign-policy implications: The genius of what happened in Tugela Ferry wasn't that it happened in Tugela Ferry. It was that it could happen anywhere.

5. The Christmas-Box Rule

In a way, what I am about to propose as the last part of our deep-security immune system, the revolutionary spread of power, will probably seem inevitable at this point. But it's worth stopping for a moment to remark how far we have come from that older hat-on-the-floor picture of our world at the start of this book. We've now left behind the idea that only states matter, that the futures of nations should be determined only by looking at leaders in rooms, that we can make policy as if we were making a cake: just add democracy or capitalism and get prosperity. We've changed how we look at the world, begun to obsess about resilience, started to see threats as systems, not objects. We've seen practical ideas about how such deep security might work in practice, changing how we create Middle East peace, for instance, or how we confront Iran, nuclear proliferation, and complex nations such as China. And now, as a last adjustment, we will move to the extreme opposite of the old way of looking. Instead of worrying about big objects (states) and expecting them to be predictable, instead of obsessing about heads of state or terrorist leaders, what I want to propose is that we focus our attention also on the very smallest parts of the system, on *people*, and bet that the one thing we know for sure is that we can't predict what they'll do. In other words, the last step to deep security in a world of unthinkable granular surprise is to push — as hard as possible — for even more unthinkable granular surprise.

Our goal now should be to empower as much of the world as we can, even if at times that means encouraging forces that make us uneasy at first glance: political systems that look different from our own, for instance, or economic notions like redistributing wealth to some of the poorest (and angriest, most polluting, sickest) people on the planet. This means placing, right at the heart of our international policy, a goal of giving everyone basic survival rights. These are the sorts of things most of us take as a given every morning when we wake up: education, some control over what we do for a living, enough to eat. This new approach doesn't mean junking our military in the hope that the world will become a peaceful place (though, as we have seen, it does mean using it more wisely). It also doesn't mean jamming people into democratic systems and thinking that's enough — and then giving up when democratic experiments backfire. Instead, it suggests elevating to the highest level of grand strategy — the same level where we put warfare and ballistic missiles and thinking about whether we should embrace or bomb Iran — the quality of the lives of people who have been largely ignored in mainstream strategic thinking. I am betting that empowered people will act like T cells in our global immune system. The more of them we have, the more likely we are to spot and control and fight deadly but inevitable outbreaks before they spread. And, like T cells, empowered people are not optional.

We can't control the sort of growth we need to foster, can't dictate what it will look like or force it into existing models. Trying to do that would kill the very spirit of innovation we're looking for. We need to accept the charming Christmas-morning law that kids often get more joy out of the leftover boxes than from the toys that were once inside and apply it globally: the more something lends itself to invention and imagination, the more enduringly useful it becomes. This is as true for human lives as it is for software, music, or children's toys. Practically, this means a dramatic, globe-defining effort to touch the lives of billions of people. It means moving away from the government-to-government connections that dominate our policy and toward broad, aggressive attempts to deal with the basic obstacles to personal power. "What can we do to make these people peers?" is the question that matters. A peer-produced world offers hope that local innovation and a flowering diversity of ideas can begin to cope with everything from water shortages to terrorism. Writing about managing a world of chaos in the early part of the twentieth century, Hannah Arendt once defined power as "the ability to act in common." This is where we've got to aim now, but our acting in common will be as people and peers, not only as nations, as it was in Arendt's time. The rights we need to ensure at first are not complex: the chance to go to school, to find a job that lets you grow, to live with some assurance of health care—all the pieces of a stable life. And we also need to add as many connections as possible between people and global sources of information and ideas.

The Brazilian intellectual and politician Roberto Unger has called what lies ahead of us the creation of a "caring economy." Our current approach to the world, he has said, has been "reduced to the passing of checks through the mail"—a danger that means our generosity is often wasted and always isolates us from a world that we need to feel and not simply see or touch at a distance. "This is far too thin a social ferment," Unger has said.

"On the contrary, the universal principle must be established that every able-bodied adult must in the course of his life hold a job in both the production systems and the caring economy and participate in some part of his working life or working year in the responsibility of caring for the old, the young and the infirm beyond the limits of the family." Unger is right. This is our only hope for matching distributed action against the distributed risks we now face. How to do this? Well, we'll turn to that next. But certainly we know that our new direction should be guided by the words of the sociologist Immanuel Wallerstein, who has said, in what is surely one of the simplest calls to action in an interconnected world, "What we do to others, we do to ourselves." This is as true for good as it is for ill.

6. "No one knows how many people we employ"

In the late 1980s a young Brazilian businessman named Ricardo Semler took over the operation of his family's thirty-year-old marine equipment company, Semco. In ordinary circumstances, in almost any country, this would have been a natural rite of passage. But Brazil in the 1980s was in the midst of a period of hyperinflation that was rare in economic history. In a good year prices would double. The bad years were much, much worse. In 1990 prices rose more than 1,000 percent. The situation was so bad that the finance minister, in a less-than-totally-lucid moment, decided to seize 80 percent of the cash in the Brazilian system. Somehow this had the effect of driving prices up further.

"In Brazil," Semler wrote as he looked back on this chaotic decade, "no state of the economy is permanent. Few last long enough to be called temporary." Running a business in Brazil, he said, was like riding a Brahma bull during an earthquake: "Some of the worst jolts come not from the bull but from the landscape."

Semco was among the best engineering firms in Brazil, with customers as far away as Los Angeles and Oslo. But, Semler discovered, the quality of Semco's products and its international client base were no protection against those earthquakes. Simply borrowing money to finance upcoming orders, for instance, required paying a premium of 30 percent over the rate of inflation. One day Semco took out a loan with an interest rate of 930 percent. It will not surprise you that between 1990 and 1994, one in every four Brazilian manufacturing firms went bust. Industrial output fell to the same level as in 1977. Semler, in short, had inherited a business that, no matter how well it might be run, was probably doomed.

Semler felt tremendous pressure to keep the firm alive. He brought in management techniques from American business schools. They didn't help. He reorganized the firm along the lines of a Japanese kanban (just-in-time) management system. That failed too. Following the government's decision to seize the bank accounts of most Brazilians in 1990, Semler and his managers met with employees in groups of one hundred at a time and confessed they were out of ideas. There appeared to be only two options: cut salaries, which would devastate many of the workers, who were narrowly surviving as it was, or lay off employees, sacrificing some of the company's workers to save the rest. No one liked either choice. "We went on desperately searching for a third way out," Semler recalled. Finally, after some careful consideration, Semler's employees proposed an alternative. They would agree to a dramatic pay cut in exchange for three things: a larger share of the profits; a 40 percent pay cut for Semler and the management team; and, to make sure they knew where the money was going, a member of their union cosigning every check the company wrote. "At that moment," Semler wrote, "we *had* no profits to share, so there was nothing for us to lose and everything to gain."

The results were transformative. Within two months, Semco was running at breakeven. To save money, employees started handling work the firm had once contracted out. They served as security guards and janitors and helped cook in the Semco cafeteria. The union official who shared check-writing duties challenged almost every expense. "For four or five months," Semler recalled, "we made a small profit in the worst economic times any of us had ever seen. But we kept on looking for a better solution." When the Brazilian economy began to right itself and the firm passed from near-death to mere crisis, Semler and his fellow managers sat back to consider what had happened. They knew they could now afford to go back and reclaim their old way of working, to get the union out of their bank accounts. But when they were honest about it, they knew that what had just happened at Semco was more than a simple matter of survival; it was a corporate miracle. In contrast to the desperate environment at other firms or even to the toxic fiscal atmosphere of the Brazilian economy in general, at Semco there had been "an explosion of energy, enthusiasm, and flexibility." And since Semler was well aware that the Brazilian economy, even in its best years, was "lunatic," he wondered: was there a way to run the business over a longer period of time by these new rules?

Semler began considering a radical new way of organizing his firm. Instead of running it along the lines of manufacturing policies that had been around for centuries—a top-down, centralized approach to making and selling products, with power resting in the hands of an imperial CEO—Semler decided to build what he called a "free-for-all" corporation. He would have as little structure and management as possible. Semler turned most of his employees into independent contractors, whom he called "satellites." He let all of his employees set their own salaries and working hours. He broke the firm into tiny pieces, ensuring that no work unit had more than one hundred or so employees, even though this meant redundant costs for things like buildings and administration. He made every element of company life, from executives' salaries to profit margins to corporate secrets such as product design, available to all employees. He let Semco's line workers decide for themselves how and when they would produce new products—and how much they would charge for them. Once, when he needed to open a new plant, he let his employees scout for locations, then bused them from site to site so they could see what their future might hold. Finally, he asked them to vote for the place where they wanted to work. And when, after looking at all the options, they decided on a location directly across the street from a plant that was home to some of the most persistent labor unrest in Brazil, Semler went ahead and followed their decision anyhow. "With two tough unions of our own," he wrote later, "we were not looking forward to front-row seats for every labor dispute that came along."

Instead of striking more often, Semler's employees struck less. They quadrupled their productivity. The employees took such care in building and managing the new plant that when he came for a visit, Semler often felt more like a guest at someone else's company than the owner. And because Semco let its employees do what they wanted when they wanted, they were constantly inventing new businesses, finding efficiencies in production, and refining products. When one group of production workers wanted to start work at 7:00 A.M., they found they couldn't because the forklift drivers did not arrive until 8:00 A.M. So everyone on that production line learned how to drive a forklift. When a group of engineers asked Semler if they could take a pay cut and just look around for projects to work on in exchange for a percentage of the profits from those projects, Semler agreed. Within a year the group was the fastest growing at Semco. By the time Semler's system — if you could even call such a loose pudding of management a *system* — was fully implemented, he was able to observe that "no one in the company really knows how many people we employ." It was at this point that Semco became one of the fastest-growing companies in Brazil.

What Semler and his workers had discovered in their furious search for a way to survive was a way of thinking and, frankly, living that was ideally suited to a world of rapid change. In a country like Brazil in the 1990s, nothing — not how many reals you had in the bank, not how good your products were, not how many customers swore by your brand — mattered as much as your ability to adapt. You had to ride both the bull *and* the earthquake. Semco's best businesses were ones that employees invented themselves in reaction to some opportunity they saw right at the ground level of their work. Over time these bottom-up businesses were so much more successful than the ones chosen by top management that Semler closed down most "strategic planning" at Semco. "I think that strategic planning and vision are often barriers to success," he explained. You needed a general sense of where you were headed, to be sure, but the moment you became too fixated, you were likely to miss an opportunity or chase a bad idea into bankruptcy. In any event, you deprived yourself of the chance to change as quickly as the world around you. What kept Semco alive was the fact that, whether he knew it or not, Semler wasn't building a business so much as he was, in every decentralizing act, building an immune system.

The ecologist C. S. Holling once wrote that in really complex systems, wealth should be measured, not in money or power but rather in the ability to change and adapt. This sort of wealth, he explained, "sets limits for what is possible—it determines the number of alternative options for the future." You should measure what you have, in other words, by what you can do. It's the reason that a Christmas box can have more entertainment power than a Barbie: there's more you can do with it. In an earthquake-prone ecosystem like Brazil, Semler understood that the ability of an institution, be it a bank or a government, to accumulate options was the difference between survival and extinction. And it wasn't simply accumulating these choices; it was shuffling bad old ideas out of the way and replacing them with new ones as fast as possible. "I own a $160-million South American company," Semler observed, "and I have no idea what business it's in. I know what Semco does—we make things, we provide services, we host Internet communities—but I don't know what Semco is. Nor do I want to know." The minute you pinned yourself down, he feared, you put your company and your employees into a mental strait-jacket. It took a near-deadly crisis for Semler to make that leap to giving away so much power. It could just as easily, he remarked later, have killed his business before he had time to adjust.

7. Deep Security Council

Running a government is not, of course, like running an engineering firm in Brazil. But the institutions we use today to deal with the world are as mismatched to our own landscape as Semco was to Brazil's at the start of the country's crisis, fundamentally incapable of delivering the sort of dramatic, powerful ideas that match revolutionary thinking to a revolutionary age. Remember Louis Halle, the American foreign-policy thinker from the 1950s, who explained that if you were clinging to a flawed image of the world, no amount of dexterous policy execution could save you from disaster? We've seen this problem over and over again in this book. And while we've outlined to some extent how to deal with it, the reality is that the complex emergent problems of a revolutionary age are beyond the comprehension of any one man or woman. No president or foreign minister can possibly master the details of each small problem on the global stage. And while this might have been fine for many years—after all, environmental worries have had little or no effect on national power for the last few centuries—it's dangerous now. It's part of the reason we feel hopeless when we look at the long list of problems we need to deal with and, at the same time, see the accumulating history of failure to act. We're thinking too narrowly.

Today when we talk about reforming the National Security Council or the State Department, the discussion is usually about devoting more people to Asia, for instance, or deepening our capacity to operate in the Arab world. But even if we could hire the very best minds to worry about these problems, throwing them into the iced bureaucracy of our current foreign-policy establishment would deliver only slow, cold death. Our age demands different things from the men and women who are called to high office—and not least is a different context in which they can work, experiment, and take risks. Cavalier risk-taking would be a disaster in government, just as it usually is in real life. But smart risk-takers, operating in systems that permit and support risk, are among the most potent forces in the world.

I don't propose here an instant, knee-jerk, or massive overhaul of our government bureaucracy. Such an approach would create more problems than solutions. But steady, intense, relentless innovation is essential; newness of ideas and institutions should be a measure we use to see how successful we have been in adapting a deep-security outlook.

Halle's theory of image and action applies as much to our institutions as it does to our brains: as long as we're trapped in old structures, we can't adjust. So we've got to begin a process of institutional experimentation. We need to act as if we're a company in an innovation race and our products are the tools of power — everything from departments of government to treaties. Successful innovation will institutionalize as little as possible; it will create new mashup policies that combine power and expertise. It will bring new, entrepreneurial minds into government and create contexts in which they can flourish. Imagine, say, if next to the National Security Council we established an equally smart group that would look at problems from unusual and new perspectives, working to disagree with the NSC at some moments or, at others, bolstering their conclusions with different arguments. Call it the Deep Security Council. Or what if the Environmental Protection Agency was moved to Silicon Valley and staffed entirely by people under forty? What about insisting that the smartest hedge-fund managers serve three years, mid-career, regulating their peers? Or imagine closing down the State Department in phases, replacing the existing bureaus with a less hierarchical structure, in which individual departments took more authority to innovate, to propose radical solutions to problems like computer viruses, disease control, and literacy — problems so low on the list of priorities of most secretaries of state that they are usually forgotten. What if foreign aid were organized into a highly decentralized Department of Global Decency and staffed in the same way we staff the military, with the promise that joining will yield the benefits of school loans, adventure, and the chance to have a career with real, resonant meaning?

These are the sorts of ideas we've got to begin trying on — less for the specifics of these particular notions than for the spirit they suggest. It's a spirit that most old-style thinkers (even if they are thirty years old) will find chafes against the classic instinct to hoard power and tightly control policy. It militates against much of bureaucratic life. And that's precisely why it is so essential to find effective ways to bring this spirit *inside* the system and to find ways to encourage it outside. We've got to support the creation of hundreds of foreign-policy entrepreneurs, both in government and out of it, people who take complex problems and devise new, radical, and inventive approaches. This is a five- to ten-year project but, done thoughtfully, it would yield new and better institutions. The last time the National Security Council was seriously reengineered was forty years ago. The fundamental structure of the State Department has not been revamped since World War II, and today our global aid budget is incoherent. Our errors are loaded into the institutions we rely on to be smart for us, to do the work of real-time immune-system adjustment.

Once, over drinks in Japan, a former top executive of Sony told me the story of a long report about how and why Sony had failed in the video-recording business in the late 1970s, when it introduced the Betamax, which was trounced by the VHS tape. (Sony had bet that viewers wanted quality more than length on a tape, so they introduced a high-resolution cassette that ran for just one hour — too short for a three-hour movie. VHS ran longer, and consumers, it emerged, cared more about knowing what happened in the last half of a film than how clearly they saw the first half.) Reading this study was supposed to be mandatory for rising executives. It was supposed to show them the problems they were meant to avoid. So if you were a curious Sony employee and wanted to learn from the mistakes of the past—financially Betamax was a disaster—you could read through this report, learn from it, and emerge with a better perspective about what to do next. There was just one problem: the report was kept locked in a safe. Sony was simply unable to think hard about where it had failed. In fact, they didn't want to think about it at all.

Our institutions today often look too much like Sony. We may know what's killing us, the lethal Betamax errors in everything from war fighting to financial management, but we keep those errors locked away and out of view. Like Semco before the financial crisis, we remain rigidly organized, one jolt away from fracture. Working in international affairs *should* be incredibly exciting now, as much fun in its own way as inventing the iPod or producing mashup music, because it should be about transforming dreams of how the world might be into reality. "The task of imagination," Roberto Unger once wrote, in language someone should translate into Japanese and post next to the office of those poor Sony engineers who were lapped by Miyamoto's Wii, "is to do the work of crisis without crisis." That's our choice now too: imagination or crisis.

You pick.

CHAPTER ELEVEN

The Revolution and You

1. "Am I a fascist?"

Of his early paintings, it is one of the most massive. From one side to the other, it measures 267 inches; from top to bottom, 120. The canvas swallows you when you stand in front of it. But what do you expect from 200 square feet or so of layered and sculpted paint, each brushstroke pressed onto another in ridges that look still fresh? The title, *Deutschlands Geisteshelden*, is marked out toward the top in what seems an uncomfortable hand, in letters a foot high. *Germany's Spiritual Heroes* is how you would translate the name of Anselm Kiefer's painting. It took eighteen months to complete. Kiefer was twenty-seven and twenty-eight when he was working on it, all through 1972 and 1973. This was years before he would be acclaimed as a great painter of our time, decades before critics would look at this one painting and say, "Yes, this is the sort of thing they will look at in two hundred years to understand our moment in history."

The canvas shows the most typical of German architectural constructions, a Lutheran meeting hall made all of wood. In the perspective of the painting, the lines of the floorboards lead away from the viewer like railway tracks. All along the walls, carefully spaced, are burning oil lamps. Near the base of each, Kiefer has inked the name of a German hero the lamp has been lit to honor. What gives the painting a particularly disturbing tension is what has not yet started but that we sense is inevitable, what you can feel as your eyes lead you along the walls of the monumental hall, from flame to wooden beam and back again: the strange foolishness of so much fire around so much wood. This is a building on the verge of combustion.

What is Kiefer trying to tell us? The first lesson, of course, is about history. You need not pick up on the echo of a concentration camp that comes from the evocation of railway tracks in the wooden floorboards or the religious resonance of the oil lamps to pick up the echoes of Holocaust he's evoking here. You need not know the names along the walls or even much about German culture to understand the tragedy of those heroes' names. This painting shows us that what is most powerful in nations or men is often what destroys them. It is the German historical disaster we already know: how the nation's great figures lit the country up at the end of the nineteenth century only, seemingly moments later, to burn it down. This is the way in which the fierce artistic heat of Richard Wagner's operas transposed so easily into World War I Krupp cannon fire. It was the tale buried in the lives of Friedrich Nietzsche's philosophical überman Zarathustra, Thomas Mann's soul-peddling Doktor Faustus, and Hitler's architect Albert Speer, all of whom pursued incandescent greatness without seeming to mind at all what else was singed in the process.

This is a strong message, but it is not the only reason you can never walk away from *Germany's Spiritual Heroes* quite the same as before you ever laid eyes on it. No, that indelibility comes from an artist's trick Kiefer uses here to masterful effect: from where we stand, in the field of perspective of the hall, we too are *in* the painting. And there is no clear exit. We're trapped. This is not the usual thing in a historic painting. It is not Emanuel Leutze's famous *Washington Crossing the Delaware*, from which the viewer is as removed from the great general as if he were behind glass in a museum diorama. And it's not the image of Napoleon on the back of a rearing horse we know from Jacques Louis David's painting. We are *in* Kiefer's painting; we're part of the action too. When those walls in the wooden heroes' hall finally do catch fire, they will do so with us inside. *Germany's Spiritual Heroes* resonates not because of the general question it poses about history, but because of the very specific one that Kiefer asks each of us personally. There are moments, and this is one of them, when we are not spectators to history but participants. Kiefer is asking, in every brushstroke: What do you do now? Stay? Run? What kind of spiritual hero are you?

Kiefer finished design school in 1969, and his graduation project wasn't the predictable color-field painting or abstract sculpture you might have expected from an ambitious young student. Instead it was a set of photographs of Kiefer making a Nazi salute in different places around Europe. The images were a sort of ersatz vacation portfolio. *Here I am stiff-arming the Louvre. Here I am saluting the English Channel.* If the photographs enraged his evaluation committee—they failed him—the members were at least so perplexed that they could only retreat into the narrowest cave of artistic defense. Kiefer's work, they said, "lacked distance." But this was exactly Kiefer's point. How on earth was one, a German after all, to have any distance from the country's recent past, from its murderous cultural and historical habits? The lone committee member who voted in favor of Kiefer was Rainer Küchenmeister, a painter who had survived a concentration camp, a man with no distance, at any moment thereafter, from what Kiefer was trying to evoke. He understood the message of those pictures, that there is finally no way to walk away from history or stick it behind glass like some diorama. It comes to find you, as it had found Küchenmeister and his family.

Later, explaining the photos, Kiefer said it was best to think of them in these terms: he wondered, as a German, precisely what sort of political DNA he carried, wanted to feel if anything in him *moved* when he raised his arm like that. Would just the right combination of historical conditions bring out a dormant fascist instinct, like some invisible, hereditary, fatal disease? He wondered what he might do if a moment in history collided with his life. It is the same problem that emerges for us now as we look at this fast-changing world, where history is happening to us and to the people we love, not contained in a museum diorama that we can study coldly on the way to the gift shop. *You think this canvas is swallowing you?* Kiefer is asking on that massive painted slate. Well, wait until you're swallowed by history.

2. The Demand

My friend Li once told me a story from 1967, the very early part of the Cultural Revolution, when he was fifteen or sixteen. One day he was discovered to have a stash of illegal books: Plato, Baudelaire, I can't recall what else. Anyhow, it was all banned. Li is of an irrepressibly intellectual bent. He had collected those books with great care over several years, gathered them from hidden parts of the secondhand bookshops he frequented. Though the Cultural Revolution was then in full swing, Li and his best friend had managed, until someone stumbled on those books, to avoid the fury of the local Red Guards, teenaged bullies hopped up on patriotic righteousness. This was unusual. Geeks like Li were the first targets of these gangs, but he and his friend had survived by a quirk of fate: they had once kept the leaders of the local Guards from failing out of school. But the books? Baudelaire in the middle of 1967? Well, that was inexcusable.

The Red Guards who found his books knew Li wasn't alone. They wanted the names of his friend and the booksellers and anyone else. *Did his parents know?* they asked. Li had a choice: slip into the general mindless madness of the moment or stand by himself, take a beating, and perhaps worse. *Give us the names,* they demanded. Li took the beating.

What should I do? This is the question Li faced in that moment. It was the question his friend, a few years afterward, faced and answered: he jumped off a building. Later, after Li became very successful in China, people who had been Red Guards decades earlier, often under assumed names, would invite him to dinners and holiday parties. They had risen to important positions. They could help him advance even further. Li remembered every single one of them. He recalled what they had done in great detail. He remembered their assumed names and their faces. *What should I do?* he wondered. He never attended the dinners.

What does this revolutionary age demand of each of us? In trying to answer that, what matters most is to keep in mind that crucial distinction between us and the grains of sand on Per Bak's slippery piles: we *can* act. We're not just passive. We can choose what to do and what not to do. We don't have to take what we're being told unquestioningly. We don't, and can't, let the same people who got us into this disastrous misalignment with our world pull us further into danger. But making a difference demands that we do, in fact, act. We can no longer outsource our security or our foreign policy the way we might once have. The line between our lives and the world is ever more permeable. In our comfortable cars and houses, in our wealthy-looking nations and our secure-feeling businesses, we can't delude ourselves about the facts: we're *in* history now.

One could in fact fill an entire book with interesting experiments to be tried in coming years as we wrestle with this new order: fresh ways to boost national savings rates; international efforts to reduce sugar consumption; plans to use the Web to make a catalogue of every person in the world dying of AIDS. These and ten thousand other ideas need to be offered and tried—tried free of the cynicism of "we've done that" or "it won't matter." The fact is, we can't know if what didn't work yesterday will work today; we can't predict the impact of our attempts to make change, and that is why we have to keep trying. It's tempting to feel that the forces at work now are so big that there is no point in action at all. But in fact the opposite is true. Even small changes can have an impact on our future—and this is why we all must get involved. We are at the start of a profound crisis that is going to demand radical changes. It is a struggle that, as Immanuel Wallerstein has written from his perspective as a historian, may "continue for twenty, thirty, fifty years and the outcome is intrinsically uncertain. History is on no one's side. It depends on what we do."

Change in our world isn't going to feel like something far away from us. As I said at the opening of this book, it is a contagious force that is going to infect every part of our lives. It presents, in the same instant, cause for great hope and great fear. We are living in one of those moments when history is going to reach into each of our lives. Yet—and this *is* truly unthinkable using any of the old ways of dreaming about our lives—now we can touch history too.

For all the bad that a dozen hedge-fund traders or a few terrorists can do, it is also possible that each of us, *any of us,* can unleash powerful and permanent change. Some of this change will be simple. We can each start to live more resiliently: saving more, eating better, driving smart, educating our children to be global and competitive, volunteering, reaching out to neighbors and new friends. Such things are essential elements of deep security. But far more of the change will be difficult. It will involve tremendous sacrifice. At times it will involve profound discomfort, when we won't know if our sacrifices will succeed or be worth the effort. It requires a psychological shift from being certain about our future to being uncertain, a transformation that is as stressful as it is productive. It will mean learning to react differently to threats we face, the difference between responding to an attack like 9/11 with a war or spending at least as much money at the same time on schools or hospitals. At the times we're most scared we'll need to replace the habit of striking back with new efforts to connect to the world instead of alienating it and isolating ourselves. This is as true for trade and economic policy as it is for our work in defense and diplomacy. All this will require a new sort of patience, something hard to understand in a culture that emphasizes instant gratification.

What matters is beginning to explore the idea that we can do unthinkably decent things with our lives, from starting schools to leaping into that "caring economy" Unger described to investing years of our lives to understand cultures different from our own. Ultimately no one can tell you exactly what to do, any more than anyone can say "go start an amazing Internet search company" or "go bomb a building"—events that emerge naturally from a system of spontaneous creation, in which the good can no more be predicted than the bad. Specific aims, like building moderate Muslim nations or providing global hospice care, matter, but mostly we must just engage with a world that is now touching us in so many ways. Energy will emerge from the friction of all of our good works, though we can't predict precisely where real heat will appear or where the flames will illuminate or what they will burn down. What this sort of progress surely demands is that we sharpen our instincts to rebel against what is and against what we are told can never be. As Niels Bohr remarked in later life, "Every valuable human being must be a radical and a rebel, for what he must aim at is to make things better than they are." Conformity to old ideas is lethal; it is rebellion that is going to change the planet.

We stand now like viewers of that Kiefer painting, aware that something dramatic is happening to the world around us. The people and institutions we might once have relied on to rescue us can't. But what we decide to do now, the decisions we make as history touches each of us, will mark the future for all of us. The power of individuals has never been greater. This is the energy we've seen animating people as indecent as those Hizb'allah guerrillas and as virtuous as Tony Moll. It's the spirit that prompted me to write this book, to see what we could do once we understood the nature of the tsunami coming our way. But answering this call requires, finally, a leap of faith. It means accepting—because this can never be proved in advance—that change will always produce more good than bad. This is the hope without which the great acts of self-sacrifice and imagination that we now require will be impossible. It is the optimistic spirit buried, finally, in the answer to the question everyone asks at those moments when history bursts through its diorama case, when it unthinkably appears in front of us, when it threatens much that we cherish. It is the question Kiefer was trying to answer, the question my friend Li had to come to terms with. And now it is also the one we must all confront every day of our lives in this unstable, terrifying, and hopeful new order, the one, yes, you must, in two seconds, answer for yourself and for the people you love:

This age, what does it demand of me?

Afterword to the Paperback Edition

There are, generally speaking, two questions I get most often from people who have read *The Age of the Unthinkable*. The first has less to do with the book itself, and more to do with the short biographical note at the end of the book: "How do you live a life divided between New York and Beijing?" And while I think the general intent of this question is logistic, the better, more important answer has a great deal to do with the second question I usually hear: "That last line in your book, about what we should do now, well, what *should* we do?"

How to live between New York and Beijing? Well, amazed, mostly. What you notice most if you live half the time in a country that is creaking with the strains of rapid growth and the rest in a nation that is struggling with the groans of a system that seems not as spry as it once was, is the glaring difference in urgency. Beijing these days is electric. It is electric with worry, with opportunity, with a fevered rush to make sense of the challenges China faces and to solve them knowing that, once solved, the answers simply breed more problems. How do we raise rural incomes? the Chinese ask. Move farmers to cities, they answer. And then they undertake a task that in scale and complexity is historic: to urbanize 300 million people in fifteen years.

This is not to offer slack-jawed praise of that process because, honestly, that solved problem is simply a machine for generating new puzzles, new opportunities for criticism: How do you manage megacities? How do you find urban work for farmers? How do you handle the cacophonous economic ambitions of city dwellers—cars, air conditioning—without blackening the planet? And, of course, how do you do all this while reshaping your politics on the fly? Urgency in China is honestly earned.

In the United States, where there is no shortage of problems to be solved, it's rare to find a similar level of ambition or energy. The president struggles to accomplish one thing in a year—and even then is attacked for taking on too much. If the Chinese, with their creaky political system, can tackle health care, stock market reform, education, water policy, unemployment, education, and a host of other issues all at once, isn't it possible the United States might manage to try for more than one accomplishment a year? It's popular in some circles to joke that the United States should be "China for a day" to jam through new laws, new force-fed rules for economics. But that's too cute. The U.S. system is still far better than the Chinese system for the sort of world we face. American democracy is more robust, better capable of managing the fundamental national task of helping turn citizens' dreams into reality. But, honestly, it runs best when amped up by urgency, and this is one thing that seems most lacking now.

This lack of urgency infects almost every aspect of our foreign policy, which today is lazy-minded and seems to run on nearly unsupervised even as the world becomes more complex. The country operates now, for instance, without a Grand Strategy—the sort of clean, big vision for the future of America and the world that is a precursor for sensible progress. Without such a prescription, no policy in areas like Iran, cyberweapons, China, or foreign aid can possibly make sense. This baffled blundering shouldn't be a surprise if you've read *The Age of the Unthinkable*. Befuddlement in the face of newness is a perennial problem, as true for royalty of the 1800s as it is for media executives of the 2000s. But it is not inherently necessary when facing a landscape of disruption. It is possible to find ideas that can guide you through periods of rapid change. Revolutions, we must keep reminding ourselves, don't only wipe out the old order. They also create new heroes, new champions, new fortunes.

This all suggests to me many tasks we should now take up, but let me just list three here, ranging from the top of the system to the operations of our government to our own lives.

The first, highest-level problem, is that the United States cannot continue to operate as we do at this moment with no clear strategy. It is critically important that we not only settle on a grand vision for our actions but that we encourage a fresh, diverse debate about what that vision should be. Partly this means rejecting an old way of looking at the world that put our own national interest first, as if to say, "Well, if the United States is taken care of, then the rest of the world will be fine." What we need instead is a complete reconception of the international system, one that thinks of it as a system, not a discrete collection of colliding parts. This is exciting work; it is also crucial.

The operational-level task we should undertake is the reworking of our tools of foreign policy. The American Department of State is a striking example of bureaucratic paralysis. You can criticize the U.S. military for many things, but a lack of creativity and urgency isn't one of them. Because it has people being killed every day, the U.S. military has adopted an eager experimentalist ethos, one apparent in the Twitter feed it uses to monitor IED explosions or in the bold new army "Capstone" concept for a risk-oriented force. The Department of State needs to become a center of gravity for great thinking about global affairs, not simply an overstretched and overstarched execution arm. It should become a magnet for the best minds of the country, not, as it is often now, a basin of political reward.

Finally, at the level of our own lives, what to do? This is a long list, of course, but I'd propose two ideas: First, take a hard look at your own resilience. Are your financial alignment and your educational posture best directed for an unstable world? And, second, commit to increasing the volunteer work you do. In an age of shrinking government capacity, the energy we all devote to the foundations of our society is irreplaceable.

In the year since the hardcover release of this book, I have seen that *The Age of the Unthinkable* has found real resonance on the forefront of change, places as different as the bottom lines of big corporations and the battle plans of the U.S. Army. I've been asked often to bring out-of-the-box thinking to everything from how the army fights to how hedge fund managers think about markets. And I've seen the electric effect the ideas of the book have when people hit that "aha" moment of understanding why the way the world is changing now is different from what we might have predicted a few years ago, how the things we thought would make the world stable are in fact spreading risk all around us. But too often the reaction to that moment isn't profound enough. In the end, our current lack of urgency reminds me a great deal of a trope from my old days as a journalist, when I used to cover technology for *Time* magazine. I would go to Internet conferences and invariably some speaker would ask the audience, "How many of you believe the Internet is going to change your business?" Many hands would go up. "And how many of you are doing something about it?" the speaker would then ask. Many fewer hands.

All of which leads me back to that question about living between New York and Beijing. (The real secret to this, by the way, is green tea.) When I first moved to China in 2002, most people I knew thought I was a little nuts. It seemed China was a distant irrelevance, likely to be important, everyone knew, but not anytime soon. Most of the world was waiting for a 1989-style collapse in Beijing or betting that China would eventually pursue an economic model that looked like America's. Today, of course, we know that is not the case. But eight years ago when I came to China I had the privilege of being here early, in a sense. It reminded me often of my work covering Silicon Valley as a journalist in the early 1990s, that feeling of being present at the very early moments of a seismic shift. You could see the world was going to change. And when that imaginary voice asked, "Are you doing something about it?" I thought the best answer was: Yes, I am going to try to understand China.

What I saw in Silicon Valley in the 1990s, what I have seen in China in the last decade, all of that has given me a sense of confidence about the fact that we now face a moment in global politics as profound as the rise of the Internet or the emergence of China have been on a smaller scale. What lies ahead of us is a world whose complexities and puzzles will make the simple black-and-white challenges of the Cold War look like a distant fantasy of an easy-to-comprehend world order. The puzzles my generation of policy makers will need to manage are as momentous as the nuclear problems of the 1950s but far more unstable. We are living at a moment of potentially enormous change. This will not all be change for good. And this evolution of the world is already presenting us with questions about how our core values—liberty, justice, opportunity—will survive in an era of constrained resources, increased political pressure, and the inevitable blossoming of fear we can expect in many countries. We don't yet know the answer to these questions. We are living in a time that demands that we, with our every action, prepare to sacrifice for what we believe in. The time for empty words, policy that has no basis in facts, and the quiet corruption of our system has come to an end. We could afford it for the last decade or so. But the price now has become too expensive, I think, because that price is nothing less than our future.

ACKNOWLEDGMENTS

No attempt to do something as ambitious as rethinking grand strategy could ever be done as a solo act. This book is no exception, and I'm incredibly grateful to the people who made it possible.

My editor at Little, Brown, Geoff Shandler, poured his own energy into this book with a generosity and patience that surpasses anything an author could ever hope for. He served as both an enthusiastic supporter and a disciplined, creative, and brilliant critic. My agent, Binky Urban, was limitlessly helpful in sharing advice and handling the demands of an intense author.

The whole team at Little, Brown offered tremendous support for the idea of this book from the very beginning. Michael Pietsch and David Young were both ardent boosters, and Heather Rizzo and Heather Fain, along with their hardworking teams, brought elegance and sophistication to the challenge of bringing the book out on a compressed time frame. Peg Anderson, Peggy Freudenthal, and the entire staff of copyeditors helped make sure the book looked good and read clearly—though any errors that remain are, of course, the author's fault. Joe Pierro, who read every line of the book and offered priceless corrections and insights, was a backstop I could not have done without.

The intellectual freedom and encouragement to write the book came from many sources, not least my good friend John Eastman, who was instrumental both in helping me frame my ideas and in finding a home for them. Henry Kissinger, Stape Roy, and Paul Speltz at Kissinger Associates were generous with their time and support—and in helping me to have the space I needed to finish composition of the book. My close friend and book coach, Bruce Feiler, offered what can only be called a heroic level of counsel—sometimes on an hourly basis—and in the process not only made this a better book but by his example made me a better person.

My friends in China and around the world, along with my family in New Mexico, gave me a constant and reassuring foundation from which to write and think courageous and out-of-the-box thoughts. And my mentors, the people who have taken risks on me over the years in the hope I would pay them back by making the world better, gave me a sense of confidence and of obligation without which this book would never have been written. I owe them everything, including the promise to never stop working to make the dream of a more decent world real.

SELECTED SOURCES

CHAPTER ONE   THE NATURE OF THE AGE

Edmund L. Andrews. "Greenspan Concedes Error on Regulation." *New York Times,* October 3, 2008.

Per Bak. *How Nature Works: The Science of Self-Organized Criticality.* New York: Copernicus, 1996.

August Fournier. *Napoleon I: A Biography.* Translated by Annie Elizabeth Adams. London: Longmans, Green and Co., 1911.

Alexander L. George. "The 'Operational Code': A Neglected Approach to the Study of Political Leaders and Decision-Making." *International Studies Quarterly* 13, no. 2 (June 1969): 190–222.

Louis Halle. *American Foreign Policy.* London: G. Allen, 1960.

Francis Heylighen. "Technological Acceleration." March 1998 at Principia Cybernetica Web, pespmc1.vub.ac.be.

George F. Kennan. "Diplomacy Without Diplomats?" *Foreign Affairs* (September–October 1997).

George F. Kennan. "Measures Short of War: The George F. Kennan Lectures at the National War College, 1946–47." Available at ndu.edu.

CHAPTER TWO   THE OLD PHYSICS

Dean Babst. "A Force for Peace." *Industrial Research* 14 (April 1972).

Peter J. Boettke, Christopher J. Coyne, and Peter T. Leeson. "High Priests and Lowly Philosophers: The Battle for the Soul of Economics." *Case Western Law Review* 56, no. 3 (spring 2006): 551–568.

Bruce Bueno de Mesquita, James D. Morrow, Randolph Siverson, and Alastair Smith. "An Institutional Explanation of the Democratic Peace." *American Political Science Review* 93, no. 4 (December 1999): 791–807.

Margit Bussmann and Gerald Schneider. "When Globalization Discontent Turns Violent: Foreign Economic Liberalization and Internal War." *International Studies Quarterly* 51 (2007): 79–97.

E. H. Carr. *The Twenty Years' Crisis: An Introduction to the Study of International Relations.* New York: Palgrave Macmillan, 2001.

Inis L. Claude, Jr. "The Common Defense and Great-Power Responsibilities." *Political Science Quarterly* 101, no. 5, Reflections on Providing for "The Common Defense" (1986): 719–732.

Raymond Cohen. "Pacific Unions: A Reappraisal of the Theory That 'Democracies Do Not Go to War with Each Other.'" *Review of International Studies* 20 (July 1994).

Michael C. Desch. "America's Liberal Illiberalism: The Ideological Origins of Overreaction in U.S. Foreign Policy." *International Security* 32, no. 3 (winter 2007–2008): 7–43.

Michael C. Desch. "Democracy and Victory: Why Regime Type Hardly Matters." *International Security* 27, no. 2 (fall 2002): 5–47.

Bernard I. Finel and Kristin M. Lord. "The Surprising Logic of Transparency." *International Studies Quarterly* 43 (1999): 315–339.

Christoph Frei. *Hans J. Morgenthau: An Intellectual Biography.* Baton Rouge: Louisiana State University, 2001.

Azar Gat. "The Democratic Peace Theory Reframed: The Impact of Modernity." *World Politics* 58 (October 2005): 73–100.

Robert Gilpin. "The Richness of the Tradition of Political Realism." In *Neorealism and Its Critics.* Edited by Robert Keohane. New York: Columbia University Press, 1986.

Nicolas Guilhot. "The Realist Gambit: Postwar American Political Science and the Birth of IR Theory." *International Political Sociology* 2 (2008): 281–304.

Friedrich August von Hayek. "The Pretence of Knowledge." The Sveriges Riksbank Prize in Economic Sciences in Memory of Alfred Nobel 1974—Prize Lecture—Lecture to the memory of Alfred Nobel, December 11, 1974, at nobelprize.org.

Ole R. Holsti. "The Belief System and National Images: A Case Study." *The Journal of Conflict Resolution* 6, no. 3, Case Studies in Conflict (September 1962): 244–252.

Samuel P. Huntington. "American Ideals versus American Institutions." *Political Science Quarterly* 97, no. 1 (spring 1982): 1–37.

Robert Jervis. "Hans Morgenthau, Realism, and the Scientific Study of International Relations." *Social Research* 61 (winter 1994): 853–854.

Robert Jervis. *Perception and Misperception in International Politics.* Princeton, NJ: Princeton University Press, 1976.

Cédric Jourde. "The International Relations of Small Neoauthoritarian States: Islamism, Warlordism, and the Framing of Stability." *International Studies Quarterly* 51 (2007): 481–503.

Miles Kahler. "Rationality in International Relations." *International Organization* 52, no. 4, International Organization at Fifty: Exploration and Contestation in the Study of World Politics (autumn 1998): 919–941.

Robert O. Keohane. "The Globalization of Informal Violence, Theories of World Politics, and the 'Liberalism of Fear.'" *Dialog-IO* (spring 2002): 29–43.

David A. Lake. "Fair Fights? Evaluating Theories of Democracy and Victory." *International Security* 28, no. 1 (summer 2003): 154–167.

Zeev Maoz. "The Controversy over the Democratic Peace: Rearguard Action or Cracks in the Wall?" *International Security* 22, no. 1 (1997).

John J. Mearsheimer. *The Tragedy of Great Power Politics.* New York: W. W. Norton & Company, 2003.

Jennifer Mitzen. "Reading Habermas in Anarchy: Multilateral Diplomacy and Global Public Spheres." *American Political Science Review* 99, no. 3 (August 2005).

Jonathan Monten. "Thucydides and Modern Realism." *International Studies Quarterly* 50 (2006): 3–25.

Hans J. Morgenthau. *Politics Among Nations: The Struggle for Power and Peace.* New York: Knopf, 1949.

Hans J. Morgenthau. *Scientific Man vs. Power Politics.* Chicago: University of Chicago Press, 1946.

Harold Nicolson. *The Congress of Vienna.* New York: Harcourt, Brace and Company, 1946.

Brian C. Rathbun. "Uncertain about Uncertainty: Understanding the Multiple Meanings of a Crucial Concept in International Relations Theory." *International Studies Quarterly* 51 (2007): 533–557.

Richard S. Ruderman. "Democracy and the Problem of Statesmanship." *The Review of Politics* 59, no. 4 (autumn 1997): 759–787.

Scott Turner. "Global Civil Society, Anarchy and Governance: Assessing an Emerging Paradigm." *Journal of Peace Research* 35, no. 1 (January 1998): 25–42.

Ole Waever. "The Sociology of a Not So International Discipline: American and European Developments in International Relations." *International Organization* 52 (1998): 687–727.

Kenneth Waltz. "Structural Realism after the Cold War." In *America Unrivaled: The Future of the Balance of Power.* Edited by G. John Ikenberry. Ithaca, NY: Cornell University Press, 2002.

Wesley W. Widmaier. "Constructing Foreign Policy Crises: Interpretive Leadership in the Cold War and War on Terrorism." *International Studies Quarterly* 51 (2007): 779–794.

Arnold Wolfers. "'National Security' as an Ambiguous Symbol." *Political Science Quarterly* 67, no. 4 (December 1952): 481–502.

Fareed Zakaria. "Realism and Domestic Politics: A Review Essay." *International Security* 17: 177–198.

Chapter Three   The Sandpile

W. Brian Arthur. "The End of Certainty in Economics." In *The Biology of Business*. Edited by J. H. Clippinger. Newark, NJ: Jossey-Bass Publishers, 1999.

P. Bak and K. Chen. "Self-Organized Criticality." *Scientific American* 264, no. 1 (1991): 46–53.

Jacqueline Best. "Ambiguity, Uncertainty, and Risk: Rethinking Indeterminancy." *International Political Sociology* 2 (2008): 355–374.

"Countering Bioterrorism: The Role of Science and Technology." Panel on Biological Issues, Committee on Science and Technology for Countering Terrorism, Institute of Medicine, the National Academy of Sciences.

Monica Czwarno. "Misjudging Islamic Terrorism: The Academic Community's Failure to Predict 9/11." *Studies in Conflict & Terrorism* 29 (2006): 657–678.

Paul K. Davis and Brian Michael Jenkins. "Deterrence and Influence in Counterterrorism: A Component in the War on Al Qaeda." RAND, 1997.

Dennis M. Egan. "The Challenge of Biological Terrorism." *Journal of Homeland Security and Emergency Management* 3, issue 2 (2006): article 12.

T. X. Hammes. "Fourth Generation Warfare Evolves, the Fifth Generation Emerges." *Military Review* (May–June 2007).

Michael I. Handel. "The Yom Kippur War and the Inevitability of Surprise." *International Studies Quarterly* 21, no. 3 (September 1977): 461–502.

G. A. Held, D. H. Solina, H. Solina, D. T. Keane, W. J. Haag, P. M. Horn, and G. Grinstein. "Experimental Study of Critical-Mass Fluctuations in an Evolving Sandpile." *Physical Review Letters* 65: 1120–1123.

C. S. Holling. "Understanding the Complexity of Economic, Ecological, and Social Systems." *Ecosystems* 4 (2001): 390–405.

Brian M. Jenkins. "Defense Against Terrorism." *Political Science Quarterly* 101, no. 5, Reflections on Providing for "The Common Defense" (1986): 773–786.

Simon Levin. "Complex Adaptive Systems: Exploring the Known, the Unknown and the Unknowable." *Bulletin of the American Mathematical Society* 40, no. 1 (2003): 3–19.

Simon Levin. *Fragile Dominion: Complexity and the Commons*. Reading, MA: Perseus Publishing, 1999.

"Making the Nation Safer: The Role of Science and Technology in Countering Terrorism." Report of the National Academy of Sciences, 2002.

William Wohlforth. "The Stability of a Unipolar World." *International Security* 24, no. 1 (summer 1999): 5–41.

Chapter Four   Avalanche Country

John Lewis Gaddis. *The Cold War: A New History*. New York: Penguin Press, 2005.

John Lewis Gaddis. "International Relations Theory and the End of the Cold War." *International Security* 17, no. 3 (winter 1992–1993): 6.

John Lewis Gaddis. *Strategies of Containment: A Critical Appraisal of American National Security Strategies During the Cold War.* New York: Oxford University Press, 2005.

John Lewis Gaddis. *Surprise, Security, and the American Experience.* Cambridge, MA: Harvard University Press, 2004.

John Lewis Gaddis. *We Now Know: Rethinking Cold War History.* New York: Oxford University Press, 1998.

Andrei Grachev. *Final Days: The Inside Story of the Collapse of the Soviet Union.* Boulder, CO: Westview Press, 1996.

William D. Jackson. "Soviet Reassessment of Ronald Reagan, 1985–1988." *Political Science Quarterly* 113, no. 4 (winter 1998–1999): 617–644.

David Kotz with Fred Weir. *Revolution from Above: The Demise of the Soviet System.* New York: Routledge, 1997.

Mark Kramer. "The Reform of the Soviet System and the Demise of the Soviet State." *Slavic Review* 63, no. 3 (autumn 2004): 505–512.

Robert M. May, Simon A. Levin, and George Sugihara. "Complex Systems: Ecology for Bankers." *Nature* 451 (February 21, 2008): 893–895.

Joseph S. Nye. *Bound to Lead: The Changing Nature of American Power.* New York: Basic Books, 1991.

Joseph S. Nye. "Soft Power." *Foreign Policy* no. 80 (autumn 1990): 153–171.

CHAPTER FIVE   BUDWEISER

Karen Ruth Adams. "Attack and Conquer?" *International Security* 28, no. 3 (winter 2003–2004): 45–83.

Richard B. Andres, Craig Wills, and Thomas E. Griffith, Jr. "Winning with Allies: The Strategic Value of the Afghan Model." *International Security* 30, no. 3 (winter 2005–2006): 124–160.

Chinese Views of Future Warfare. Edited by Michael Pillsbury, U.S. G.P.O., Supt. of Docs., Congressional Sales Office. Revised edition, 1998.

James W. Davis, et al. "Taking Offense at Offense Defense Theory." *International Security* 23, no. 3 (winter 1998–1999): 179–206.

Johan Eriksson and Giampiero Giacomello. "The Information Revolution, Security, and International Relations: (IR)relevant Theory?" *International Political Science Review* 27, no. 3 (2006): 221–244.

Robert Jervis. "Cooperation under the Security Dilemma." *World Politics* 30, no. 2 (January 1978): 167–214.

Alastair Johnston. "China's New 'Old Thinking': The Concept of Limited Deterrence." *International Security* 20, no. 3 (winter 1995–1996).

Martin Kramer. "The Moral Logic of Hizballah." In *Origins of Terrorism:*

Psychologies, Ideologies, Theologies, States of Mind. Edited by Walter Reich. New York: Cambridge University Press, 1990.

David Lei. "China's New Multi-Faceted Maritime Strategy." *Orbis* 52, issue 1 (2008).

Keir Lieber. "Grasping the Technological Peace: Offense Defense Balance and International Security." *International Security* 25, no. 1 (summer 2000): 71–104.

Andrew Mack. "Why Big Nations Lose Small Wars." *World Politics* 27, no. 2 (January 1975): 175–200.

Angel Rabasa, et al. "Beyond Al-Qaeda: The Global Jihadist Movement." RAND, 2006.

Scott D. Sagan. "1914 Revisited: Allies, Offense, and Instability." *International Security* 11, no. 2 (fall 1986): 151–175.

Jack Snyder. "Civil-Military Relations and the Cult of the Offensive, 1914 and 1984." *International Security* 9, no. 1 (summer 1984): 108–146.

Martin van Creveld. *The Transformation of War.* New York: Free Press, 1991.

Stephen Van Evera. "The Cult of the Offensive and the Origins of the First World War." *International Security* 9, no. 1 (summer 1984): 108–146.

Stephen Van Evera. "Offense, Defense and the Causes of War." *International Security* 22, no. 4 (spring 1998): 5–43.

Frank Zagare and D. Marc Kilgour. "Asymmetric Deterrence." *International Studies Quarterly* 37, no. 1 (March 1993): 1–27.

Mao Zedong. *On Guerrilla Warfare.* Translated by Samuel Griffith. New York: Praeger, 1961.

Chapter Six Mashup

Ulrich Beck. "War Is Peace: On Post-National War." *Security Dialogue* 36, no. 5 (2005).

Ulrich Beck and Mark Ritter. *Risk Society: Towards a New Modernity.* Newbury Park, CA: Sage, 1992.

Seyom Brown. "An End to Grand Strategy." *Foreign Policy* no. 32 (autumn 1978): 22–46.

John Lewis Gaddis. "A Grand Strategy of Transformation." *Foreign Policy* no. 133 (November–December 2002): 50–57.

Stephen Kern. *The Culture of Time and Space, 1880–1918.* Cambridge, MA: Harvard University Press, 2003.

John Maynard Keynes. *The Economic Consequences of the Peace.* New York: Harcourt, Brace and Howe, 1920.

Walter Lippmann. *Public Opinion.* New York: Harcourt, Brace and Company, 1922.

Harold G. Nicolson. *Peacemaking, 1919.* Boston: Houghton Mifflin, 1933.

Carl E. Schorske. *Fin-de-siècle Vienna: Politics and Culture.* New York: Vintage, 1981.

Gertrude Stein. *Picasso.* New York: Dover Publications, 1984.

Bijal Trivedi. "Toxic Cocktail." *New Scientist* (September 1, 2007): 44.

Chapter Seven   The General and the Billionaire

Deborah G. Barger. "Toward a Revolution in Intelligence Affairs." RAND, 2005.

Sir Isaiah Berlin. *The Hedgehog and the Fox.* New York: Simon & Schuster, 1953.

Paul K. Davis. "Strategic Planning Amidst Massive Uncertainty in Complex Adaptive Systems: The Case of Defense Planning." RAND Graduate School, 2006.

David C. Gompert and Jeffrey A. Isaacson. "Planning a Ballistic Missile Defense System of Systems: An Adaptive Strategy." RAND, 1999.

Michael I. Handel. "The Yom Kippur War and the Inevitability of Surprise." *International Studies Quarterly* 21, no. 3 (September 1977): 461–502.

Richard Nisbett. *The Geography of Thought.* New York: Simon & Schuster, 2004.

Philip Tetlock. *Expert Political Judgment: How Good Is It? How Can We Know?* Princeton, NJ: Princeton University Press, 2005.

Masako Watanabe. "Styles of Reasoning in Japan and the United States: Logic of Education in Two Cultures." Ph.D. Thesis at Academic Commons.

Chapter Eight   The Management Secrets of Hizb'allah

Brad Allenby and Jonathan Fink. "Toward Inherently Secure and Resilient Societies." *Science* 309, no. 5737 (August 2005): 1034–1036.

Derek Armitage and Derek Johnson. "Can Resilience Be Reconciled with Globalization and the Increasingly Complex Conditions of Resource Degradation in Asian Coastal Regions?" *Ecology and Society* 11, no. 1 (2006): 2.

Daniel Barbee. "Disaster Response and Recovery: Strategies and Tactics for Resilience." *Journal of Homeland Security and Emergency Management* 4, issue 1 (2007): article 11.

Johan Colding. "Ecologists as the New Management Elite?" *Ecology and Society* 4, no. 2 (2000).

Anne-Sophie Crépin. "Using Fast and Slow Processes to Manage Resources with Thresholds." *Environmental & Resource Economics* 36 (2007): 191–213.

Thomas Dietz, Elinor Ostrom, and Paul C. Stern. "The Struggle to Govern the Commons." *Science* 302 (2003): 1907–1912.

Lance H. Gunderson and C. S. Holling. *Panarchy: Understanding Transformations in Human and Natural Systems.* Washington, DC: Island Press, 2002.

Francis Heylighen. "The Science of Self-Organization and Adaptivity." Center "Leo Apostel," Free University of Brussels, Belgium.

C. S. Holling. "Resilience and Stability of Ecological Systems." *Annual Review in Ecology and Systematics* 4 (1973): 1–23.

C. S. Holling. "The Resilience of Terrestrial Ecosystems: Local Surprise and Global Change." In *Sustainable Development of the Biosphere.* Edited by W. C. Clark and R. E. Munn. New York: Cambridge University Press, 1986.

C. S. Holling. "Understanding the Complexity of Economic, Ecological, and Social Systems." *Ecosystems* 4 (2001): 390–405.

Brian A. Jackson, et al. "Economically Targeted Terrorism." RAND, 2007.

John Kambhu, Scott Weidman, and Neel Krishnan. "New Directions for Understanding Systemic Risk: A Report on a Conference Cosponsored by the Federal Reserve Bank of New York and the National Academy of Sciences" (2004).

Henry Kissinger. *The Necessity for Choice: Prospects of American Foreign Policy.* New York: Anchor, 1962.

P. A. Larkin. "An Epitaph for the Concept of Maximum Sustained Yield." *Transactions of the American Fisheries Society* (January 1977).

P. H. Liotta. "Boomerang Effect: The Convergence of National and Human Security." *Security Dialogue* 33 (2002): 473.

Per Olsson. "Shooting the Rapids: Navigating Transitions to Adaptive Governance of Social-Ecological Systems." *Ecology and Society* 11, no. 1 (2006).

Martin Scheffer, et al. "Slow Responses of Societies to New Problems: Causes and Costs." *Ecosystems* 6, no. 5 (August 2003): 493–502.

Chapter Nine The Limits of Persuasion

Ephraim Asculai. "Rethinking the Nuclear Non-Proliferation Regime." Jaffee Center for Strategic Studies, monograph 70 (June 2004).

Simon Atkinson and James Moffat. "The Agile Organization: From Informal Networks to Complex Effects and Agility." U.S. Department of Defense (2005), at dodccrp.org.

Nora Bensahel, et al. "After Saddam: Pre-War Planning and the Occupation of Iraq." RAND, 2008.

Jarret M. Brachman and William F. McCants. "Stealing Al Qaeda's Playbook." *Studies in Conflict & Terrorism* 29 (2006): 309–321.

Carl von Clausewitz. *On War.* Princeton, NJ: Princeton University Press, 1989.

Erik J. Dahl. "Warning of Terror: Explaining the Failure of Intelligence Against Terrorism." *The Journal of Strategic Studies* 28, no. 1 (February 2005): 31–55.

Paul K. Davis. "Effects-Based Operations: A Grand Challenge for the Analytical Community." RAND, 2001.

Michael Dillon. "Network Society, Network-Centric Warfare and the State of Emergency." *Theory, Culture & Society* 19, no. 4 (2002): 71–79.

Robert Herndon, et al. "Effects-Based Operations in Afghanistan: The CJTF-180 Method of Orchestrating Effects to Achieve Objectives." *Field Artillery* (January–February 2004).

Michael Horowitz and Stephen Rosen. "Evolution or Revolution." *The Journal of Strategic Studies* 28, no. 3 (June 2005): 437–448.

Stephen Hosmer. "Why the Iraqi Resistance Was So Weak." RAND, 2007.

Robert Hunter, et al. "Integrating Instruments of Power and Influence, Lessons Learned." RAND, 2008.

François Jullien. *Detour and Access.* Translated by Sophie Hawkes. New York: Zone Books, 2000.

François Jullien. *The Propensity of Things.* Translated by Janet Lloyd. New York: Zone Books, 1995.

Dan Kaminsky. "Dan Kaminsky on the DNS Bug of 2008 at O'Reilly FOO Camp." Available at youtube.com.

David Lane and Robert Maxfield. "Foresight, Complexity and Strategy." Conference Paper, December 1995.

Thomas Melia. "How Terrorism Affects American Diplomacy." Institute for the Study of Diplomacy, 2005.

Thomas Metz, et al. "Massing Effects in the Information Domain: A Case Study in Aggressive Information Operations." *Military Review* (English) (May–June 2006).

David Ochmanek and Lowell H. Schwartz. "The Challenge of Nuclear Armed Regional Adversaries." RAND, 2008.

V. P. Österberg. "Military Theory and the Concept of Jointness: A Study of Connection." Monograph of Fakultet for Strategi og Militaere Operationer, 2004.

David Pendall. "Effects-Based Operations and the Exercise of National Power." *Military Review* (January–February 2004).

Edward Allen Smith. "Complexity, Networking, and Effects-Based Approaches to Operations." U.S. Department of Defense (2006), monograph at dodccrp.org.

CHAPTER TEN   RIDING THE EARTHQUAKE

John Arquilla and David Ronfeldt. "Swarming and the Future of Conflict." RAND, 1997.

Yochai Benkler. "Coase's Penguin." *Yale Law Journal* 112 (2002).

Raymond E. Miles, et al. "Organizing in the Knowledge Age: Anticipating the Cellular Form." *Academy of Management Executives* 11, no. 4 (1997).

Barry R. Posen. "Command of the Commons: The Military Foundation of U.S. Hegemony." *International Security* 28, no. 1 (summer 2003): 5–46.

Eric Raymond. *The Cathedral and the Bazaar.* Cambridge, MA: O'Reilly, 1999.

Ricardo Semler. "Managing Without Managers." *Harvard Business Review* (September–October 1989).

Ricardo Semler. "Why My Former Employees Still Work for Me." *Harvard Business Review* (January–February 1994).

Roberto Unger. "The Future of the Left and Economic Policy." Miliband Lecture, 2006.

Roberto Unger. *What Should the Left Propose?* New York: Verso, 2005.

Eric von Hippel. *Democratizing Innovation.* Cambridge, MA: MIT Press, 2005.

Index

About the Author

Joshua Cooper Ramo is a managing director of Kissinger Associates, one of the world's leading strategic advisory firms. Before entering the advisory business, Ramo was an award-winning journalist, working as senior editor and foreign editor of *Time* magazine.

Ramo, a Mandarin speaker who divides his time between Beijing and New York, has been called "one of China's leading foreign-born scholars." His papers on China's development, including "The Beijing Consensus" and "Brand China," have been widely distributed in China and abroad. In 2008, Ramo served as China Analyst for NBC during the Summer Olympics in Beijing.

Ramo has been a member of the Asia21 Leaders Program, a cofounder of the U.S.-China Young Leaders Forum, and a Young Global Leader of the World Economic Forum. He served as cochair of the Santa Fe Institute's first working group on Complexity and International Affairs. An avid flyer, Ramo has written a book, *No Visible Horizon*, about his experiences as a competitive aerobatic pilot. Trained as an economist, Ramo holds degrees in Latin American studies from the University of Chicago and economics from New York University.

BACK BAY · READERS' PICK

Reading Group Guide

THE AGE OF THE
UNTHINKABLE

• • •

WHY THE NEW WORLD DISORDER
CONSTANTLY SURPRISES US
AND WHAT WE CAN DO ABOUT IT

by

Joshua Cooper Ramo

A conversation with
Joshua Cooper Ramo

In this age of immense technological reach — whereby most everyone has at least the potential to access the same information — do you think that there is still a fundamental difference in the way that people think depending on where they're from?

Absolutely. One of the biggest mistakes we make is thinking that technology can sort of wipe away initial conditions. Not only does it not — we shouldn't want it to. Nothing is more important for really thriving than diversity: of ideas, of background, even of motive. Ecosystems that get whittled down to a single strain or two of a plant or animal tend to get wiped out very easily. So it's only natural that there are tremendous differences in how we think — you might even say it is not only historically inevitable (after all, global connection is a pretty new thing) but also a precursor to survival. That's why our goal shouldn't be to homogenize the planet so that everyone looks like us (and who is "us" anyhow?), but rather to encourage as much diversity as possible. That means empowering people from different backgrounds to define success their own way, to disrupt the world for good in whatever way moves them. It also means resisting the forces that might want to homogenize us for silly commercial reasons or dangerous ideological reasons. If we want to raise children who are resilient, the first step should be making sure we encourage them to be different.

Are rapidly developing countries such as China and India better pre-pared to face the "unthinkable" because they've been forced to think cre-atively for longer? Do you think that the global financial crises could change them into superpowers? If so, how?

Well, it's dangerous to lump China and India together. They are very different places. I do think that places that are habituated to constant rapid change are a bit better prepared to think out of the box—because they have to in order to survive. China, for instance, is going to urbanize several hundred million people in the next few decades. That can't be done using any sort of off-the-shelf think-ing. The hunt for new ideas is what makes China so exciting now.

You speak often of the importance of "resilience" in society. What exactly do you mean by this and what are some key things that people can do to foster such an attitude? What role do you see technology playing in our ability to maintain resilience?

Resilience is the ability not only to stretch in reaction to stress—instead of snapping—but also to get stronger. That's one thing that makes it different than, say, resistance. Resistance is about preparing for risks and dangers we do know about. For a nation, that might mean hardening roads against a nuclear attack; for an individual, it might mean saving up money in case you lose your job. But resilience is something else. It's a kind of learning-on-the-fly crisis reaction in which you emerge stron-ger. So if you lost your job, say, resilience would mean that you would end up with a better and more suitable one because you had prepared yourself by learning new skills, establishing new networks, and so on. This need to prepare yourself in very basic ways in advance is a crucial part of resilience.

It's a bit worrisome then when you look at nations like the United States that are missing some of the basic infrastructure that would allow us to survive a prolonged economic crisis, say, and not only resist it but change and grow from it: our low savings rate, lack of health care, poor education system. Frankly, the United States is the most resilient nation around for other reasons, mainly the deep psychological optimism of Americans, but there are many things we could do to be an even more resilient society. Technology, of course, is a part of this, but many of the risks we face come from technology, like financial systems or biological engineering that we want and need, so technology in and of itself isn't a tool for resilience.

What are some of the things that the revolutionary age has already fostered? Who are the "virtuosos of the moment"?

The most important thing this age has delivered—and will continue to deliver—is the profound sense individuals have of being able to change their lives in ways that were unimaginable for their parents. This basic act of self-invention is profoundly important and is an unstoppable human trend. It means the ability to think revolutionary thoughts isn't just confined to masses of people, but is more and more handed over to individuals. We are given power to disrupt the patterns of our lives in really wonderful ways. The idea of the American Dream, that you can create a life for yourself that exceeds your dreams, is now becoming possible for more people around the world. Now, many of these people may invent lives that we find abhorrent or align their personal revolutions with ideologies that are very dangerous for us—but that is unavoidable. The core reason our world will be ever more disruptive is that the spread of this desire to create a new life for yourself is—and should be—unstoppable. What we've got to do is not try to stop it but to direct it so that more and more people invent ways of living that are good for all of us.

Do you believe that a total collapse is necessary in order to fully reimagine our place in the global community and grow into it?

No. We can learn a lot from my friend Simon Levin and his studies of ecosystems here. If we get to the point of total collapse, we're probably too late. What you need instead is energetic regeneration. This should be pretty merciless in some respects, in the sense that we can't be sentimental about old ideas that are now imperiling us—like the notion that everyone should have a gas car or that unrestrained capitalism is a good idea. But we don't want to throw out the good, useful parts of our past: personal transportation is great, markets are super mechanisms for setting prices. So what you need to do is poke very hard at systems and find where the rust is. This goes on very intuitively and naturally in nature and in bleeding-edge businesses in technology, where newness and innovation are unstoppable. But we're pretty bad at applying this sort of thinking to most of our ideas. We often don't want the hassle of rethinking the world, even if we are wrong.

There are parallels between the most successful, innovative companies and the deadliest, most cunning terrorist groups of the past decade; but, as you say, one doesn't "dare mention a moral equivalency between Hizb'allah and, say, the innovations of Google" (page 5). In our attempt to master a revolutionary attitude toward the changing world, is there a line—as individuals and as nation— that we can cross?

The line is sentimentality. I think it's great and important to hold on to traditions (like reading books!), but it's also true that when some traditions outlive their usefulness they are, inevitably, going to be discarded by the world. It's crucial to hold on to old ideas, to our history, so that we can learn from the past. And, of course, one of the great joys of being alive is that sense of being part of a human chain stretching back and forward, so we never want to sever that link. But I do think we have to be willing to say "this is not working" when ideas are clearly failing. Today we end up in these very extreme debates between clinging to old ideas and embracing new ones, a sort of revolutionary versus reactionary view of progress. And we should instead be asking how we can frame these inevitable changes as evolutions and see the excitement about new ideas even as we hold on to the core wisdom of old notions.

We have just survived a decade whose theme seems to be not just that of extraordinary deception but of the mass acceptance of that deception. Do you think that we're heading in the right direction now or are we settling back into old habits?

I think that's a good point and gets again at our unwillingness to ask hard questions, at the habits of intellectual laziness we aren't quite ready to kick yet. I think we are heading in the right direction because the world is shoving us that way. We're starting to see all the evidence we need that our old ways of thinking were delusional and dangerous, that we were mistaking a very unstable world for something that was getting more stable.

But I also think there is a struggle, as there always is at historical moments like this, between people who have a huge interest in holding on to those ideas and the reality of the shifting world around them. It's not fun to give up your old ideas about the world — particularly if those ideas were part of how you justified the way you lived your life or how you did your work. But when those ideas begin to break under the pressure of change, it's best really to give them up, not try to defend them. And that is what you see a lot of today, people trying in a very unreasonable way to defend ideas that the last decade has taught us are not only wrong but dangerous.

Questions and topics for discussion

1. In *The Age of the Unthinkable*, Joshua Cooper Ramo argues that we are in a revolutionary age with a global order that is changing around us exponentially faster than ever before. What does Ramo think has caused the global landscape to shift over the course of the past century, and how large a role do you think technology has played in this transformation? Does Ramo believe that this change was inevitable? Do you agree or disagree?

2. Consider the significance of Louis Halle's observation that "foreign policy is made not in reaction to the world but rather in reaction to an image of the world in the minds of the people making decisions" (page 13). In light of Ramo's argument, what is the fundamental problem with this approach to foreign policy?

3. What does Ramo mean by "We Won the Cold War!" illusions? Discuss some reasons why this mode of thinking could prove detrimental in a revolutionary era.

4. Explain the implications of Friedrich August von Hayek's 1974 acceptance speech, "The Pretence of Knowledge," for the Nobel Prize for Economics.

5. What was radical about Per Bak's theory of a sandpile and its avalanches, and how does Ramo use "the sandpile effect" to further his argument? Can you think of some recent events in our history that exhibit similar patterns?

6. Ramo discusses the excessive provisions that governments often take to protect their countries from every possible danger—even going as far as to say that such small-scale efforts make countries *more* vulnerable to disaster than they had previously been. What, according to Ramo, is the difference between "resistance" and "resilience," and which does he think should be adopted in today's changing world?

7. Does Ramo believe that the chaos of the past decade— terrorism, war, recession—has had any kind of positive influence on our society? If so, what form has it taken?

8. What does Ramo mean by the term *mashup* and how does it relate to luminaries such as Gertrude Stein, Pablo Picasso, Michael Moritz, and Shigeru Miyamoto, about whom he writes? What do they all have in common?

9. History, both personal and collective, is a subject that necessitates a particularly careful balance in the minds of world leaders and individuals alike. In two instances Ramo writes that "history became data; the future became output" (page 23) and that "there is finally no way to walk away from history or stick it behind glass like some diorama" (page 258). In order to think and act like a revolutionary, to master an "instinct for cataclysm," what role does history play in our

ability to adapt and move forward? Which aspects of the past must we bring with us, and which must we forsake?

10. What does Ramo think that this revolutionary age demands of each of us? Discuss his ideas about how we can learn to anticipate the unexpected and begin to live more resilient lives.